Family and Community

FAMILY AND COMMUNITY

Italian Immigrants in Buffalo, 1880-1930

Virginia Yans-McLaughlin

University of Illinois Press

URBANA AND CHICAGO

Illini Books edition, 1982
By arrangement with Cornell University Press

Manufactured in the United States of America
P 5 4 3

This book is printed on acid-free paper.

Library of Congress Cataloging in Publication Data

Yans-McLaughlin, Virginia, 1943–
Family and community.

Reprint. Originally published: Ithaca: Cornell University Press, 1977.
Bibliography: p.
Includes index.
1. Italian Americans—New York (State)—Buffalo—Economic conditions. 2. Family—United States. 3. Buffalo (N.Y.)—Economic conditions. I. Title. II. Title: Italian immigrants in Buffalo, 1880–1930.
F129.B819189 1981 305.8'51'074797 81-11475
ISBN 0-252-00916-9 AACR2

For my mother and father

Fanciulli piccoli, dolor di testa
fanciulli grandi, dolor di cuori.

Once the Malavoglia were as numerous as the stones on the road to Trezza; . . . and good and brave seafaring folk, quite the opposite of what they might appear to be from their nickname of the ill-wills, as is but right. . . . Now at Trezza there remained only Padron 'Ntoni and his family. . . . The tempests, which had scattered all the other Malavoglia to the four winds, had passed over the house by the medlar-tree and the boat anchored under the tank without doing any great damage; and Padron 'Ntoni, to explain the miracle, used to say, showing his closed fist, a fist which looked as if it were made of walnut wood, "To pull a good oar the five fingers must help one another." He also said, "Men are like the fingers of the hand—the thumb must be the thumb, and the little finger the little finger."

And Padron 'Ntoni's little family was really disposed like the fingers of a hand. . . . Padron 'Ntoni was in the habit of using certain proverbs and sayings of old times, for, said he, the sayings of the ancients never lie: . . . "Be content to be what your father was, then you'll be neither a knave nor an ass," and other wise saws. Therefore the house by the medlar was prosperous, and Padron 'Ntoni passed for one of the weighty men of the village.

Giovanni Verga, *The House by the Medlar-Tree*
Translated by Mary A. Craig

Acknowledgments

Many friends and colleagues contributed their ideas, interest, and spirit to this book. Eric Foner, Herbert Gutman, Richard Sennett, Charles Tilly, and Silvano Tomasi read the entire manuscript. Their criticism was invaluable for clarification and discovery. Rudolph Bell, Allen F. Davis, John Gillis, James Henretta, Alice Kessler Harris, John Krause, W. David Lewis, Arno Mayer, Lawrence Stone, Louise Tilly, Rudolph J. Vecoli, Dana F. White, and E. A. Wrigley read parts or all of earlier versions of the manuscript. Special thanks are due Herbert Gutman for knowing how to learn and to teach at the same time. Bernhard Kendler of Cornell University Press provided many votes of confidence. Several Italian-Americans in Buffalo, identified by fictitious names in this book, welcomed me into their homes and spent hours relating personal experiences to me. Their interviews added a human dimension to already explored written records. The humanity, trust, and wisdom of these immigrants served to remind me that as a historian I am, after all, studying people. I hope I have done justice to them and to their history. I am grateful to all of these individuals for sharing their time, talents, and sensitivities so generously.

The Woodrow Wilson Foundation Dissertation Fellowship Program and the American Philosophical Society Research Grants program provided financial assistance. The City College of the City University of New York and Princeton University awarded Faculty Research fellowships. The State University of New York at Buffalo contributed funds for research assistance.

I have used material from earlier versions of sections of this book. Passages have been taken from "Italian Women and Work: Experience and Perception," *Class, Sex, and the Woman Worker,* Milton Cantor and Bruce Laurie, editors, reprinted by permission of the publisher, Greenwood Press, a division of Williamhouse-Regency, Inc. Other passages are reprinted from "Patterns of Work and Family Organization: Buffalo's Italians," *Journal of Interdisciplinary History,* II (1971), 303, 304, 305, 306–312, by permission of *Journal of Interdisciplinary History* and the M.I.T. Press, Cambridge, Massachusetts. Passages from "A Flexible Tradition: Immigrant Families Confront New Work Experiences," *Journal of Social History,* June 1974, pp. 429–441, are reprinted by permission of the editors. The Indiana University Press has granted permission to quote from Carla Bianco, *The Two Rosetos.*

Others deserve special mention. Gladys Hartman patiently typed the manuscript; Ann Adelman and Lisa Turner provided editorial assistance. Joe Ellis, Helene Freeman, Robin Goldberg, Carol Groneman, Judith Mara Gutman, Marilyn Yans Hanlon, Norma Holt, Kyla Marion, Bella Mirabella, Rosemary Poulos, and Frank Yans, Jr., occupy hidden places in these pages. My greatest debts are to my mother and father, whose lives inspired the writing of this book. For their generation, the language of gratitude to one's family was hard labor; for mine, it can be writing a book. There are countless ways in which they made that transition possible. I hope they understand that I appreciate many I know about, and know about many I should appreciate more.

Just weeks before this book appeared, my father died suddenly. These words of appreciation remain unread by him. But, then, he always seemed to understand words unsaid, and I think he knew without reading it that this book is for and about him.

VIRGINIA YANS-MCLAUGHLIN

New York, New York

Contents

Tables

Abbreviations

BE	*Bollettino dell'Emigrazione* (Italy, Ministry of Foreign Affairs)
COS	Charity Organization Society of Buffalo
FIC	*Report of the Factory Investigating Commission* (New York State)
IC	*Il Corriere Italiano* (Buffalo, N.Y.)
La F	*La Fiaccola* (Buffalo, N.Y.)
NYSMC, 1905	New York State Manuscript Census, 1905
NYSMC, 1925	New York State Manuscript Census, 1925
USFMC, 1900	United States Federal Manuscript Census, 1900

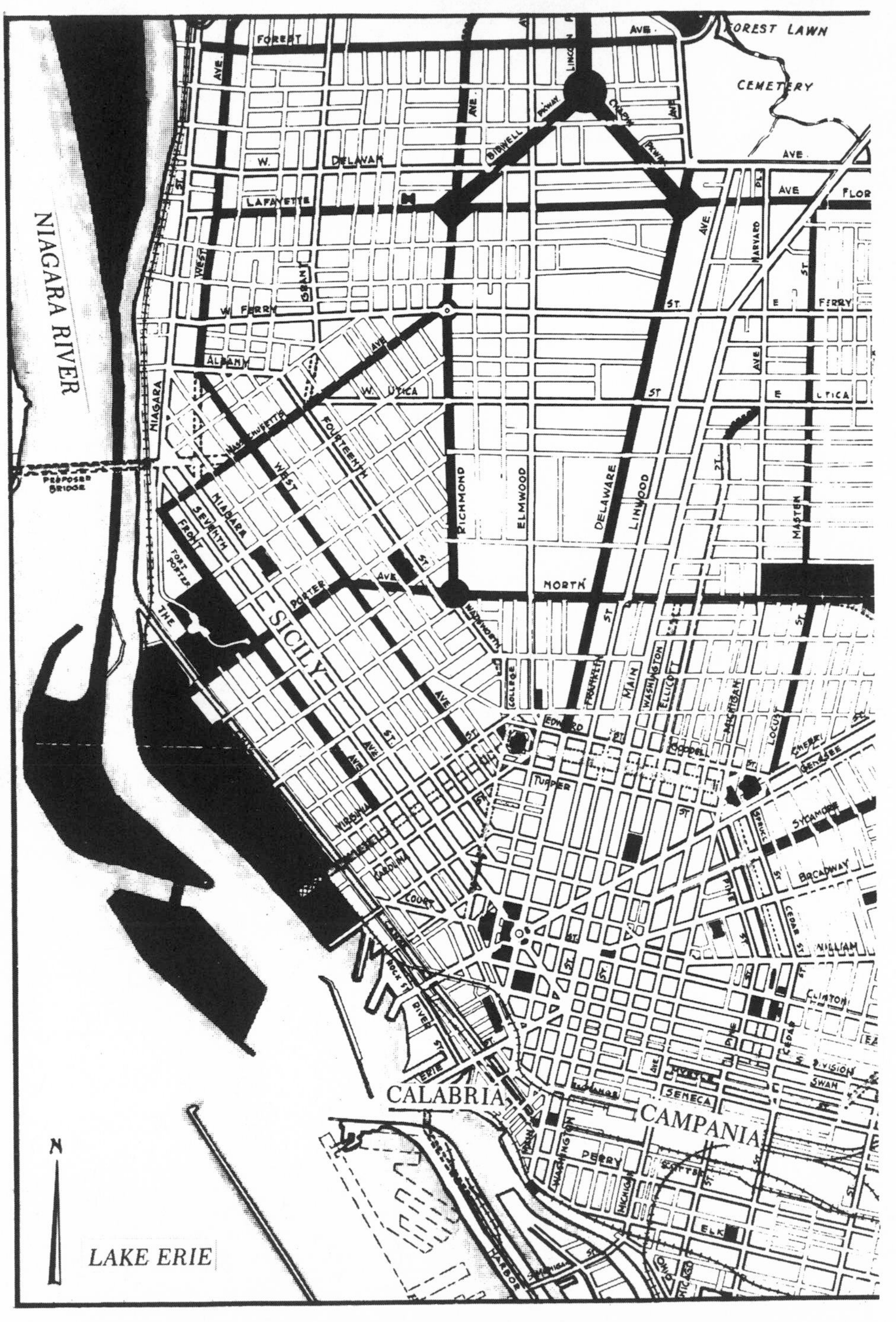

Main areas of Italian settlement in Buffalo, 1880–1930

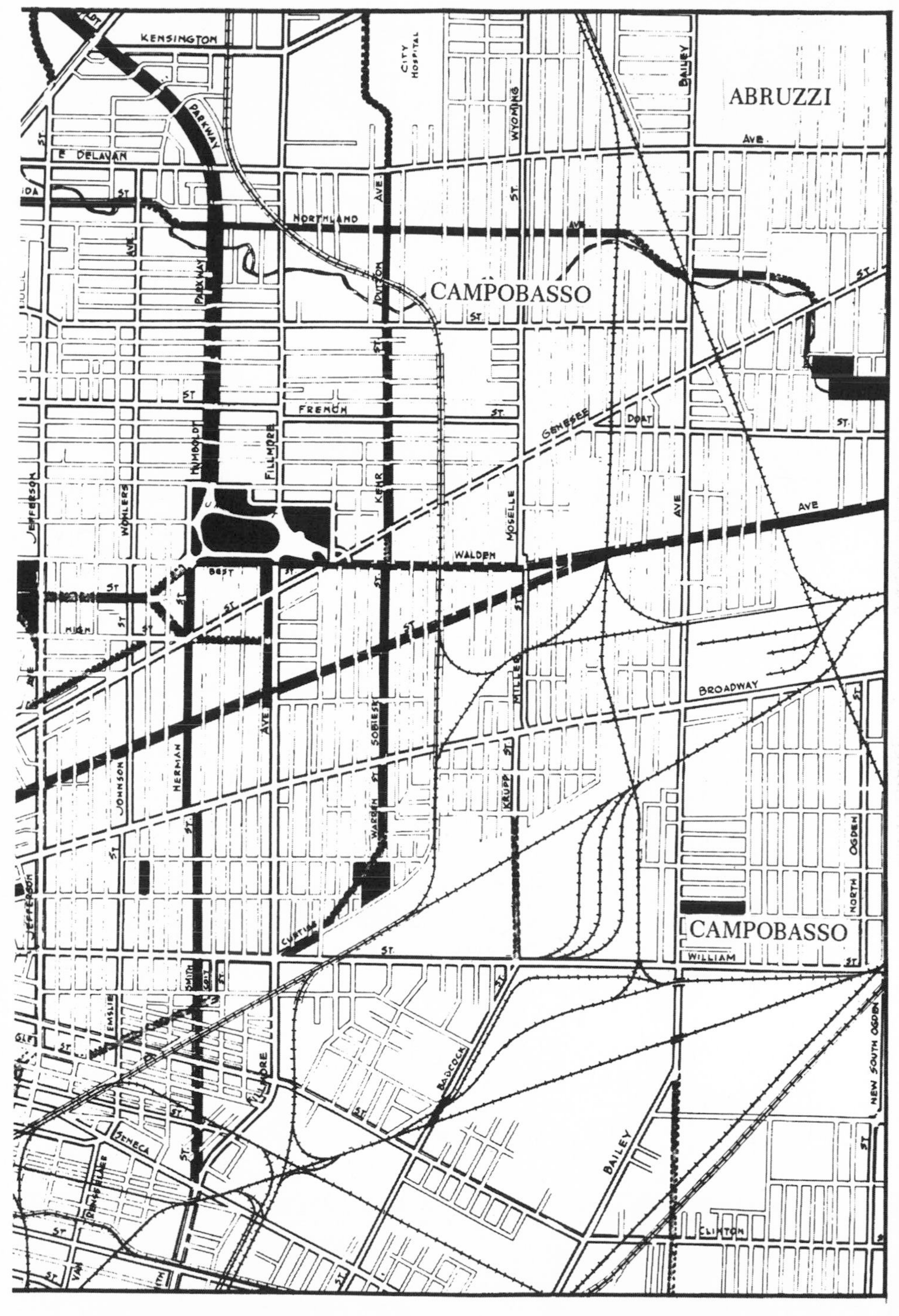
KENSINGTON
CITY HOSPITAL
BAILEY
ABRUZZI
PARKWAY
WYOMING
E DELAVAN
NORTHLAND
DUTTON
CAMPOBASSO
HUMBOLDT
FILLMORE
KEHR
FRENCH
GENESEE
DOAT
JEFFERSON
WOHLERS
MOSELLE
WALDEN
BEST
HIGH
BROADWAY
JOHNSON
HERMAN
SOBIESKI
WARREN
KRUPP
MILLER
NORTH
OGDEN
CAMPOBASSO
CURTISS
WILLIAM
SMITH
EMSLIE
SENECA
BABCOCK
BAILEY
CLINTON
NEW SOUTH OGDEN

Family and Community

ITALIAN IMMIGRANTS IN BUFFALO, 1880–1930

Introduction

In 1887, at age twenty-one, Francesco Barone left his home in Valledolmo, a Sicilian agricultural town with a population of about eight thousand. He ultimately settled in Buffalo, New York, working, stinting, and saving for a number of years until he managed to establish himself as a saloonkeeper. Having done well and being impressed with the opportunities Buffalo offered, he wrote to friends, relatives, and neighbors in Valledolmo encouraging them to join him. This small Sicilian town, troubled by underemployment and poor living standards, had discharged several respected family men like Barone to find appropriate settlements abroad. By 1947 a total of eight thousand Valledolmesi had settled in Buffalo.[1]

The Buffalo branch of the Barone family increased in number. Signore Barone was joined by his wife, Antoinetta. By 1905, eighteen years after Francesco settled in Buffalo, more than fourteen of his relatives and their families, encouraged by Francesco's optimism, had joined him. Most of the Barones settled in the city's first and nineteenth wards, which contained heavy concentrations of immigrant Italians. The Barones continued to help one another in a variety of ways.

How can the Barone family's history be explained? What is its significance? How did the Barones' decision to settle in Buffalo,

[1] Michael Augello, "A History of Italian Immigrants in Buffalo, 1880–1925" (unpublished M.A. thesis, Canisius College, Buffalo, N.Y., 1960), pp. 15–16; and New York State Manuscript Census (hereinafter NYSMC), Buffalo, N.Y., 20th Ward, Third Electoral District, p. 19, contain information on Barone. City of Buffalo, *The People of Buffalo* (Buffalo, 1947), p. 29, discusses the Valledolmo immigrants.

a rapidly expanding center of heavy industry, affect the family's fortunes and those of other Italian immigrants like them?

This book focuses on such questions, but its implications extend beyond the particular story of Italian immigrant families in one industrial city. Their experience is important because of its relation to a nexus of broader historical questions. What happens when peasants migrate to industrial cities? How did immigration affect the family's internal and external relationships? How did families from agricultural societies relate to the factory and to other new types of work? How did they cope with charitable and other urban agencies? How did they go about organizing a group and institutional life that supported and protected their Old World family traditions?

The standard answers which a generation of scholars gave to these questions paint a grim picture of immigrant family life. Their work, most notably that of Oscar Handlin, was grounded in a conventional sociological model implying a clear dichotomy, as well as abrupt discontinuities, between folk and urban societies. The family figured prominently in this scheme. Its disorganization was viewed as one consequence of the transition from peasant village to industrial nation. Industrial work patterns, in particular, were associated with the erosion of Old World family ways.[2]

Yet the evidence that we have on the Italians in Buffalo seriously challenges this conventional model. These families made a relatively smooth transition from the Old World to the New. Strain and conflict occurred certainly, but not disorganization. The nuclear family pattern proved extraordinarily resilient; unstable male employment, for example, rarely resulted in desertion or diminished male control. As the Barone clan's history implies, the extended family not only survived but actually aided the adjustment to the New World.

The Italians in Buffalo made their adjustments while they ex-

[2] Oscar Handlin, *The Uprooted*, 2d ed. (Boston, 1973), is the most famous example of an immigration historian adopting the folk-urban dichotomy. Rudolph Vecoli, "*Contadini* in Chicago: A Critique of *The Uprooted*," *Journal of American History*, 51 (1964), 404–417, is an important article calling for a revision of this approach.

perienced precisely those conditions which the "disorganization" school considered inevitably destructive to traditional family relationships. These Italians confronted the usual problems experienced by families migrating to cities. Certainly, they found a very different society from the one they had left—more complex, more stratified, politically and technologically more sophisticated, and more anonymous. They were prevented or discouraged from participating in established social and political institutions. As the last large European group to enter Buffalo, the Italians were harshly discriminated against by both the upper- and the working-class citizens. Economic discrimination limited their employment opportunities.

The specific pressures that could have produced family instability were considerable. First, there was the process of immigration itself and the temporary family disruptions this sometimes required. Until the prosperous 1920's, Italian families in Buffalo experienced the hardships of urban poverty. Segregated into substandard, overcrowded housing, they were constantly exposed to infectious disease. High infant mortality rates resulted from the low living standards and inadequate diet. Italian families were large nevertheless, and this meant a constant struggle to meet daily living expenses. Most of the men found employment in low-paying, insecure occupations, and worked only five or six months out of the year. The severe economic depressions of 1893 and 1915 added to their problems. Immigrants left Italy hoping to escape economic difficulties and to make a better life for their families; in Buffalo, they found problems of a different kind. The Sicilian proverb warned correctly, as folk proverbs always seem to do in retrospect: "Chi lascia la via vecchia per la nuova, sa quel che perde e non sa quel che trova" ("Whoever forsakes the old way for the new knows what he is losing, but not what he will find").

In the face of harsh conditions, these Italian immigrant families made a series of adjustments. The "disorganization" model does not accurately describe or explain them. Alternative approaches and methodologies seem more promising. Rudolph Vecoli maintains, for example, that the south Italian familial culture survived the transoceanic journey and aided adjustment to the city.[3] Shifting the focus from either disorganization or cultural continuity, another model stresses the emergence of new "functional" family forms which emerged to replace outmoded patterns. The transition from the old country to the new molded the Old World family into a mobile, detached, nuclear form whose roles and relationships fit the demands of a more "rational" industrial economy.[4]

For a historian attempting to understand changes in family life over a period of time, each of these approaches is inadequate. The first implies a linear view of human behavior. It has the virtue of de-emphasizing disorganization and alienation, themes that have too long dominated immigration history. But it assumes too simply that Old World culture was transported to America, that past experiences determined present behavior. The "functional" model is flawed in another way. It assumes too facilely that a people's culture—their values, norms, and world views—and their persistent social behavior are static "mirror images" or "simple reflexes" of one another.[5] If the functional model explains how a society works at one historical moment, it fails to explain how social change occurs over time. In order to understand fully the family changes among the Italians in Buffalo or any other group, past traditions, historical context, and particular situations (which exclude some possibilities and include others) all require examination. In this case neither a simple functional model nor a linear model will suffice. What we are observing is a dynamic process of give and take between new conditions and old social forms as the immigrant families made their transition from Europe to America.

The theoretical perspective and methodology used in this book differ from those used by pioneering immigration historians and contemporary quantitative historians.[6] Because the

[3] "*Contadini* in Chicago."

[4] Talcott Parsons is the most noted exponent of the functional view. See, for example, his "Kinship System of the Contemporary United States," *American Anthropologist*. 45 (1943), 22–38.

[5] Clifford Geertz, "Ritual and Social Change," *American Anthropologist*, 59 (1957), 32–54, offers a critique of such a position.

[6] Stephan Thernstrom, *Poverty and Progress: Social Mobility in a Nineteenth Century City* (Cambridge, Mass., 1973), has written one of the more notable examples of the new quantitative history.

differences influence the use and interpretation of historical evidence, they merit exploration. The older school of immigration historians stressed the alienating aspects of migration from rural towns to industrial cities. They typically assumed that family stability and consensus were the norm and that immigration disrupted them. I began with different assumptions. The question that prompted the writing of this book was not why do immigrant families become disorganized, but why and how did such families stay together? In the case of immigrant Italians, I hope the book will make clear some of the reasons for this cohesion. Families gave emotional, practical, and financial support during the immigration crisis and long after. Further, remaining outside the family was not a realistic or comfortable option for these immigrants.

The inadequacy of quantitative evidence alone for defining the family experience of working-class Italians will become apparent at several critical points in this book. The form and availability of statistical evidence determine the kinds of questions posed, and narrow the historian's vision. It is not enough to know that Italian families experienced low rates of dissolution or illegitimacy, high population turnover, and significant male unemployment. By themselves, these facts give us a one-dimensional view of Italian immigrant life. I hope that even though this book views Italians from only one perspective—through the lens of their family experience—it provides a less myopic view. The use of both quantitative and qualitative evidence permits an understanding of the subtle ways in which family, culture, and class can interact and adapt, suggesting a wholeness of experience that one-dimensional quantification cannot describe.

Other dangers lurk behind the use of quantification in writing family history. I think it is wrong to assume that family stability—measured statistically by low rates of desertion, divorce, and illegitimacy—implies family consensus, or indeed to assume that family consensus was the norm. This point can be argued on theoretical grounds alone.[7] From a methodological

[7] Jetse Sprey, "The Family as a System of Conflict," in Joann S. and Jack R. Delora, eds., *Intimate Life Styles* (Pacific Palisades, Calif., 1972), pp. 184–195. contains a critical discussion of the consensus model.

viewpoint, social historians relying heavily upon quantitative data must more modestly come to terms with the limits of their evidence. Census and other statistical data inform us of structure, not content. If families stay together, it does not necessarily follow that they did so without conflict and strain. At best quantitative evidence can describe certain objective aspects of family life. But neither actual behavior nor cultural and subjective attitudes can be safely deduced from statistical descriptions. For this reason I have utilized literary evidence and oral interviews to verify, negate, or interpret the statistical record.

Because both the quantitative and the more conventional approaches seemed so inadequate to explain the historical evidence, I turned instead to the social scientists, particularly those concerned with examining the transition from traditional to modern societies as a historical process. Clifford Geertz and Lloyd and Susanne Hoeber Rudolph provide a dynamic model that seems more apposite to historians attempting to account for family change.[8] They emphasize that tradition—familial or otherwise—interpenetrates and facilitates social change; that it continues to satisfy basic human needs, even in modernizing societies. Social change, these and other critics of standard modernization theory argue, does not necessarily imply the dissolution of traditional family forms or a systematic fit of institutions, but rather the adaptation of one institution to another. The relationship between modernity and tradition, then, is neither dichotomous nor linear but dialectical.[9] From this perspective the

[8] Rudolph and Rudolph, *The Modernity of Tradition* (Chicago, 1967), are specifically concerned with Indian politics, but they adopt the flexible approach used by several cultural anthropologists. Geertz's anthropological studies stress the role of tradition in social change. See his "Ritual and Social Change" and *Peddlers and Princes: Social and Economic Modernization in Two Indonesian Towns* (Chicago, 1963).

[9] I am indebted to Rudolph and Rudolph for this approach. Critiques of more simplified modernization theory are plentiful. Dean C. Tipps, "Modernization Theory and the Comparative Study of Societies: A Critical Perspective," *Comparative Studies in Society and History*, 15 (1967), 216, presents a particularly acute analysis. He points out that much of the literature has been "tempocentric . . . in its conception of history as a unilinear process of progressive change toward a model of modernity patterned after a rather utopian image of 'Western' Society." See also Reinhard Bendix, "Tradition and Modernity Reconsidered," ibid., 9 (1967), 292–346.

family is a flexible organization, which, while adapting to new social conditions, may continue to rely upon traditional forms and ways of relating. Using this approach, I was able to understand not only how the family was transformed but how the traditional Italian family transformed itself.

Such an approach can explain both the continuities and the incongruities that exist in transitional cultures such as Buffalo's Little Italy. Italians immigrating to Buffalo found themselves in a new situation with a variety of options, and they adapted their Old World traits accordingly. Some old modes matched the situation; others did not. Those that did match were retained more easily. Thus, the Italian-American culture and the Italian-American family were certainly influenced by the new social situation in Buffalo and are best understood within its context. But cultural change did not occur automatically, and disparities appeared in the process. Given their economic position and urban situation, it may, for example, have been "rational" or "functional" for Italian women to enter the work force, but strong cultural traditions inhibited most of them from doing so. And if extended family ties limited the Italian occupational achievement by restricting immigrants and their children to the local community, kinship structures also adapted to immediate immigrant needs; established relatives, for example, helped inexperienced newcomers to find local employment in the urban labor market. Such behavior can be explained: socially, first-generation Italians had become urbanites; culturally, they remained folk.

Of course, people in transition eventually relinquish many old practices and beliefs, but they do so hesitantly and painfully. Is it indeed so surprising that in the interim human beings should want to relate to the world in familiar ways, to respond to it with forms and meanings significant to them? An interpretation of social change which recognizes this human need for continuity explains much that is important and indeed much that is human about human behavior. It provides a useful tool for understanding what happened to Buffalo's Italian families, how they adjusted to American society, and how they made the transition from peasant to urban working class.

What role did the immigrant family play in the transition from Old World to New? As an important economic unit, chief socializing agent, and tradition's custodian, it had its own power to inhibit, counter, or adapt to a variety of social pressures. Different family systems, moreover, seem to have varying capacities to sustain themselves when confronting stress. Urbanization, immigration, and industrialization did not have the same impact on all people everywhere. The Italians in Buffalo reacted differently than the Poles; they may also have responded differently than their New York City *paesani*. Interactions among ethnicity, class, and family over a period of time and within different socioeconomic contexts require further study before sweeping generalizations can be made about such highly varied circumstances. Comparative studies of a variety of immigrant groups in different cities are essential. This book simply describes what happened to one group of families in one situation over a period of fifty years.

1 Work Experiences and Opportunities: From Italy to Buffalo

The southern provinces of Italy, especially Sicily and Basilicata, sent the most immigrants to Buffalo. Although some immigrants named cities as their birth places, most actually lived in nearby villages. In 1881, soon after the first great migration began, many of these towns ranged in population from eight thousand to twenty-one thousand.[1] Some places of origin are identifiable: Valledolmo, Caltavuturo, Montemaggiore Belsito, Misilmeri, Bagheria, Cefalù, and Termini Imerese in the Palermo area, and Vallelunga Pratameno and Riesi in southern

[1] "Italians in Buffalo," Buffalo *Express*, Aug. 27, 1901; "Little Italy of Buffalo," Buffalo *Times*, June 26, 1903. The following contain information on the origins of Buffalo's Italians: Ferdinand Magnani, *La città di Buffalo, New York e paesi circonvicini e le colonie italiane* (Buffalo, 1908), best account of the movement of Italians into Buffalo by province, especially pp. 27ff.; Stephen Gredel, "Immigration of Ethnic Groups to Buffalo, Based upon Censuses of 1850, 1865, 1875, and 1892," *Niagara Frontier* (Summer 1963), pp. 42–56; and Gredel, "Italian Pioneers of Buffalo" (unpublished manuscript, Buffalo and Erie County Historical Society, March 1961), describe the earliest Italian settlers. See also an interview with the Italian Consular Agent in "Buffalo's Little Italy," Buffalo *Illustrated Times*, Jan. 4, 1903, pt. 5, p. 35; references to and descriptions of the towns in a series in Buffalo's *Il Corriere Italiano*, "Da dove vengono gli Italiani di Buffalo e dintorni," from July 31 to Dec. 4, 1909 (hereinafter referred to as *IC*); see also the report of the Italian consul to Buffalo, G. Banchetti, "Gli Italiani in alcuni distretti dello stato di New York," in Italy, Ministry of Foreign Affairs, *Bollettino dell'Emigrazione*, No. 5 (1902), pp. 20ff. (hereinafter cited as *BE*); Italy, *Atti della giunta per l' Inchiesta Agraria e sulle condizioni della classe agricola*, Vol. 13, Tomo 2, Fas. 4 (Rome, 1885), *passim*. Population figures are from Italy, Istituto Centrale di Statistica, *Comuni e loro popolazione ai censimenti dal 1861 al 1951* (Rome, 1960).

and central Sicily. Avigliano, Potenza, and San Fele in Basilicata were key sources; Torre dei Passiere and Campobasso were important points of origin in Abruzzi.

Oscar Handlin has characterized the European immigrants as former peasants, whose "livelihood sprang from the earth." [2] But Italian immigrants were distinguished by the relatively complex socioeconomic structure of the towns they lived in and by the variety of their former work experiences. The stereotypical yeoman farmer with his own self-sufficient homestead rarely appeared on the Mezzogiorno's rocky landscape.[3] Peasants, whether they were smallholders, day laborers, sharecroppers, or tenants, resided in hill towns. Both owners and tenants daily walked long distances, sometimes five or more miles, to their scattered fields below. Day laborers seeking work wherever they could find it often experienced long separations from their village homes.

Even those who lived in the towns belonged to "part-cultures" in that they had significant social, economic, and cultural ties to the surrounding agrarian regions and nearby urban centers. Laborers, craftsmen, and peasants from an entire region, for example, would meet one another on a town's street, negotiate the sale of their produce or labor in its marketplaces and fairs, marry one anothers' sons and daughters, and sometimes even migrate to neighboring villages.[4]

The occupational background of Buffalo's immigrants reflected a wide range of employment. A fortunate few had been professionals, village craftsmen, or itinerant provision merchants; some had labored in railroad and public utility construction; Sicilian sulphur miners and fishermen also emigrated. A few immigrants once tended Basilicata's pastoral lands. The majority of the male immigrants, however, were former Sicilian ag-

[2] Handlin, *Uprooted*, p. 7.

[3] Vecoli, "*Contadini* in Chicago," attacks this and other stereotypical images of Italian peasants.

[4] Josef J. Barton, *Peasants and Strangers: Italians, Rumanians, and Slovaks in an American City, 1890–1950* (Cambridge, Mass., 1975), pp. 40f.; Anton Blok, *The Mafia of a Sicilian Village, 1860–1960: A Study of Violent Peasant Entrepreneurs* (New York, 1974), p. 23, observes that even the relatively isolated central Sicilian village he studied had connections with its wider region.

ricultural workers primarily employed in grain, citrus, grape, and fruit production. Their wives sometimes joined them in the fields at harvest time, but usually the women concentrated on household tasks, including spinning and weaving. Even these peasant town-dwellers were affected by their connections to the surrounding regions and cities. Many peasants became migrant laborers following the harvests in neighboring areas. Off-season unemployment drew them to such varied occupations as sulphur mining,town industry, quarrying, and construction work. The towns themselves provided occasional employment in agricultural and other small-scale industries. Peasants who lived near larger settlements like Palermo, Bagheria, Potenza, San Fele, and Cefalù could work in the local cheese, olive, canned goods, wine, cord, flax, or silk factories.[5]

Those few immigrants who had engaged in manufacturing did not compose an industrial proletariat. The southern industries were usually small-scale enterprises employing only a few workers; craftsmen controlled most of the work processes. Moreover, even if the peasants labored occasionally in industry, mining, or construction, their primary commitment was to the land. Underemployment, a chronic southern problem, always forced peasants to move from one occupation to another. Even today, the Sicilian *braccianti* (seasonal contract laborers) work only 110 days annually on the land; and the available evidence indicates a similar pattern for the late nineteenth century.[6] At

[5] John W. Briggs, "Return the Immigrant to Immigration Studies: A New Appeal for an Old Approach" (unpublished paper, delivered at the Conference of the Canadian Association of American Studies, 1972), p. 5, points to the highly diversified occupations of south Italian immigrants. Yet the largest proportions of southern Italian immigrants were agricultural laborers. See, for example, *BE*, No. 18 (1910), pp. 20–21. On fishermen, see Phyllis H. Williams, *South Italian Folkways in Europe and America* (New Haven, 1938), p. 25; and *IC*, Jan. 23 and 30, 1904. On sulphur miners, see William Chazanof, "The Sicilians of Fredonia" (unpublished paper, American Community Life Class, New York State University College of Education at Fredonia, May 15, 1961), p. 6. See also Italy, *Inchiesta Agraria*, 13: 20; and the series in *IC*, "Da dove vengono gli Italiani di Buffalo e dintorni," which provides information on the large towns.

[6] Paolo Sylos-Labini, ed., *Problemi dell'economia siciliana* (Milan, 1966), p. xxi; Andrea Saba Sebastiano Solano, "Lineamenti dell'evoluzione demografica ed economica della Sicilia dall'Unificazione ad oggi" in Sylos-Labini, p. 41; Robert Foerster, *The Italian Immigration of Our Times* (Cambridge, Mass., 1919), p. 85.

that time the peasant day laborer, sharecropper, or smallholder could not anticipate stable continuous employment from agricultural work alone or even in combination with domestic work or other industry.

Underemployment, on the rise since the middle of the nineteenth century, contributed to the peasant's decision to leave the Mezzogiorno. But his fluid, unstable work experiences are important for another reason. Once in Buffalo, Italians usually worked in outdoor jobs which also left them underemployed. Many compensated for the seasonal unemployment just as they had in Italy; they took any available day laborer's job in the city or drifted around the Niagara Frontier region seeking work as construction, railroad, or agricultural laborers. Thus, their Old World patterns enabled these immigrants to deal effectively with underemployment: exploring alternatives, accepting shifts in jobs, and even moving from one home to another in order to obtain work.

Yet despite their varied work experiences, the overwhelming majority of south Italian immigrants were involved either primarily or marginally in agriculture.[7] Thence a deeper exploration of that sector of the Mezzogiorno's economy, and particularly of the late nineteenth-century peasant occupational structure and property distribution patterns, is essential if we are to understand these immigrants and their reasons for leaving.

Fluid employment patterns, unstable tenancy, and simultaneously held land contracts make it difficult to describe the

[7] *BE*, No. 18 (1910), pp. 20–21. Passport applications from 1901 to 1914 for two towns which sent many residents to Buffalo illustrate the predominance of agricultural occupations. Termini Imerese, a north Sicilian coastal town with a diversified economy, produced the following adult male applicants: *contadini*, 36 percent; agricultural day laborers, 5 percent; truck farmers, 4 percent; town laborers and industrial workers, 18 percent; fishermen, 12 percent; skilled workers, 17 percent; large and small merchants and gentlemen, 6 percent. Altogether 46 percent stated agricultural employment. Serradifalco, a central Sicilian sulphur mining community, produced a different pattern: 56 percent of its applications were from miners, and 12 percent from skilled workers and townsmen. Still, about a third stated agricultural employment. We do not know if Buffalo Italians from these towns represented a fair sample of these emigrating populations. Serradifalco sent a disproportionate share of artisans to Rochester, and Termini sent more than its share to Baltimore. See Briggs, "Return the Immigrant to Immigration Studies," pp. 7–13.

peasant occupational structure.[8] Land was the Mezzogiorno's most valued capital investment. But an individual's relationship to it as owner, renter, or sharecropper only roughly determined his economic position and the opportunities open to him. The same peasant might work different plots simultaneously under different arrangements. He could hold his own land in one field and maintain a sharecropping arrangement in another; or he might have different functions throughout the year, being a sharecropper one month, a laborer another, and a herdsman another.[9] No matter what his status—smallholder, sharecropper, or day laborer—the underemployed peasant hired himself out for wages.[10] And no matter what his status, he hoped to maintain or purchase a plot of land.

The *contadini*, or owners of small private holdings, had no guarantee of economic independence. A typical holding was only 2.5 acres—often widely scattered and fragmented, uneven in quality, and difficult to place under any capital intensive system—which failed to provide family sustenance. Mortgages, taxes, and declining prices added to the *contadini's* hardships. Smallholders supplemented their earnings with day laborer's wages, sharecropping contracts, and by mining or fishing. The Inchiesta Agraria's director aptly described them as a "proletariat of proprietors." [11]

Those tenants and sharecroppers who worked on large estates enjoyed neither job security nor permanent tenacy. The *gabellotto*, a land agent or speculator, leased large parcels from absentee owners and subdivided them into small rental plots. The sharecroppers, who rented their parcels under varying contractual forms, did poorly. Small, scattered plots and short, insecure contracts prevented them from applying rational agricultural

[8] For this reason Blok, p. 67, questions official statistics on the South's occupational structure.

[9] See, for example, Blok, p. 46.

[10] Foerster, pp. 84–85.

[11] Quoted in Foerster, p. 84. In 1901 only one-fourth of Basilicata's agricultural population and only one-sixth of Sicily's cultivated their own lands. See Leonard Covello, "The Social Background of the Italo-American School Child: A Study of the Southern Italian Family Mores and Their Effect on the School Situation in Italy and America" (Ph.D. dissertation, New York University, 1944), pp. 70ff. (Although subsequently published by E. J. Brill [Leiden, Netherlands, 1967], all references to Covello herein apply to the dissertation.)

techniques. Landords typically kept two-thirds of the crop, leaving little to the tenants. Irregularly or partially employed, most sharecroppers sought other income as day laborers.[12] Renters struggling to maintain their status saw their contracts as a possible means of entry into the landholding class.[13]

The *giornalieri* or day laborers, who composed the bulk of south Italy's work force, fared worst of all. Without even small plots to rely upon, they were totally dependent upon the low wages offered by the large or medium-sized estates. These itinerants moved from place to place seeking employment, and frequently spent days or weeks on distant manors far from home. Driven by an insatiable land hunger typical of Italian peasants, many *giornalieri* hoped to save enough money to rent small holdings.[14]

Lack of crop diversification, population pressure, low wages, and the poor diet all added to the underemployed peasants' difficulties. Entire regions focused on one crop such as grain or citrus fruits; a bad year brought disaster, especially for sharecroppers who had no part in production decisions. Despite high emigration rates, population pressure strained the South's inefficiently utilized resources. Both birth and death rates had been declining since 1881. A sharp decline in child mortality between 1880 and 1910 contributed significantly to the population pressure, as improved prenatal and child care resulted in higher fertility and survivial rates.

Until relatively recent times, southerners continued to have large families, although the explanations for their preference vary.[15] Some argue that peasants, who neither understood nor

[12] Foerster, p. 84; Gustav Schacter, *The Italian South* (New York, 1965), pp. 107ff., discusses some land contract forms.

[13] Barton, p. 38.

[14] Covello, p. 79; Foerster, pp. 85–87, claims that day laborers composed half of Basilicata's and two-thirds of Calabria's and Sicily's cultivators.

[15] On the demographic situation, see Shepard B. Clough and Carlo Levi, "Economic Growth in Italy," *Journal of Economic History*, 16 (1956), 350; George H. Hildebrand, *Growth and Structure in the Economy of Modern Italy* (Cambridge, Mass., 1965), pp. 287ff.; Associazione per lo Sviluppo dell'Industria nel Mezzogiorno, *Statistiche sul Mezzogiorno d'Italia, 1861–1953* (Rome, 1954), p. 61, gives the following figures for birth rates: for 1881–1885 and 1896–1900 birth rates were 40.5 and 35.8. Comparable northern figures for

practiced family limitation, considered large numbers of children an economic asset. Others describe a more complex process. Before 1880, when infant and child mortality reached 70 percent or more, peasants had no need to practice family limitation. When these rates dropped sharply after 1880, some used traditional contraceptive measures—*coitus interruptus*, abortion, and vaginal ablutions of herbs and vinegar. According to this view, the majority continued to prefer large families because they considered children "potential bearers of good fortune" who might possess some quality or asset that would "dramatically alter the family's lot in the future." Children "were not an 'economic asset' in terms of a straight forward income-versus-expense calculation, but families without any 'assets' had little cause to worry about such calculations. Instead, they risked all on their hope that one of the children would somehow bring good fortune. More children meant more chances in this cruel lottery."[16]

Laborers' wages, typically paid in kind, scarcely supported the large southern family. Hunger existed only in times of severe unemployment, but the average diet resulted in chronic malnutrition, predisposing the peasant population to tuberculosis, malaria, and pneumonia. Dry bread soaked in oil, pasta, vegetables, and fruit were the staple fare, as meat was available only occasionally. Those who lived in the coastal areas could, of course, turn to the sea for sustenance and fortunate peasants grew vegetables in their family gardens. Many families owed their survival to these supplements. Total deprivation was rare because even the most disinterested southern landlords responded to desperate pleas for life's essentials.[17] Thus the

---

these years were 35.0 and 33.3. Southern death rates for 1881–1885 and 1896–1900 were 28.8 and 25.1; comparable northern figures were 26.2 and 21.8. Although official statistics indicate declining southern birth rates, Rudolph Bell, in a letter to the author, March 5, 1976, argues that birth rates per thousand married females with husbands at home may not have declined at all in the South until the 1930's. Before then, improved health resulted in greater fertility which offset early contraception efforts.

[16] Bell, letter to the author. The more traditional view that children were considered economic assets is found in Covello, p. 355.

[17] Foerster, pp. 85, 95; further wage and diet information is in U.S. Cong., Sen., *Reports of the Immigration Commission*, IV, *Emigration Conditions in*

average family could eke out its existence; yet between 1880 and 1913, almost four million southerners left for the United States, effectively demonstrating their belief that their efforts could be more profitably expended elsewhere.[18]

Unemployment, backward agricultural organization, population pressure, and low living standards had created daily dilemmas for the families who finally emigrated to Buffalo. But these were chronic problems in the Mezzogiorno, shared by peasants in developing economies throughout the world. They do not elucidate the particular motives of Italians who decided to emigrate; nor do they explain the specific timing of emigration, the massive surge that began after 1880.

Why did so many peasants choose the strategy of migration, and why did they choose it when they did? In the first place, the availablility of inexpensive, convenient, and efficient steamship passage began in the 1870's to make the intercontinental voyage possible for thousands of people. A variety of conditions encouraged them to take that journey.

Between 1870 and 1900, demographic shifts, agricultural depression, and contractions in mining, domestic, and artisanal production upset the Mezzogiorno's precarious economic stability. A late nineteenth-century agricultural crisis that extended throughout Europe brought falling prices and reduced the South's agricultural exports.[19] Out-migration, a shift to labor-intensive vegetable crops, and a reduction in fallow time effected by the use of fertilizers increased the number of employment opportunities for some agricultural laborers. Increased cereal production in the United States and central Europe and certain technological and agricultural innovations meant unemployment for others. In the same period, the declining child

---

Europe (Washington, D.C., 1911), 163; Williams, p. 24; Italy, *Inchiesta Agraria*, 13: 14. Although some peasants probably supplemented their diets with fish, these sources do not mention this practice; Paul Radin, *The Italians of San Francisco: Their Adjustment and Acculturation*, II (San Francisco, 1935), 120, comments on help offered by landlords.

[18] Associazione per lo Sviluppo dell'Industria, p. 117; and Foerster, pp. 22ff., gives figures on emigration rates.

[19] Solano, pp. 21, 41.

mortality rates increased competition for both land and work.[20] The alternate employment upon which peasants and their families depended—mining, domestic, artisanal, and other small scale industrial work—became hard to find. The Sicilian sulphur mining industry, subject to erratic price fluctuations in the 1890's, suffered serious export and production losses after 1901. Artisanal and household production and some food and textile industries experienced cutbacks after 1870. The Sicilian figures illustrate the resultant labor market conditions: active employment in industry declined from 50 percent to 40 percent. The number of workers exclusively involved in industry was not the only group affected. The proportion of women who contributed to peasant family resources as domestic weavers of silk and cotton also dropped significantly.[21]

The demographic and economic changes occurring after 1870, then, upset the close interdependence of peasant agricultural and household production on the one hand, and domestic, artisanal, and small-scale industry on the other. Thus the reduced opportunities for alternate work, coupled with an increasing demand for scarce land, encouraged young individuals and ultimately entire families to emigrate.[22]

The competition for small holdings figured prominently in the decision to leave. Regional out-migration rates were related directly to property distribution patterns. By the mid-1860's marked geographical differences had resulted from a state redistribution of Church and feudal lands.[23] Large estates (*latifondi*)

[20] Solano, p. 18; Andrea Saba, "Movimenti della popolazione e struttura economica," p. 75, in Sylos-Labini, ed., *Problemi.* See Rudolph M. Bell, "Old World Influences on New World Experiences: The Demography of Italo-American Migration" (unpublished paper, Rutgers University, Sept. 1975), pp. 15, 22, for relationships between out-migration and underemployment, wage levels, and weather conditions.

[21] Solano, pp. 53, 23, 26; Sylos-Labini, "Il problema dello sviluppo industriale nella particolare situazione siciliana," p. 991, and pp. xviiff. On southern industry, see Barton, pp. 39f.

[22] Barton, pp. 39f.; Solano, p. 26; Sylos-Labini, "Sviluppo industriale," p. 992.

[23] John S. and Leatrice D. MacDonald, "Institutional Economics and Rural Development: Two Italian Types," *Human Organization,* 23, No. 2 (Summer 1964), 114, 117; John S. MacDonald, "Italy's Rural Social Structure and Emigration," *Occidente: Rivista di Studi Politici,* 12 (Sept.–Oct. 1956), 441ff.;

assembled by absentee entrepreneurs and worked by gangs of laborers dominated central Apulia and the Sicilian interior. There the out-migration rates remained relatively low because landless laborers chose to remain behind. They hoped to improve their economic circumstances through militant organizations and cooperatives.

In the "typical South"—Sicily's coasts, Campania's interior, Basilicata, Abruzzi-Molise, parts of Apulia, and most of Calabria—wide land distribution, finer gradations of property holdings, and more varied forms of tenure emerged by the 1860's. Here, the owners of large estates, the owners of small holdings, and landless day laborers coexisted. Compared to Sicily's and Apulia's central areas, where relatively few peasants owned property, this was a region of smallholders who expected to pass property on to the next generation. Late in the nineteenth century, fragmented inheritances and increasing competition for land in the typical South's crowded villages frequently caused peasants to opt for emigration. Out-migration rates soared.[24]

Because most Italian-Americans, including those in Buffalo, came from villages like these, Italian immigration is appropriately understood as a selective process: those individuals who were preoccupied with immediate family needs, and those who lacked experience with or commitment to institutions outside the family predominated. They chose the familistic strategy of migration rather than any cooperative or class effort as their means to achieve or maintain security. Many originally thought of their American sojourn as a temporary measure. They hoped to accumulate money abroad, to return home, and then to purchase land and homes.[25] Their ultimate goal was decidedly family-oriented.

Emigration was not so much an escape from misery as an attempt by thousands of families to maintain or to improve their

---

Sydel Silverman, "Agricultural Organization, Social Structure, and Values in Italy: Amoral Familism Reconsidered," *American Anthropologist*, 70 (Feb. 1968), 1–20; Italy, *Inchiesta Agraria*, 13, and Barton, pp. 27ff., describe land tenure and general peasant conditions.

[24] MacDonald, "Italy's Rural Social Structure and Emigration."

[25] Foerster, pp. 22ff., documents the temporary character of Italian immigration.

economic position. Those who settled in Buffalo and other American cities were not the poorest, the least motivated, or the dropouts of south Italian society. On the contrary, their contemporaries judged them to be more "frugal, thrifty . . . energetic" and better educated than the peasants who remained behind.[26] These immigrants did not originate from the most destitute areas, nor were they the most destitute themselves.[27] Many had roots in the higher and middle echelons of the agricultural working class; they were people who had once been concerned with economic improvement, property ownership, and capital accumulation. The smallholders had directed their own farms and sold their own produce. Even miners and fishermen saw themselves as entrepreneurs. Some miners, who considered themselves artisans, hired their own labor forces and provided capital in the form of mules and tools. Sicilian fishermen owned their own boats or worked with the owner for a share of the catch.[28] These immigrants obviously differed from the other nineteenth-century "men in motion" whom historians classify as economic failures, passively drifting from place to place seeking work.[29]

After their arrival in the United States, most of the immigrant families joined the ranks of an impoverished working class; but their motives for emigrating and their occupational roots left an imprint that influenced their economic aspirations and their choice of work. Italians saw emigration as a way to avoid loss of

[26] Briggs, "Return the Immigrant to Immigration Studies," p. 4, quoting an American consul at Palermo; Briggs, "Italians in Italy and America: A Study of Change within Conformity for Immigrants to Three American Cities, 1890–1930" (unpublished Ph.D. dissertation, University of Minnesota, 1972), *passim*, contradicts usual assumptions about the south Italian's lack of education.

[27] Foerster, pp. 103–104; interviews with immigrants Roberta Salerno and Thomas Angelico, Buffalo, N.Y., April 16, 1973, confirmed this suggestion. Bell, "Old World Influences," p. 13, observed in his study of three Italian towns that "the threat of lowered living standards, not the absolute level of those standards, . . . induces emigration."

[28] Briggs, "Italians in Italy and America," pp. 6ff.

[29] See, for example, Stephan Thernstrom and Peter Knights, "Men in Motion: Some Data and Speculations on Urban Population Mobility in Nineteenth Century North America," *Journal of Interdisciplinary History*, 1 (Autumn 1970), 7–35. Barton, pp. 45f., documents the mobility aspirations of south Italians.

status and to fulfill their desire to own property. These hopes had some effect on the routes to success that they chose in America. The men who originally intended to return—the majority—sought good wages; they had little interest in businesses or careers that required permanent residence. Others transferred their dreams to America and selected goals that matched their family orientation. Shunning such individualized routes to success as the professions or higher education, the average immigrant family coveted a home or a petit bourgeois business (a shop or saloon) so that their children might inherit property. For many, the determination to obtain family property, an extension of the peasants' hunger for land, was ultimately satisfied in Buffalo. The price they paid was limited occupational mobility.[30]

A heavy demand for unskilled labor created by industrial growth and brisk commercial enterprise attracted Italians and other job-seeking immigrants to Buffalo. It was one of the nation's major immigrant centers, and its population more than doubled between 1880 and 1910, reaching almost one-half million. Italians were not alone in finding this rapidly growing metropolis attractive. In 1910 about three-quarters of Buffalo's residents were foreign immigrants and their children. Poles, Germans, Italians, Canadians, Irishmen, Englishmen, and Russians were well represented. Buffalo ranked only beneath such major immigrants cities as New York, Philadelphia, Chicago, Boston, Newark, San Francisco, Pittsburgh, and Jersey City as an Italian-American city. Between 1900 and 1920 the Italian-born population increased almost three-fold from six thousand to sixteen thousand. In 1920 Italo-Americans represented 10 percent of the city's foreign stock and about 7 percent of the total city population. Italians and Canadians were the only foreign groups that continued to immigrate in large numbers after 1920.[31]

Early twentieth-century Buffalo earned prominence as a

[30] See Ch. 6 for discussions of occupational mobility and homeownership.

[31] *Twelfth Census of the United States, 1900, Population*, I, Pt. 1, cxi, 238; Peter Roberts, *The Foreign Population Problem in Buffalo* (extracts), (Buffalo, 1908); L. H. Weir, *Recreation Survey of Buffalo* (Buffalo, 1925), pp. 358–360; Foerster, p. 329; *Fourteenth Census of the United States, Population, 1920*, II, 933.

major eastern rail terminus and center of heavy industry. It was one of the world's great ports; tons of grain were handled annually in the massive elevators and bins lining Lake Erie's waterfronts. The most rapidly expanding sectors of Buffalo's economy—heavy industry, transportation, and construction—created an unprecedented demand for unskilled and semiskilled male laborers.[32] Steel and related industries provided jobs for thousands of unskilled workers.

Figures for sectors employing more than two thousand men reveal the character of the city's job market in 1910 and 1920.[33] The occupations that maintained a relatively stable demand over this ten-year period were those of clerical personnel and retail dealers, carpenters, and metal workers. Although the census classifications of steam railroad laborers and building or general laborers maintained two thousand or more workers, from 1910 to 1920 each occupational category suffered a loss of half or more. Demands for other kinds of workers rose steadily. The numbers of electrical engineers, factory foremen and laborers in blast furnaces or steel mills increased by 50 to 100 percent. The census recorded increments of 100 percent or more in three occupations: semiskilled operatives in auto factories and steel mill furnaces, and chauffeurs.

Because they chose different styles of entry into this job market, a comparison of the Italian immigrants with the Polish immigrants is illuminating. The Poles, a much larger group, began entering Buffalo about ten years before the Italians. Both groups involved themselves immediately in outdoor labor. But the Poles' previous industrial experience in European cities partially explains why, unlike the Italians, they also chose foundry work and manufacturing. A survey in 1910 reported that 87 percent

[32] For a discussion of Buffalo's economic development, see John Horton, "Old Erie," *History of Northwestern New York*, I (New York, 1947), 219ff. Occupational statistics reflecting the move from commerce are in *Twelfth Census of the United States, 1900, Special Reports: Occupations*, 494–638; and *Fifteenth Census of the United States: 1930, Population*, IV, *Occupations by State* 423–429, 689–698, 1085–1086, 1239.

[33] Young Women's Christian Association (Buffalo, New York), the City Business and Industrial Department, and Students of the Department of Sociology, University of Buffalo, "Some Facts Concerning Women in Buffalo Industries" (unpublished report, Buffalo, N.Y., 1925), pp. 9ff.

of Polish males were employed in manufacturing; 12 percent worked in railroad and lumber yards or in contracting. Like many of their countrymen in other cities, the immigrant Italians typically found their initial employment in outdoor jobs resembling those they had done in Italy—construction, dock, and railroad work. Before 1930 only a handful moved to jobs connected with the briskly expanding heavy industries.[34] As the United States Immigration Commission reported in 1911, "South Italian laborers [in Buffalo] are for the most part engaged in labor outside the factories. Polish laborers are in the majority of cases in the factories." [35] In these respects the Italian experience within this industrial metropolis was unique.

The early twentieth-century national surveys characterized Italian-Americans as "general laborers," men lacking permanent connections with any industry.[36] Italians took any obtainable job. Before 1930, in many cities including Buffalo, they found themselves confined to outdoor, seasonal employment. Longshore work, construction projects, railroad development,

[34] Ellen Taussig, "The Polish Community," Buffalo *Evening News*, Nov. 13, 1971; see also Stephan Gredel, *Pioneers of Buffalo—Its Growth and Development* (Buffalo, 1966), p. 26. Scanning NYSMC, 1925, indicated that only a small minority of Italians had entered heavy industry by that date. George W. Gillette, "The Tenement Situation in Buffalo," *Charities and the Commons*, 17 (Oct. 1906), 71, notes that the Italians' chief connection with the steel industry was plant construction, not manufacturing.

[35] *Reports of the Immigration Commission*, XXVI, *Immigrants in Cities*, 652. Contemporary reports supported the Commission's findings. A 1910 survey reported 87 percent of employed Polish men working in manufacturing. A search of. NYSMC, 1905, revealed few Italian men in such positions. Not until the 1920's, some forty years after their immigration commenced, did a few Italians enter factories. See Taussig, "The Polish Community," and NYSMC, 1905, 1925. This pattern repeated itself in other cities, including Chicago; see Humbert S. Nelli, *The Italians in Chicago: 1880–1930* (New York, 1970), p. 74. The majority of Buffalo Italians became building workers; see "Virtus," "I manovali," *La Fiaccola*, Aug. 20, 1911, p. 1 (hereinafter cited as *La F*). See also "Maria," "Ai manovali," *La F*, Oct. 15, 1910, and Magnani, *La città di Buffalo*, p. 46.

[36] For a discussion of the national employment patterns of Italians, see E. P. Hutchinson, *Immigrants and Their Children* (New York, 1956), pp. 137–138, 178–179, 258–259, and *Reports of the Immigration Commission*, XXVIII, *The Occupations of Immigrants*, 169–170. Gerd Korman, *Industrialization, Immigrants and Americanizers: The View from Milwaukee, 1866–1921* (Madison, Wis., 1967), pp. 35–36, documents seasonal unemployment among Milwaukee Italians.

and factory building originally attracted many Italians to Buffalo. Hundreds took positions as excavators, hod carriers, bricklayers, and assistants to skilled workers; a few fortunate craftsmen obtained work in the higher ranks of the building trades. Increased public spending on construction, sanitation, and education facilities presented other alternatives for unskilled immigrants. Italians labored as city street cleaners, garbage collectors, or street maintenance men. Erie County employed some on construction jobs.[37]

Steady work in outdoor occupations depended upon long, clement seasons, something that Lake Erie's icy, windswept shores did not offer. By December of each year, the port traffic dwindled and cold weather inhibited construction projects.[38] But the arrival of good weather in spring carried no employment guarantees. Permanently settled immigrants faced extra competition in a market already amply supplied with cheap labor when temporary Italian migrants came to work during the warmer seasons.[39]

These conditions resulted in chronic underemployment for Italians who were engaged in outdoor occupations: many worked only five or six months annually.[40] Thomas Angelico's

[37] For a discussion of physical expansion and public utilities in Buffalo, see "Healthy Boom on in Building Industries," Buffalo *Courier*, April 1, 1901; Richmond C. Hill, *Twentieth Century Buffalo*, Pt. I (Buffalo, 1902), p. 151; James Malcolm, comp., *A Record of Failure: History of Asphalt Pavement in Buffalo* (Buffalo, n.d. [1901?]). For the Italians' part in construction projects, see Banchetti, pp. 20–21; "I lavoratori," *La F*, Oct. 28, 1911; "Regular Men on Street Work," *Courier*, March 26, 1901, describes the seasonal nature of the city's maintenance contracts. For a description of the seasonal nature of freight handlers' work, see L. E. Moss, "Where to Go in Buffalo: Among the Freight Trains," *Express*, Aug. 1, 1909. The Buffalo-based Lake Shore Rail Road, employed 11,000 men, one-quarter of them Italians. See *Reports of the Immigration Commission*, XVIII, *Immigrants in Industry*, Pt. 22, *The Floating Immigrant Labor Supply*, especially p. 21.

[38] U.S. Dept. of Commerce, *Seasonal Operation in the Construction Industries: Summary of a Report and Recommendations of a Committee of the President's Conference on Unemployment* (Washington, D.C., 1924), p. vi; Banchetti, p. 21.

[39] *BE*, No. 1–3 (1920), p. 70.

[40] Amy Bernardy, "L'emigrazione delle donne e dei fanciulli italiani," *BE*, No. 1 (1909), p. 17, reports that Italians in eastern cities usually worked only six of twelve months; see also Maria Maddalena De'Rossi, Segretariato Femminile per

experience was typical: "I helped build roads. To find work you carried your shovel around and went from one place to another seeking work. I would find work for a month or two. World War I made it possible for me to obtain more steady work. The steel mills needed workers. After the war, the Italians got fired first."[41] Like Angelico, the average unskilled laborer of this era typically experienced periods of unemployment and irregular work. Some, like the Poles, dealt with this situation by shifting from one job sector to another. But the Poles in Buffalo had established a niche for themselves in both the factory and outdoor labor markets, whereas the Italians could not be so optimistic about year-round employment until the 1920's, when a few factories offered them temporary winter employment.[42]

Underemployment was a fact of life with which Italians and their families had to cope; they dealt with it just as they had as peasants in Italy. They sought alternate opportunities in the city. When none existed, they extended the search for jobs beyond Buffalo to the surrounding regions. The construction of intercity highways, railroads, and aqueducts scattered Italians, a floating immigrant labor force, throughout the Niagara Frontier. Some found construction work in smaller cities or utilized skills learned abroad in local quarries. Others traveled to Pennsylvania's coal fields. Many Sicilians and their families, repeating their earlier experiences, worked seasonally as migrant agricultural laborers. The Niagara and Chautauqua County vineyards, fruit and vegetable farms, and processing plants attracted them. Other Italians journeyed to nearby Brant, Falconer, and Dun-

---

la Tutela delle Donne e dei Fanciulli Emigranti, *Relazione*, "Le donne ed i fanciulli italiani a Buffalo e ad Albion" (Rome, 1913), pp. 11, 6; Myron Adams, *The Buffalo Newsboy and the Street Trades Bill* (Buffalo, 1903), p. 6.

[41] Interview with Thomas Angelico, Buffalo, April 16, 1973.

[42] Caroline Golab, "The Impact of the Industrial Experience on the Immigrant Family: The Huddled Masses Reconsidered" (delivered at the Eleutherian Mills Historical Society Conference on Immigrants in Industrial America, Nov. 1973), pp. 13, 15, points out that the Pennsylvania Department of Labor and Industry, Division of Immigration and Unemployment, showed that between June 1913 and June 1914 about one-fourth of the men surveyed were either unemployed or forced to change occupations. Philip Taylor, *The Distant Magnet* (New York, 1971), p. 207, also stresses the "double jeopardy" of low wages and cyclical unemployment faced by unskilled immigrants.

kirk for temporary work, and eventually created permanent colonies. A few actually achieved their Old World dreams by purchasing small farms nearby.[43]

But these journeys to Buffalo's hinterlands were usually temporary measures; most immigrants returned to the city and outdoor employment. Why did Italians choose this unsteady work in Buffalo, a city of expanding heavy industry? Their decisions must be understood within the context of parallel Old World experiences. The seasonal nature of casual outdoor employment and the occasional opportunities to alternate types of work according to the time of year produced familiar work rhythms for the former peasants, many of whom had supplemented their agricultural wages by mining, fishing, railroad construction labor, or occasional work in domestic industries. Interpersonal networks among Italians supported their continual entry into outdoor occupations; in Buffalo, as in other cities, the immigrants relied upon employed friends and relatives to help them find work.[44]

Most Italian men chose outdoor work, to which their cultural background permitted a ready adjustment. In this sense their choice was a rational adaptation to undesirable alternatives. In many western nations rural migrants have found the move into general labor or service occupations easier than a direct shift into factory work. Unlike the Poles, Italians knew only rural, construction, or small-scale industrial work routines; the modern factory's unnatural, relentless tempo did not appeal to them. "My husband," said Mary Sansone, "would not work in an automated factory, even though his training as a tailor could have

[43] For a discussion of Italians in areas surrounding Buffalo, see Banchetti, pp. 21–24; Kate Burr, "The American Spirit Speaks," *Times*, Nov. 19, 1905; Samuel Alessi, "The Coming of the Italians to Chautauqua County" (paper delivered to the Chautauqua County Historical Society, Westfield, N.Y., Aug. 6, 1960); "Problema degli Italiani in America," *IC*, Sept. 5, 1908 and Aug. 1902. Discussion of Italian farm purchases are in *IC*, June 3, 1905. Real estate advertisements for farms are frequent in *IC*. See, for example, Nov. 5, 1904, and Jan. 15, 1925. When farm size was mentioned, offerings ranged from 10 to 83 acres; prices varied from $3,600 to $6,000.

[44] Kinship and friendship networks are discussed in detail in the following chapter. Korman, pp. 65f., establishes that Old World connections helped Milwaukee Italians to find jobs at International Harvester.

brought him such work. He did unskilled work in a radiator shop because he did not like machines." [45] Mr. Sansone's attitude was not unusual. An Italian government investigator also observed her countrymen's aversion to factory labor. She said that the "fear of [possible] disgrace" or embarrassment caused by the misuse of implements they could not handle and hesitated to use brought anxiety to the former peasants.[46] A well-informed social worker from New Haven, Connecticut emphasized both the Italian's aversion to rigorously disciplined factory employment and his hesitancy to seek year-round work. Attempting to understand this antipathy within the context of past experiences, she observed that the drastic change in climate and the "new and rapid movement of life" placed a great strain on Italians and required a drastic adjustment in their "leisurely way of life." Some never adjusted to factory work. The most ambitious attempted to fulfill their Old World dreams by establishing small business, but, she continued, "failure dogs them and their debts pile higher and higher." Many who had worked in factories for years "suddenly give up and are found in their homes complaining of a vague indisposition with no apparent physical basis." Others, after years of diligent work, suffered "frequent minor accidents." "Their fundamental problem," she concluded, "is that despite years of struggle, they have never been able to adjust to the high pressure of the American industrial system and can no longer spur themselves to the point of meeting the heavy demands made upon them." [47] The south Italian experience had simply not prepared immigrants to function effectively as industrial workers.

The Italians' choice of seasonal outdoor labor, even if it meant long winters of unemployment, stemmed from personal concerns as well. Many immigrants feared that they might contract pneumonia, rheumatism, or tuberculosis, diseases of tragic consequence for Italian families. Working during Buffalo's merciless winters predisposed them to such long-term illnesses, and

[45] Interview, Buffalo, April 16, 1973.

[46] De'Rossi, "Le donne ed i fanciulli," p. 11; Korman, pp. 65ff., observes the same tendency in Milwaukee.

[47] Williams, pp. 30, 32.

poor living standards made the immigrants highly susceptible. The anxieties which family men felt about year-round work, therefore, were not entirely unrealistic.

Furthermore, the established citizens in Buffalo tended to project ethnic stereotypes upon Italians which prevented those who sought indoor work from obtaining it. A 1920's survey of employers in the industrial and mechanical trades affirms this suggestion. Some immigrants implied that the slight Italian physique disqualified them from these jobs,[48] but manufacturers did not offer this excuse. Employers stated that they found Italians unsuitable for "inside" jobs or shop work. With some justification, they thought these immigrants preferred and excelled in outdoor occupations, notably in building, street work, and farming. Three claimed that Italians simply did not like the "hot work" of Buffalo's mills and blast furnaces. Another put it more plainly—they are not, he said, "foundry men." Still another was disgruntled by their tendency to "desert *en masse*" for outside work in the spring, a complaint echoed by employers in other cities. Two manufacturers complained that injured Italians loafed and demanded high compensation awards. Commenting on what he believed to be their temperamental qualities, one employer found Italians "very excitable;" another declared them "so susceptible to the opposite sex that they could not satisfactorily be employed . . . especially with girls of their own nationality." Finally, most employers claimed that men of Italian and Polish backgrounds could not get along in work situations. In these instances, they preferred to use Polish workers.[49]

A comparison of Italians with other immigrant groups who more easily entered the Buffalo factories produced revealing results. Employers considered the Polish men heavy drinkers, agitators, and overly anxious for holidays; but like employers in other industrial cities, they preferred them to Italians. They

[48] Interview with Vincent De Bella, Buffalo, April 20, 1973.

[49] Employers' attitudes towards Italians are described in Niles Carpenter, "Nationality, Color, and Economic Opportunity in the City of Buffalo," *The University of Buffalo Studies*, 4, No. 4 (Buffalo: University of Buffalo, 1927), 108ff.; Korman, p. 45, documents Milwaukee employers' complaints that Italians were itinerant, lazy, quarrelsome, and overly fond of liquor.

characterized Negroes as gamblers, inclined to take days off, but nevertheless capable of doing hard "hot work." All the employers favored the Germans, whom they described as good, skilled workers able to get on with all other ethnic groups. The Irish, also considered good workers, were thought well qualified for supervisory positions.[50]

A closer look at the Italian labor force at the beginning of the twentieth century confirms the somewhat impressionistic evidence of restricted opportunities. Census figures indicate a bottom-heavy class structure and little evidence of upward mobility (Table 1). A small upper class, 1 percent of working-age first-generation males, headed the occupational hierarchy. Macaroni manufacturers, who exploited Buffalo's importance as a grain port, and produce merchants, who profited from the city's location near northwestern New York's fruit belt, were in this elite group.[51] Little Italy's most successful entrepreneurs benefited from their Italian experience. The Mezzogiorno was, after all, an important fruit- and grain-producing center. Real estate dealers in this elite group sold homes in the Italian quarter to Italians; doctors, lawyers, and a few bankers and businessmen served the expanding needs of the immigrant community and established their reputations within its confines. A whole spectrum of occupations—financial, business, industrial, public, and institutional administration—were not represented in the Italian upper class. Little Italy's most successful men owed their achievements to expertise obtained abroad or to the tastes and needs of the ethnic community. Very few distinguished themselves in the world outside the ghetto.

Only 12 percent of the male working-age population were small shopowners by 1905. Italians achieved middle-class status, then, through property acquisition, not through education. Most of this group of small entrepreneurs fulfilled their dreams of acquiring property by investing in shoe repair or tailor shops. The most prosperous of this group served the native population. Vincent De Bella, shoemaker and proprietor of a shop catering

[50] Carpenter, pp. 108–110; Korman, p. 68, indicates that Milwaukee employers also believed Poles to be good factory workers.

[51] Augello, p. 37.

Table 1. Age and occupation of Italian-born males, 1905

	Age								
Occupation	15–19	20–29	30–39	40–49	50–59	60–69	70–79	Percentage in each occupation *	Number in each occupation
Officials, professionals, semiprofessionals	3	16	15	15	2	1	0	1	52
Manufacturers, wholesalers, contractors, bankers, real estate dealers	0	6	10	3	3	1	1	less than 1	24
Small retail shopowners	24	93	145	90	49	17	3	12	421
Clerical and sales	18	19	8	8	2	1	0	2	56
Skilled workers	46	130	91	74	34	8	1	11	384
Personal service workers	60	77	26	17	5	2	0	5	187
Laborers	236	816	693	391	258	49	10	69	2453
Percentage in each age group *	11	32	28	17	10	2		100	
Number in each group	387	1157	988	598	353	79	15	Total	3577

* Figures are founded to the nearest percent.
Source: New York State Manuscript Census, 1905.

to non-Italians, offered a simple explanation for his achievements: "People could accept an Italian as a shoemaker. It was an 'Italian job'." He exhibited a sharp consciousness of the ways in which American attitudes subtly dampened dreams and limited achievement for more ordinary immigrants. De Bella, himself a well-educated, trained craftsman, observed: "An American woman once said to me: "You are not a shoemaker, but a cobbler.' " "A cobbler," De Bella chided with a dignity unabated by fifty years of serving clients insensitive to preindustrial attitudes toward craftsmanship, "is one who repairs shoes, but I was trained to make shoes. . . . I was a shoemaker. . . . My shop to me was like a temple." The more typical Italian shopkeepers—butchers, grocers, bakers, liquor dealers, and confectioners—achieved petit bourgeois status within the ghetto by relying on immigrant tastes and traditions.

The lower echelons of the occupational hierarchy, men with no property investment or formal education, included 87 percent of working-age males. Skilled workers headed this group. Even though a small shop required only a minimal cash outlay,[52] most skilled workers lacked the means to acquire one. The majority were employees in tailoring, shoemaking, and building enterprises, trades locally associated with Italians. Clerical and sales personnel belong to this group simply because they did not have the education normally associated with white-collar employment. The majority were actually street vendors or men who worked in Italian-owned stores, usually for some relative. Most personal service workers were barbers without their own businesses. Barbering was also recognized as an "Italian occupation" in Buffalo, and Italian barbers, like local shoemakers, appear to have dominated their craft.[53] The majority of adult Italian-born males (69 percent) were, of course, unskilled laborers working in the outdoor, seasonal occupations already described.

Census returns confirm that Italians did not enter the rapidly expanding industries, replace older immigrant groups in semiskilled jobs, and eventually follow them up the occupational lad-

[52] Interviews with Vincent De Bella and Thomas Angelico.
[53] Banchetti, p. 24.

der. Neither is there any evidence of serious job competition between Italians and other ethnic groups; indeed, by 1905 the Italians were already confined to and identified with certain occupations within the working class. This restriction of movement even across lower occupational levels obtained well into the 1920's. A sample of 10 percent of the households headed by second-generation males in 1925 revealed that time, language, and literacy skills did not significantly alter this pattern.[54] The unskilled and uneducated sons of immigrants repeated their fathers' careers in building, general labor, and service occupations. They found new opportunities in transportation, driving taxis and trucks, but not in Buffalo's growing steel and auto industries.

The pattern of limited mobility up the occupational ladder, established in 1905, also continued throughout the 1920's. Although some intergenerational upward mobility occurred, by 1925 mobile second-generation sons had not achieved the status of small entrepreneurs carrying some title to property, which their parents had coveted. Most became salesmen, clerks, electricians, and printers.[55] A survey of Buffalo and its industrial suburbs in 1927 revealed that Italians could not obtain high-ranking executive positions; only a few had secured ordinary white-collar jobs[56] In the late 1920's Little Italy was still predominantly a working-class community.

Neither the immigrant generation nor its children conformed to the American ideal of occupational success. But they had their own standard of achievement, namely, the acquisition of family property, usually a home. And in this sense by the 1920's Italians and their children in Buffalo had indeed reached the promised land. Thousands had become homeowners, often sacrificing their children's education and career prospects to do

[54] NYSMC, 1925. [55] Ibid. (based upon a 10 percent sample).

[56] Carpenter, surveyed more than 14,000 men and women workers. He established a probability scale on which first- and second-generation Italians ranked zero in terms of high ranking office and managerial positions. The comparable figure for native whites born of native parents (based upon an index of 1.0) was .07; for the Irish, .04; for the Germans, .03; for the Poles, .00. The probability of first- and second-generation Italians obtaining ordinary office jobs was also .00; the comparable figure for the native whites born of native parents was .06; for the Irish, .03; for the Germans, .01; for the Poles, less than .01.

so.[57] Economically pressed Italians had to make this trade-off, and their choice was entirely consistent with their familistic mentality.

Other characteristics of the Italian immigrant population, including length of residence, age, family status, and commitment to remain in the United States, also contributed to its particular career patterns and to its poor occupational performance. A lack of interest in remaining in the United States could be the key to the immigrant generation's undistinguished occupational achievement. The immigrants' determination to own property only rarely manifested itself in practical business terms. Many Italians originally intending to return to their homeland saw no point in investing the amount of time required to establish a business. Though large sums were not necessary, the 1905 Buffalo census data confirm that establishing even a small business within Little Italy was not a quick enterprise; only 12 percent of its shopkeepers managed to do so within five years.[58] And education for the professional standing which so few Italians acquired demanded an even longer investment.

Length of residence, citizenship status, and the decision to bring a family here or to create one after arrival can be used as indices of commitment to remain in the United States. The length of time an Italian male resided in the United States related directly to his achievements in Buffalo.[59] More than half the unskilled laborers had been in the United States five years or less by 1905; at the other extreme, only 4 percent of the manufacturers, wholesalers, contractors, bankers and real estate dealers declared so short a residence. The youthfulness of the Italian population makes length of residence a somewhat deceptive measure of intention to remain in the United States. Like most immigrant communities, Little Italy had a large proportion

[57] This point is developed fully below in Ch. 6.

[58] See the author's Ph.D. dissertation (under Virginia Yans McLaughlin), "Like the Fingers of the Hand: The Family and Community Life of First-generation Italian-Americans in Buffalo, New York, 1880–1930" (State University of New York at Buffalo, 1970), pp. 32ff, for tables detailing the following discussion of residence, citizenship, and other immigrant characteristics.

[59] NYSMC, 1905.

of young people (see Table 1). In every occupational category a minimum of 25 percent were in their twenties or younger; and about half of the unskilled wage earners and three-quarters of the personal service workers, the lowliest occupational ranks, belonged to this age group. This heavy concentration of young men helps explain the unexceptional career records of the Italians in Buffalo—an argument that is borne out when the most accomplished groups (the manufacturer-wholesalers and small businessmen) are studied. The percentage of young people in these categories was relatively low. Time, age, and experience enabled these men to prove themselves, but unless they had been committed to settling in the United States, they would not have earned the benefits.

The correlation between citizenship and job mobility is less significant because by 1905 more than half of the men in each occupational category excepting unskilled laborers were American citizens. Nevertheless, Little Italy's most enterprising men—its property owners and investors—were more likely to be citizens. Only 36 percent of the unskilled laborers had declared citizenship, despite the fact that the city required citizenship papers for such unskilled outdoor jobs as garbage collection.[60] Since citizenship is one of the most certain indications of a person's intention to remain, the relatively low percentage of laboring men who declared it further confirms that the intent to return affected occupational status negatively.

The data on family status and migration patterns reinforce the suggestion that when people transferred their aspirations to the United States, their level of achievement rose. By 1905, Little Italy had already become a community of families. Except for the personal service workers, more than half the Italians in each occupational category had wives or wives and children with them. But the most prosperous—the property-owners and investors—were much more likely to be family men than unskilled laborers and personal service workers.[61] An analysis of

[60] Banchetti, p. 24.

[61] Eighty-five percent of the manufacturer-wholesaler group, 77 percent of the small entrepreneurs, 54 percent of the unskilled laborers, and 35 percent of the personal service workers had wives or wives and children living with them in 1905.

all first-generation Italians in 1900 indicated that of the men holding higher ranking occupations almost none were forced to come to the United States without their families. Crafts and professions learned in Italy made it possible for these men to bring their wives and children with them when they emigrated; on the other hand, men of lower status more typically left families behind.[62]

The decision made by professionals, businessmen, and skilled craftsmen to emigrate with their families or to bring them later indicates a commitment to the new land. The category of unskilled workers, likely to be single or temporarily detached from families left abroad, contained a higher percentage of transients—men more concerned with current wages than future careers. Many were temporary migrants or originally conceived of themselves as such. If the attitudes of employers and the restricted occupational opportunities locked three-quarters of all immigrant males in the ranks of Buffalo's unskilled labor force, at least their hopes of returning to the homeland made that position more bearable.

Most newly arrived immigrant men competed poorly in America's urban job market. In many cities the immigrant families attempted to supplement their breadwinners' wages with contribution from wives and even children. Buffalo—a rapidly growing industrial center, with increased markets for consumer goods and personal and domestic services—provided some work for women and children, but its developing concentration upon heavy industrial production did not create ideal circumstances for an immigrant family seeking its livelihood. Although the proportion of women employed and the demand for female labor were increasing, there was a much greater demand for unskilled immigrant males. Illiterate, unskilled, non-English-speaking women could find work in this metropolis, but other cities provided more varied and expanding opportunities. The 1910 statistics for nine industrial cities with populations of a hundred thousand or more indicate, for example, that—excluding the census category of "miscellaneous manufac-

[62] United States Federal Manuscript Census, 1900, Buffalo, New York (hereinafter referred to as *USFMC*, 1900).

ture"—Buffalo had only five manufacturing categories employing three hundred or more women. Boston had eight; Chicago, thirteen; and New York City, seventeen. Cleveland, a city closer in size to Buffalo, had eight.[63] Although the proportion of employed women had expanded by 1930, Buffalo maintained one of the lowest percentages of the nation's great cities. Only Erie, Pennsylvania, Youngstown, Scranton, and Pittsburgh—centers of heavy industrial production and transportation—trailed behind.[64]

The 1910 and 1920 figures for occupations employing a thousand or more women further reveal long-term occupational options for unskilled females. The employment categories which maintained a relatively stable demand over this ten-year period were store clerks, saleswomen, and domestic servants; the demand for literate, educated female employees steadily increased. Opportunities for bookkeepers, cashiers, accountants, schoolteachers, and nurses enjoyed an increase of 50 percent or more; positions for clerks, stenographers, typists, and telephone operators expanded 100 percent or more. As clothing and textile production became mechanized, one of the largest employers of immigrant women—non-factory dressmaking—declined almost 50 percent.[65]

Women in Buffalo could not turn confidently to the homework trades either. New York City contained the bulk of the state's homework industry, including clothing, artificial flower, and paper box manufacturing. Thousands of immigrants, especially Italians and Jews, labored in these trades in other New York State cities, but relatively few found work of this type in Buffalo. The New York State Factory Investigating Commission

[63] *Thirteenth Census*, IV, *Occupational Statistics*, 152–193.

[64] The percentage of employed women fifteen years and over in selected cities with populations over 100,000 was as follows: for 1920, Buffalo, 5; Boston 9.9; Chicago, 10.4; New York, 9.6; Cleveland, 9.6; Erie, 4.6; Scranton, 2.6; Pittsburgh, 6; Youngstown, 5.1. For 1930 comparable percentages are: Buffalo, 8.7; Boston, 10.8; Chicago, 14.6; New York, 11.8; Cleveland, 14.1; Erie, 8.4; Scranton, 4.6; Pittsburgh, 8.3; Youngstown, 7.3. Source: *Fifteenth Census, 1930*, IV, *Occupations*, 81.

[65] Young Women's Christian Association, pp. 9ff.; *Fifteenth Census, 1930*, IV, *Occupations*, 1088ff., clearly demonstrates the increasing demand for domestics.

reported that in a typical year, 1912, Buffalo claimed only seventy-two out of almost twelve thousand homework licenses. The little homework that did exist was distributed by firms throughout the Niagara Frontier area, so that Buffalo had no monopoly even on these small operations.[66]

In brief, after 1910 Buffalo offered fewer and fewer opportunities in tenement work and the non-factory clothing industry, which had been the important initial employers of peasant women and children entering urban labor markets.[67] Thousands of foreign-born and second-generation women could do laundry work at home; thousands more still worked as seamstresses in non-factory settings; and working-age women could always find work as domestics. In 1910, more than 60 percent of women working outside their homes in unskilled, semiskilled, or service occupations chose this employment. Within this group foreign-born women (42 percent) were almost as heavily represented as native-born women (58 percent). In that same year, unskilled second-generation women seeking outside employment, especially those between the ages of sixteen and twenty, preferred other options, notably factory positions. Clothing manufacture, semiskilled tailoring, laundry operations, silk, soap, and box manufacturing, and the printing and publishing industries were the most popular.[68] If language disability and child care prevented mothers from taking these jobs, the second generation was not so hampered.

The first-generation Italian women and their children adapted themselves to this job market in their own peculiar way. When they worked, they did so only part of the year; the light indus-

[66] New York City had 11,691 homework licenses. New York State, *Second Report of the New York State Factory Investigating Commission, 1913*, I (Albany, 1913), 94 (hereinafter referred to as *FIC*). See also Jeremy Felt, *Hostages of Fortune: Child Labor Reform in New York State* (Syracuse, 1965), p. 143; Charity Organization Society of Buffalo, N.Y., *23rd Annual Report, 1899–1900*, pp. 95–106; *Second Report, FIC*, II (1913), 12–13, 709, 711; see also *Preliminary Report, FIC*, II (Albany, 1912), 770.

[67] Joan W. Scott and Louise A. Tilly, "Women's Work and the Family in Nineteenth Century Europe," emphasize the importance of domestic work, home industry, and light manufacturing as initial entry points into the urban-industrial labor force for women from traditional peasant cultures.

[68] Derived from *Thirteenth Census*, IV, *Occupational Statistics*, 543.

tries such as clothing, textile, candy, and paper box manufacturing were all highly seasonal. Truly enterprising women seeking year-round wages could become domestics; but the Italian women were more likely to take in boarders because the men rarely permitted their wives to work as maids, cleaning women, or factory hands. The Italian ideal was to keep women at home.[69] So the majority of women and children who worked took advantage of another part-time occupational opportunity: every summer hundreds became migrant laborers and traveled to the Niagara Frontier's fruit-, vegetable-, and grape-growing areas to harvest or process cannery crops. Once again, this was strictly seasonal work, which minimized the gap between Old and New World experiences by offering short-term employment in a semi-agricultural occupation; the women and children thus employed never worked full-time the year round.

If the Italian families maintained their traditional ways, Buffalo's peculiar occupational structure and the place Italians occupied within it do much to explain this fact. It is true that male unemployment created difficulties for these families; but the available options limited the possibilities for new family work patterns and concomitantly for new family strains. It would have been harder to retain the traditional relationships had the city forced entirely new occupational modes upon these families. Any explanation of the parallels in family life between Italy and America must stress the similarities in the family's economic position in both places.

Yet economic opportunities and class position did not by themselves determine family work roles. Within this large, complex metropolis, Italians still had some choices of employment, and their cultural attitudes and Old World experiences had much to do with the decisions they made. The Italian woman's decision to forego readily available domestic work in middle-class homes is the most striking example of this. Culture, then, acted as an interface between family and economy, dictating which options were acceptable and which were not. This com-

[69] Bernardy, "L'emigrazione delle donne," p. 13; Walter Goodale, "The Children of Sunny Italy," *Express*, Oct. 15, 1905. This point is fully developed in Ch. 8.

plex interaction between family, work, economy, and culture suggests that we must revise our standard assumption that immigration to cities and new urban-industrial work routines inevitably disrupt traditional family relationships. If this situation occurred in other American cities, Buffalo's occupational structure did not require it and the Italians perceived other alternatives.

2 New Wine In Old Bottles: Family, Community, and Immigration

Several brothers and cousins followed Francesco Barone when he left in 1887 for America; together they formed a chain of migration from the small town of Valledolmo. Orazio, one of the first relatives to follow Francesco, emigrated ten years later at the age of thirty-seven with his wife Frances and three children. Eleven years after that fifty-two-year-old Richard Barone settled in Buffalo with his wife and three children. By 1905, Richard had retired securely; his children could support him if need arose. Still other Barone brothers and cousins came: James, his wife, and two children arrived twelve years after the trailblazing Francesco. Another Orazio and his wife settled in Buffalo two years later. The following year Frank arrived with his wife and children. Next came John, Michael, Louis, Thomas, two Josephs, Anthony and finally, yet another Orazio; most of them chose to bring their wives and children with them rather than sending for them later.[1]

Only two clan members, Tony and Anthony, had not been joined by their families in 1905. Tony rented in a boarding

[1] These branches of the Barone family are located in NYSMC, 1905, which indicates relationships between household members only. Other sources confirmed kin ties among the Barones. Mrs. Isabella Iannuzzi (interview, Buffalo, April 16, 1973), a relative, identified the Buffalo Barones as related kin from Valledolmo. Other sources confirm that Barone helped his relatives to immigrate; see, for example, Patricia M. Gorman, "The Life and Work of Dr. Charles R. Borzilleri" (unpublished thesis, D'Youville College, 1967), Borzilleri's wife was Barone's sister; Barone helped her family to immigrate.

house; Anthony joined the Nonataro family, contributing his regular food and rent payments to the household budget. Working as unskilled laborers, Tony had been in Buffalo three years, Anthony, two. They were young men in their twenties, and they had not yet established roots.

Not all the Barones achieved Francesco's success. Two brothers, Joseph and Anthony, worked as unskilled laborers. These siblings helped each other considerably during the immigration and settlement period. The first to come, Joseph, encouraged his brother's family to join him, and they arrived within a year. Neither had the special skills required by Buffalo's commercial, shipping, or industrial enterprises. Each had come with a wife and two children. Within three years, Joseph and Anthony each had two more children. Both families struggled and needed help. In this strange new city, who else could be counted upon but one's own blood? The brothers cooperated, renting one of Buffalo's many two-family homes and perhaps dreaming of purchasing it together one day.

John Barone, his two married children, and their families also cooperated. They shared the same household, but for different reasons from Joseph and Anthony. Sixty-year-old John and his sons had all come to the United States together. In 1905, John was an unemployed widower, but his married sons, watchmaker Louis and grocery clerk Joseph, brought their father into their home. Another son, a musician, contributed to his support and to the joint household budget. Less fortunate families aided each other in different ways. The older Orazio Barone and his wife waited ten years before they could help their son and his family join them, but the younger Barones found an apartment reserved for them in the overcrowded tenement which housed their parents.

This extended family's history raises important questions about people on the move. Is immigration from country to city always a traumatic and disorganizing experience? Are families always severely disrupted by such an event? Or did kinship ties, as the history of the Barone clan suggests, tend to ease the adjustment to the city by supporting the families in transition?[2]

[2] The destructive effects of immigration and of city life upon the extended family were enumerated by Louis Wirth in his classic "Urbanism as a Way of

Before approaching these questions, it is important to stress the limitations of the historical sources used to answer them. Manuscript censuses are employed here because they permit the reconstruction of certain aspects of family life—notably household formation and, to a lesser degree, family ties within neighborhoods.[3] These were not the only or even the most significant forms taken by kin relationships. The sustained informal kin relationships underlying household and neighborhood formation concern us here, but the psychological evidence—sources indicating how people perceived their kin and what such relationships meant to them over a period of time—normally eludes historians. Definitive statements on such qualities of family life cannot be inferred solely from census data fixed on one point in time; nonetheless this information, supported by other sources, can be used to hint at a possible range of human experience.

This evidence tells us that kin played an active part in both immigration and settlement. More sustained reciprocal relationships—sharing residences, becoming neighbors, aiding in education, and finding jobs or spouses—suggest a continued mutual support. From the beginning, economic, normative, and sentimental attachments all played a part. Economics figured more importantly in the early days; established Italian-Americans could afford the luxury of sentimental and ethical considerations. As the Italians migrated and settled in Buffalo, they developed elaborate and extended family ties. Their experience negates the conventional view of a number of historians that the "extensive family of the Old World disintegrated." [4]

Life," *American Journal of Sociology*, 44 (July 1938), 11. Among others, Handlin continued this tradition. Eugene Litwak denies that industrialization and geographic mobility preclude extended family cohesion in "Occupational Mobility and Extended Family Cohesion," *American Sociological Review*, 25 (1960), 9–21, and "Geographic Mobility and Extended Family Cohesion," ibid., 385–394.

[3] This chapter draws heavily upon John S. MacDonald and Leatrice D. MacDonald, "Chain Migration, Ethnic Neighborhood Formation, and Social Network," *Milbank Memorial Fund Quarterly*, 42 (1964), 82, who discuss family and chain migration.

[4] See Handlin, p. 205; Michael Anderson, *Family Structure in Nineteenth Century Lancashire* (London, 1971), pp. 8ff. and 42ff., discusses both economic and normative bases for extended family cohesion.

Like the Barones, many Italian families immigrated to northwestern New York to join relatives or village friends. These might be adopted relatives, or *compari,* ritual godparents whose formal functions consisted of religious guardianship for a baptized child, although the bond actually served to cement secular relationships between the child's parents and the godparents.[5] A local immigrant who joined his grandfather and cousins in 1906 recalled: "Immigrants almost always came to join others who had preceded them—a husband, or a father, or an uncle, or a friend. In western New York most of the first immigrants from Sicily went to Buffalo, so that from 1900 on, the thousands who followed them to this part of the state also landed in Buffalo. There they joined friends and relatives who in many cases had purchased the tickets for their steerage passage to America. After they arrived, guided and assisted by their friends and relatives, they ventured out of the city of Buffalo." [6] In 1910 Buffalo's Italian consul also emphasized the role of family and friends. "The moment an Italian immigrant arrives," he reported, "he is received by parents or a countryman who give him their support and help him get work. Generally, it is parents or very good friends who have the means to migrate here." [7]

The Italians who had arrived in Buffalo purchased hundreds of tickets for family members still in Italy; a small number bought their tickets overseas so that by the early 1900's approximately twelve to fifteen hundred Italians, directly depending on Buffalo family contacts, were entering the city annually. Immigrant banks helped thousands to save thirty or forty dollars for each relative's fare.[8] By the turn of the century a chain of

[5] S. W. Mintz and E. R. Wolf, "Ritual Co-parenthood" in Jack Goody, ed., *Kinship* (Middlesex, England, 1971), pp. 346–361, discuss this theme.

[6] Alessi, "Italians to Chautauqua County," p. 5. [7] Banchetti, p. 24.

[8] "Italians in Buffalo," *Express*, Aug. 27, 1901 and Richmond C. Hill, *Twentieth Century Buffalo*, p. 71. On immigrant banks see Beth Stewart, "Rapid Fire Rises of Buffalo Italians," *Courier*, Jan. 7, 1923. In 1904 the cost of transport from Naples, a typical departure point for many Buffalo Italians, was $26; from Palermo costs were $26 to $29. Including the trip from New York City, the entire cost was $35 to $40. See Banchetti, p. 24. Children and infants received substantial reductions; see steamship line advertisements, for example, *IC*, July 9, 1905.

migration from south Italy to Buffalo had been well established.

A columnist writing for *Il Corriere Italiano*, Buffalo's most important Italian-language newspaper, emphasized how these sustained migration chains also contributed to the formation of city neighborhoods: "Suppose he [the male immigrant] comes alone. Invariably, the wife, the sister, the brother, are soon to follow. Not infrequently the aged parents respond to entreaties to come to this great and glorious land. Here, then, we have the family. Bonds of kinship and the peculiarity of their language soon bring the families together into colonies, and often in our cities we find whole streets made up of Italian residents." [9] Buffalo's Little Italy, a mosaic of provincial clusters, was composed largely of families and individuals like the Barones who chose to settle near kin and *paesani*.

In the late nineteenth century, families from a few north Sicilian coastal towns began to dominate the important west side colony.[10] Originating on the extreme southwest corner of Main Street, by 1922 it extended from Niagara Street's northern tip westward to the waterfront. Buffalonians designated this area "Little Italy" because the immigrant social and cultural life centered here. Less important settlements also developed. Natives of Basilicata, Calabria, and Campania occupied areas farther south and east. In the 1890's when Campobasso's children worked on a railroad extension to neighboring Cheektowaga, they established their own east side neighborhoods. Abruzzesi and Marchesi settled farther north. The former, grave-monument carvers, chose this convenient location on East Delevan Avenue to be near a major city cemetery. Natives of Lom-

[9] Norman N. Britton, *IC*, Sept. 19, 1905.

[10] Magnani, *La città di Buffalo*, p. 24, provides a chronology of settlers by province. On the location of provincial clusters see Goodale, "The Children of Sunny Italy," and letter to Dr. Stephen Gredel from Charlotte I. Claflin, Oct. 16, 1961, Buffalo Historical Society, Letter File; also see Ferdinand Magnani, "Italian Population in the History of Buffalo," *Catholic Union and Times, Centenary Edition*, June 26, 1931; "Buffalo's Little Italy," *Express*, May 24, 1891; "The Italian Colony in Buffalo," *Courier*, May 8, 1898; Beth Stewart, "Buffalo's Italians Hold High Banner of Civic Pride," *Courier*, Dec. 31, 1922; Lucian Warren, "Thrift, Labor Mark Italian Rise Here," *Courier*, Nov. 17, 1940; "From Abruzzo to Buffalo," *Express*, May 25, 1908; Stewart, "Rapid Fire Rises of Buffalo Italians."

bardy, Romagna, Piedmont, Tuscany, and Lucca also formed settlements. Over the years as the west side colony expanded north and south, population turnover occurred just as it did in other cities.[11] By the 1930's some of the Italians had deserted their provincial clusters for suburbia, but most remained in their inner city neighborhoods. Until mid-century, when urban renewal destroyed much of the lower west side colony, the underlying family, village, and friendship ties maintained their hold within these city neighborhoods.

Such informal social networks, combined with neighborhood facilities and economic considerations, channelled the Barones into Buffalo's Little Italy. Italian-American institutions—church, school, bank, stores, and restaurants—had their own drawing power. Limited finances forced immigrants into low-rent districts like the lower west side.[12] Transportation costs could be saved by living near places of employment on the west side: the rail and freight yards and city docks. If more than one family member worked, the savings could be considerable. Settled relatives, *compari,* and friends who shared the newcomers' culture and language helped in many ways during immigration and settlement—searching for jobs or indicating nearby markets for pasta, red peppers, and romano cheese. Personal feelings also influenced a new arrival's place of residence. When she was reluctant to leave Italy, Marion Callendrucci's husband assured her that she could get along in Buffalo. "He told me I could get together with his sister."[13] Settling in a provincial neighborhood made emotional and practical sense to immigrants who were confronted for the first time by loneliness and the day-to-day problems of city life.

The important role that extended families played in this settlement process can best be understood within the context of past experience. After all, immigrants left the Mezzogiorno with a specific familial outlook and, while the past does not always determine future behavior, people facing a crisis like migration often seek to ascribe some familiar meaning to the world around

[11] On Chicago, see Nelli, *Italians in Chicago*, p. 49.

[12] Edward De Forest and Lawrence Veiller, eds., *The Tenement House Problem*, I (New York, 1903), p. 121; "When Canal Street Saw Its Palmy Days," *Courier*, March 23, 1902, p. 31. Housing is further discussed in Ch. 4.

[13] Interview with Marion Callendrucci, Buffalo, April 17, 1973.

them. In this case, immigrants put their Old World family ties to novel uses in America.

The society which these peasants left behind is frequently termed "familistic" because the nuclear and extended family, rather than the individual or the community, dominated social life to such an extent that an individual's primary social role was his or her role in the family. He or she might be mayor, teacher, or laborer, but each of these roles had to give way to that of husband, father, wife, mother, or child whenever a conflict existed.[14] Less concerned with the larger social world or the roles within it, peasant morality placed family before communal responsibility. Family honor (*onore di famiglia*)—a sentiment which contributed significantly to kin solidarity and to clan feuds—further defined these family boundaries.[15] South Italians resolved the potential conflicts between family and other personal ties by means of the institution of *comparraggio,* which incorporated friends into the family by making them ritual godparents (*compari*).[16]

Kinship ties were extremely significant in the Mezzogiorno, but there immediate family loyalties often took precedence. When the situation demanded, the original family unit kept to itself and governed its own affairs. A proverb expressed the southern attitude well: "Christ minds His own business." [17] The extended family, a loosely structured constellation, occupied itself more with social functions. Its obligations were typically (although not always) limited to defense of family honor and attendance at baptisms and other family rituals. In Niccopurto, Sicily, for example, it played no part in major decisions except to give advice on proposed marriages. The decisions to emigrate, to educate, or to seek employment were all made by immediate family members.[18]

The southern hill-town homes, usually one- or two-story

[14] J. Davis, "Morals and Backwardness," *Comparative Studies in Society and History,* 12 (July 1970), 345.

[15] Covello, "Italo-American School Child," 242–243.

[16] Vecoli, "*Contadini* in Chicago," p. 406.

[17] See Constance Cronin, *The Sting of Change: Sicilians in Sicily and Australia* (Chicago, 1970), pp. 50–51, 59ff.

[18] Disagreement exists over the character and importance of extended family relationships. See Cronin, pp. 24ff.

structures shared with animals, housed only the conjugal unit. In the Mezzogiorno as in many other peasant societies, scattered holdings, divided inheritance, and insecure land tenure offered little incentive for extended family households.[19] Instead of incorporating relatives into their homes, overburdened peasants hired laborers when extra work had to be done. The heavy emphasis upon single crop production made seasonal hands more economical than a permanent labor force composed of related kin in one household. These circumstances explain why the nuclear family household typically prevailed in the South. The infrequency of expanded households deserves emphasis simply because historical myths claim that immigration destroyed them.[20] This could not be true if they had rarely existed to begin with.

The extended family, then, performed social, not economic functions; and even its social obligations were minimal. There were some exceptions. In Reggio Calabria, MacDonald observed "nuclear family solidarity plus relatively strong identification with and participation in cliques of certain relatives . . . [and] friends (especially *compari* and *comari*)." These cliques cooperated to form chains of migration to foreign locations.[21] In such communities helping relatives to migrate became a family obligation.

If in most instances the extended families concerned themselves only with ritual and social obligations, why did they ex-

[19] H. J. Habakkuk, "Family Structure and Economic Change in Nineteenth-Century Europe," *Journal of Economic History,* 15 (1955), 6, and Conrad Arensberg and Solon Kimball, *Family and Community in Ireland* (Cambridge, Mass., 1940), discuss this phenomena in other peasant societies. The following document the predominance of the nuclear household in the Mezzogiorno: Edward Banfield, *The Moral Basis of a Backward Society* (New York, 1958), p. 144, provides recent figures for "Montegrano," Basilicata; Joseph Lopreato, *Peasants No More: Social Class and Social Change in an Underdeveloped Society* (San Francisco, 1967), p. 142, provides similar figures for contemporary Franza, Calabria; Donald S. Pitkin, "Land Tenure and Family Organization in an Italian Village," *Human Organization,* 18 (Winter 1959–1960), 170, offers nineteenth-century figures for Lazio in south central Italy; see also MacDonald and MacDonald, "Institutional Economics and Rural Development," pp. 114–115; Silverman, "Agricultural Organization," provides the basis for much of the following discussion.

[20] See, for example, Handlin, pp. 10, 13, 229–230.

[21] Letter from J. S. MacDonald to Edward Banfield cited in Banfield, p. 88n.

pand their operations during immigration and settlement periods? The successful migration chains, frequently offering material help as well as advice and encouragement, are best understood as elaborations of already established family connections. The process involved was complex; the suggestion that immigrants packed kinship ties along with their meager belongings and shipped them to America is too crude. Yet economic aid and other favors did not emerge as something entirely new, instituted after the immigrants' arrival in the city. Because the quality and kinds of commitment to kin varied regionally, general explanations referring to past experiences are suspect. Some villages already had active kin networks engaged in a variety of tasks; these were easily adapted to support migration chains. In other instances, the immigration crisis pushed more restricted social networks in new directions and assigned them new functions. In both cases, the links that already existed between relatives or *compari* were now expanded to include other kinds of aid.[22]

Anthropological studies indicate that kin bonds based upon blood or ritual adapt readily to particular historical contexts. The original religious basis of godparenthood, for example, expands to secular areas—to enhance relationships between parents and godparents, to provide social and economic aid, and to ensure social controls. In times of rapid change such as immigration, these adaptations seem to represent a "community's unconscious effort to answer new problems."[23] If the New World the immigrants confronted seemed hopelessly confusing, these informal social networks provided stability and security by strengthening social ties outside the immediate family. Whereas community involvement in Italy might have been insignificant, in the New World the creation of such networks involved relatives, friends, and neighbors in interdependent relationships which frequently permeated entire Italo-American neighborhoods.

[22] Such adaptations of the *compare* bond are discussed by Jack Goody, "Forms of Pro-parenthood: the Sharing and Substitution of Parental Roles," *Kinship*, p. 338.

[23] Goody, "Pro-parenthood," p. 358.

The Italian past provided other resources wholly consistent with this new kind of localism. Here etymology offers some interesting examples. Peasants in Italy frequently called anyone outside the larger kin group *forestiero* (stranger): in urban America, anyone outside the tightly knit Italian neighborhood could become *forestiero*. The immigration crisis caused more extreme adaptations. In the Mezzogiorno terms such as *paese* (meaning anything from nation to town) or *villaggio* (small town or village) had spatial rather than social connotations.[24] But in the anonymous American city, far from the homeland, the word *paesano* came to connote much more than someone born in the same geographic location; an emotional bond was implied. From an anthropological standpoint, the formation of provincial neighborhoods is quite understandable and provides a basis for exploring the larger social life. American opportunities permitted formerly impossible kin relations to become real or, for natives of some Italian villages, ideal kin relations to become possible. Immigration's pressing difficulties provided incentives for short-term aid. Kin, once only witnesses at rituals or protectors of the family honor, assumed new roles in Buffalo. They became housing, ticket, travel, and employment agents, and sometimes emotional advisors and moral censors, too. The immigrant experience infused old forms with new content—new wine in old bottles.

Once immigrants settled in Buffalo, the extended family ties expressed themselves in several new ways. Such cultural adaptations could not have survived unless they continued to fit New World conditions and fulfilled some vital need. For example, while joint residence rarely existed in the Mezzogiorno, Buffalo immigrants used it as a form of reciprocal aid. In 1905, twenty years after the heavy in-migration had begun, more complex family units existed, although most of the households were still nuclear. Of more than two thousand families, 88 percent were simple nuclear families living alone. So high a percentage is not unusual, as an independent unit of this type would more readily adapt to geographic mobility.[25] The remaining 12 percent of all

[24] Covello, pp. 240–241.

[25] In each of the surveys listed in n.19 at least 85 percent of the households were nuclear. If the 1905 Buffalo figures are related to the only comparable

households were expanded: 9 percent of the first-generation households included some relative of the husband or wife, usually a widowed parent or an unmarried sibling; 2 percent were stem households containing parents and their married children; 1 percent were joint households consisting of married siblings and their families.

The proportion of complex households was not large. A surprising number of studies indicate that it was the norm in both urban and rural communities.[26] But a sensitive reading of the census data should warn us against drawing conclusions too hastily. Even a normal percentage of extended households, depending upon the form they take, is impressive in a new immigrant community. Few immigrant households contained aging parents because old age and poverty forced many relatives to remain abroad. Middle-aged adults approaching the autumn of their lives abandoned their Italian homes only hesitantly to begin life anew in Buffalo. Like many immigrant communities, this one had more than its normal share of young couples in their twenties and thirties just beginning married life, many of whom had not yet produced children. These demographic peculiarities explain why three-generation households including grandparents and grandchildren were rare.

Crude census figures tend to underestimate the efforts of some immigrant families to extend themselves. The number and variety of reciprocal relationships occurring over the whole period of immigration are in fact greater than the 1905 census figures allow us to observe. Relatives had died or moved out of the host family household; their number is undetermined. If the criteria for household organization are modified to include coresidence at the same address, the proportion of extended house-

---

study based upon a compilation of historical data—the south central Italian village of Sermoneta in 1847—there is one difference: Buffalo had a slightly higher percentage of expanded, stem, and mixed joint households. (12 percent for Buffalo and 10 percent for Sermoneta in 1847.) Data is from NYSMC, 1905, and Pitkin, "Land Tenure and Family Organization," p. 170. This is the only significant change in household arrangements when Buffalo data are compared to pre-migration Italian figures. The south Italian data are neither plentiful nor typical. Some of it, for example, does not apply to the deep South.

[26] For a discussion of historical and sociological studies, most of which find roughly 10 percent expanded and 90 percent nuclear households, see Anderson, pp. 2, 44.

holds climbs to 16 percent. And if we include households with boarders, many of them *compari*, then the percentage climbs to 26 percent. The actual proportion of expanded households was almost certainly higher. The coresidence figures are underestimated simply because married daughters and sisters also shared homes with their original families. Their number cannot be determined because the manuscript census does not list maiden names, but other sources indicate that Italians saw the benefits of this practice. Grandmothers sitting on front stoops, gossiping, knitting, praying, and scolding and minding grandchildren along with general neighborhood business were a common feature of Little Italy's landscape.[27] If they did not share their daughters' homes, many lived nearby.

The increased percentage of complex households further proves that the immigration crisis did create new family obligations. At the very least, immigrants continued to help members of their households adjust to city life. A detailed consideration of stem family households provides one example of how these families helped one another in practical ways. About a quarter of the younger nuclear units in these households had no children or had only begun their own families, whereas most of the older families had already completed their child-rearing duties.[28] Obviously, the more established parents sought to help children who were just beginning married life. Until legal ordinances forbade overcrowding,[29] older and younger families found it economically beneficial to share living and rent expenses, even if only temporarily. In Italy, where peasants had little land to pass on to their sons, the coresidence of parents and married offspring had served no function and created heavy burdens. In Buffalo, the opposite was true.

Additional evidence suggests that the new situations encouraged new and longer-term commitments to kin, which extended beyond the initial crisis of settlement. Some immigrants, for the first time in their lives, had enough money for survival,

[27] "Buffalo's Little Italy," *Illustrated Express*, May 4, 1902.

[28] NYSMC, 1905. Of the 34 children present in the younger families, 14 were under 5; only a quarter of the older families had unmarried children.

[29] City of Buffalo, *The People of Buffalo*, p. 29.

perhaps even money to invest. They involved themselves in economic relationships with relatives that required sustained obligation. The emotional values in which some immigrants could now afford to indulge determined their relationships to kin.[30] A few examples will illustrate these points. Relatives who were employed could contribute their wages to a scanty household income, thus permitting some families to save. Although few achieved such dreams before the 1920's, homeownership and the inheritance of a house were now real possibilities for these families.[31] And they adapted their kin ties accordingly. The Ferranti family is a case in point. Explaining how his family acquired their own home, Richard Ferranti said: "Two brothers-in-law bought the house; the two families cooperated." [32] Even when the chance of owning a home remained remote, other living arrangements bound families together. A dwelling or apartment shared with relatives spread the family expenses. Mr. and Mrs. Angelico shared a flat with her parents from the time of their marriage. "No trouble. No arguments," said Mrs. Angelico. "It was hard to get a house." [33]

Other considerations were also operating, of course. Providing a home or a job for an unemployed relative—perhaps the aged, widowed parent whom a son had encouraged to immigrate—added to the economic strain, but such close kin could not be expected to fend for themselves in a strange land. Again the Ferranti family gives an illustration of family help patterns. Richard Ferranti, owner of a soda-bottling business, employed his own relatives. "We were all friends," he said, "and helped each other in business." Ferranti's mother initially financed his business, "to help her son," he said. "A lot of people tried to help their children in this way." By hiring relatives, Ferranti recognized his mother's generosity and attempted to repay her favor.

[30] Anderson, pp. 8ff., 165, calls this a transition from "short-term calculative" to "normative" kin relations, usually made possible by economic improvement.

[31] Although Hill, *Twentieth Century Buffalo*, p. 71, claims that by 1902 many Italians were homeowners, more reliable sources contradict this opinion. See, for example, *Twelfth Census, 1900, Population*, II, P. 2, p. 751. Homeownership is discussed in Ch. 6.

[32] Interview with Richard Ferranti, Buffalo, April 16, 1973.

[33] Interview with Rose Angelico, Buffalo, April 16, 1973.

In this way, family ties supported the Ferranti family business activities.

Although many Italians still expected to return home in 1905, individual and *padrone*-sponsored migration by then had dwindled in importance. The census listed only 9 percent (651) of first-generation Italian men as "roomers" or "boarders," most of them unskilled laborers. Almost always recent arrivals,[34] many had not yet committed themselves to sending for a family or establishing an American-based household. "Sometimes," immigrant housewife Mary Sansone recalled, "the boarders would stay for a very short time, sometimes for two or three years. Then they would send for their wives. The boarders were men seeking work where they could find it, so they would go from place to place. Sometimes they would go to *paesani* who would help them find work." But these men were more than marginally attached to the local community. Three-quarters (507) lived with a family, in many instances with relatives or *compari*.[35] "Many people," Mrs. Sansone tells us, "had boarders in their house at one time or another. They came from the same town. They didn't want to get in with the wrong kind of people."

If a family could not ask newly arrived relatives into its already overcrowded household, it referred them to friends with more living space. In turn, such references provided the host families with a security that would have been unobtainable in more anonymous neighborhoods lacking personal ties. Because most boarders were single men in their teens and twenties or married men not likely to remain long, their presence was tolerable to host families. Although an alternative—the urban boarding house—existed, even the young and unattached rarely opted for it. Very few families found it necessary to live in boarding houses until they had established roots. The fact that so many could bypass rooming houses again indicates how strongly personal ties between adults used in novel ways cemented this community together. By 1905 these Italians had es-

[34] Eighty-four percent had lived in America five years or less and only 13 percent had declared citizenship. Source: NYSMC, 1905.
[35] NYSMC, 1905.

tablished a personal, familial community. They intended to settle down and get on with their lives.

Other patterns substantiate these assumptions. Early in the century family, rather than individual, migration had become the predominant form. The census classified almost 90 percent of Italian-born residents in Buffalo as family members. More and more men sent for their wives and children, and many families migrated as whole units.[36] More than two thousand natural families included in the 1905 manuscript census reported sufficient information to explain underlying migratory patterns. About half (1021) had migrated together; the rest (1096) had not.[37] Because early Italian immigration is frequently described as a movement of unattached men, so high a percentage of migrating families is unusual. Considerable family and social stability already existed roughly twenty years after the great movement to Buffalo had begun. An explanation for this relatively rapid settlement is not simple. Why did so many families take the risk of coming together rather than assume the more

[36] NYSMC, 1905. Ninety-one of the unit-migration families and 64 of the non-unit-migration families were broken in 1905. Because many of the following calculations characterize both husband and wife, only unbroken families are described in discussions of unit- and non-unit-migration unless otherwise specified. The discussion on household formation is not included in this generalization because it considers households, not families.

This data was originally analyzed and census accuracy discussed in Appendix I of Virginia Yans-McLaughlin, "Like the Fingers of the Hand." Sampling errors were corrected whenever possible for data contained in this book.

[37] This figure refers to broken *and* unbroken families. The 1905 manuscript census data on families not migrating as a unit include a few cases in which children preceded parents and an undeterminable number of couples not actually married in Italy by the time emigration commenced. The 1905 census does not provide needed information to ascertain their exact number. The most we know is that 14 percent of these couples (143) were not married, because the wife lived in the U.S. longer than her husband (or because she was born in the U.S. or another foreign country). Italians rarely chose this migration style. The 1900 Federal Manuscript Census, which does describe family migration patterns, confirms this assumption. Only 4 of 546 non-unit-migration families in that cohort had wives preceding husbands. We can extrapolate further from that cohort to estimate the accuracy of the 1905 data. Thirty-one percent of the 1900 couples not emigrating together were not actually married when emigration commenced; 11 percent married on arrival; 58 percent left Italy married. This suggests that the 1905 figures overestimate the proportion of non-unit-migration couples actually married when emigration commenced.

conventional pattern of husband first, wife and children later? The immigrants themselves tell us that this serious decision depended heavily on friends and relatives already in Buffalo who supplied advice and encouragement. "We knew where to go in America because we had cousins and friends here." "My parents had friends here." [38]

Household formation patterns tell us more about both the nuclear and the extended family style of migration. About half of all family households (1,135) had one relative who preceded the others to America. A few of these households formed after all members had immigrated, but the remaining cases say much about the methods relatives used to help one another. Because most Italians lived in nuclear households, we can learn a great deal about their genesis, but a study of the more complex households shows how and why more distant relatives got help.

Who were the first Italian-born household members to come to America and what sort of person helped others to migrate? Eighty-one percent (916) of the earliest migrants were husbands and fathers in their twenties and thirties who by 1905 had established or sent for their families. The wives of family heads represented the next largest group, 12 percent (139).[39] Because Italian mores forbade it, few women traveled and settled in America without their husbands or a chaperone. So deeply engrained was this attitude that it found lyrical expression in a popular Italian folk song:

> "Mother, mother, give me a hundred lire
> For to America I want to go."
> "I won't give you the hundred lire
> And to America no, no, no!"

[38] Interviews with Frank Iannuzzi, Buffalo, April 16, 1973 and Thomas Angelico.

[39] NYSMC, 1905. The proportion of males who actually initiated immigration is probably slightly overestimated. See n. 42 in Ch. 3. Households containing brothers and sisters living without their parents are included in this discussion. They represent 3.5 percent of the Italian population (275). One-third of these had been in the U.S. longer than their siblings, whom they probably helped to come. However, they could have been sons and daughters of deceased parents. The parents, not they, could have initiated family migration. It is not possible to determine which alternative is correct.

"If you don't let me go to America,
Out of the window I shall jump."
"I won't let you go to America,
Better dead than dishonored."

Her brother is at the window:
"Mother, mother, let her go."

. . .

"Go ahead, evil daughter,
May you drop in the deep, deep sea!"

The girl eventually left for America and drowned at sea.[40] Perhaps heeding this song's warning, less daring single girls tended to emigrate to Buffalo only to marry a particular young man.[41] Most of these women who had lived in America longer than their husbands had not actually initiated family migration. They had either arrived with first husbands who had since died or, more likely, they had come with their own original families. Unmarried or widowed relations—sisters, brothers, aunts, uncles, and various in-laws—rarely began households; rather, established families welcomed them as homeless newcomers and as lonely relatives temporarily separated from their loved ones.

The initiators were a stable group, individuals who determined quite early to settle down in America. Three-fourths of them had been in the United States at least seven years (having arrived in 1897 or before). A large proportion had become citizens: 65 percent of the men and 72 percent of the women. Even though declaration of citizenship may have been a tactical maneuver to obtain public employment or a street-vending li-

[40] Folk song "Mother, Give me a Hundred Lire," transcribed by Carla Bianco in Roseto, Pennsylvania, and quoted in *The Two Rosetos*, (Bloomington, Ind., 1974), p. 37.

[41] The marriage announcements in *IC* provide many instances of brides and grooms giving the same address as their respective residences. Consensual marriages and illicit love affairs were rare among Italians. Therefore, these represent instances of men who sent for their future brides, whom they immediately married and took into their homes. See, for example, the marriage licenses in *IC* for 1908. Bernardy, "L'emigrazione delle donne," pp. 7–8, noted that Italian girls rarely immigrated to the U.S. unaccompanied by some relative, unless they were certain that some relative or friend would provide security and housing. Unlike Irish and Scandinavian women, she claimed, they came to America for personal and family reasons, not to earn a living.

cense—two occupational categories popular with Italian males—so high an overall percentage for men and especially for women suggests a permanent commitment to the new country. The first men to arrive had not risen spectacularly in the employment hierarchy; their occupational distribution hardly differed from that of all male family heads. Even though most had been in the country at least seven years, the majority (64 percent) still worked as unskilled day laborers.[42] So occupational success as measured by a higher-status job played a minor role in their decision to establish families or to bring relatives to Buffalo. Other considerations must have induced them to act as initiators. The fact that they had established households and sent for their wives and children indicates a commitment to remain in the United States. As settled married men with wives, they could provide the simple hospitality of a home for relatives or friends. Further, they could expect to benefit from these personal ties; the economic burdens of supporting a family encouraged invitations to newly arrived relatives because they contributed toward the household expenses.

Who were the "outsiders," those who were welcomed into established households? In 1905, 4 percent (473) of all related individuals living in Italian households enjoyed such hospitality. Because the census does not specify *comparraggio* relationships, discussion is restricted to blood ties. Siblings or brothers- and sisters-in-law, parents, parents-in-law, and sons-and daughters-in-law were the most heavily represented; these immediate collateral relatives of the household head and his wife were the most likely to receive help regardless of when they came.[43] Only a few more distant relatives (male cousins, nephews, nieces, aunts, and grandmothers) got aid. In a few cases, an entire family joined the host household to form the stem and mixed joint families mentioned earlier.

Immigrant families admitted kin into their homes, whether permanently or temporarily, for several reasons. Many new arrivals got temporary help until they became oriented to their new life. This does not explain the presence of some 15 percent of relatives who were born in the United States; however, 61

[42] NYSMC, 1905. [43] Ibid.

percent of all Italian-born relatives had been in the United States two years or less.[44] Probably only some 39 percent, then, were taken into these households on a long-term basis. Feelings of charitable obligation explain why some families offered their relatives homes—a large number of unemployed women who made no financial contribution to their host families fell into this category. Employed people who had been city residents for some time but without immediate families of their own helped to defray household expenses; but a charitable impulse toward unattached relatives also explains their presence. Several motivations, then, among them social obligation, charity, sentiment, and economic considerations, explained the continuation of expanded households long after migration.

Did the host families wish to help relatives, to be helped, or to engage in a relationship of mutual benefit which might continue on a permanent basis? In households containing relatives who had migrated after the head, aid in migration and settlement undoubtedly constituted an important consideration. But relatives who came before the household head obviously did not receive this type of aid; they either donated money toward the household expenses or relied upon their hosts for support. Those who came to the United States at the same time as the household head could have represented a mixture of these motives. Any working relative, regardless of years spent in America, could contribute to the household budget; but recent arrivals were more likely to receive financial or other aid than any other group. The largest group of foreign-born relatives (48 percent) entered the United States after the foreign-born head of their household; 24 percent entered before; and 28 percent at the same time. These migration sequences confirm the earlier impression that chain migration and aid in settlement played a major part in shaping the expanded household patterns.[45]

Relatives without families (usually brothers or brothers-in-law in their teens and twenties) received help in immigrating and

[44] Ibid.

[45] Ibid. Only 380 relatives, not 473 are analyzed in the discussion of relatives who came before, after, or at the same time as the household head because 73 relatives were American-born and some household heads were not born in Italy. Both cases involve second-generation Italians who do not concern us here.

settling and joined their hosts primarily for this reason. These men, like the single boarders, were considered visitors. Other relatives lacked the resources to increase the family budget; indeed, many unemployed and widowed mothers and older female relatives added to the family burden. Some provided child care, but since Italian mothers rarely left the home to work, such help was not usually necessary. Most complex households expanded to provide homes for needy relatives, and the most likely candidates for help were the very young and inexperienced and the very old and poor.[46] The former stayed only temporarily, while the latter indicated a more serious commitment.

Most expanded households had been involved in the immigration process in some important way, yet the census data provide only a snapshot of family patterns at one historical moment. Set the image in motion and a panoramic view of Italian neighborhoods laced together by hundreds of personal bonds and mutual experiences emerges. If kinship ties strengthened the formation of ethnic neighborhoods, coresidence with relatives, *compari*, or *paesani* added another level of interaction. Its effects continued even after separate residences were established. Other personal negotiations reinforced the sense of interdependency as this immigrant community matured. The earlier immigrants often assisted their friends and relatives to find employment in construction and dock work, where jobs were frequently obtained through personal contact.[47] Their help also included such simple intangibles as advice, encouragement, and companionship.

Practices requiring an even greater commitment and responsibility reveal persistently strong family and provincial ties reaching out beyond the city itself to Italians who settled in other Niagara Frontier towns. Festivals, village and religious celebrations represented common occasions for reunion.[48] Furthermore, the individual stories of various successful Italians from Buffalo stress that they counted upon their *paesani* for educational aid. Once a person had completed his schooling, *paesani* could also be relied upon to provide him with a clientele,

[46] NYSMC, 1905. [47] Interview with Frank Iannuzzi.

[48] See, for example, *IC*, March 23, 1907 and Aug. 10, 1909.

especially for professional men. Horace Lanza came originally from Valledolmo when he settled in Fredonia (outside Buffalo) with his family. Valledolmesi helped him to become a successful lawyer-politician in Buffalo's Italian colony. To repay his obligation to his *paesani*, Mr. Lanza in turn helped their sons enter the profession; he gave advice and encouragement to many and employed some as law clerks in his office.[49]

The family of young Dr. Frank Mammana, originally Buffalo settlers and later Fredonia residents, provides another example. They sent their son to medical school in Buffalo, certain that he would be assured of the company and support of their countrymen there. The presence of family and friends in Buffalo reassured other parents from surrounding towns who sent their children to the city's colleges in the 1920's.[50] And because *paesani* and relatives lived all over western New York, a professional man could move from one town to another, or establish a practice in more than one place. This made it possible for Dr. John Ragona to transfer his office from Niagara Falls to Buffalo in 1906. For similar reasons, Buffalo lawyers Frank Miceli and Russell Borzilleri, of Valledolmo families, successfully established their office in nearby Rochester in 1909.[51]

The marriage licenses published in Buffalo's Italian press confirm that the region's Italians maintained a very high level of interaction; such unions represented efforts to marry *paesani*, for most of the out-of-towners were natives of the same towns from which Buffalo's Italians had emigrated. The marriage registers of the city's principal Italian church revealed the same endogamous pattern.[52]

Impressionistic evidence suggests that active kin networks extended even beyond the Buffalo area. Families maintained

[49] See, for example, the biographies of Michael Montesano, *IC*, June 10, 1916, and Nicholas Grisani, *IC*, June 19, 1920.

[50] For Dr. Mammana's biography, see *IC*, June 19, 1920; see also the biographies in *IC*, May 31, 1913, and the biography of Dr. Horace Lo Grasso, *IC*, July 23, 1924.

[51] *IC*, Jan. 13, 1906 and Jan. 16, 1909.

[52] See, for example, the marriage licenses in *IC*, for 1908. A 10 percent sample of the 1909–1919, 1920, 1925, 1928, and 1930 marriage registers of Saint Anthony of Padua Church revealed that one-fifth of all marriages involved individuals from the same town; intraprovincial rates were higher.

bonds with relatives in the Pennsylvania coal fields, where experienced Sicilian miners settled. These ties gave an important flexibility to immigrants who were struggling to adjust to American labor conditions. Both Mary Sansone and her husband had relatives in Buffalo and in Pennsylvania. When a Pennsylvania strike left Mr. Sansone unemployed, the family moved to Buffalo, where they lived with relatives until they could establish their own home. After a few years in the city, another strike forced the Sansones back to Pennsylvania. The cycle repeated itself and the Sansones finally made Buffalo their home.

The immigration network was not solely a one-way operation from Italy to Buffalo; many people wished to return one day to the Old World. Indeed, such expectations kept family sentiment alive. Italians had one of the highest return rates of all immigrant groups. Although the Buffalo community had stabilized by 1905, until the 1924 restriction act limited the number of single male migrants allowed to enter, the men flowed in and out of Buffalo. Many hoped to save enough to establish vineyards or wine shops in the Mezzogiorno. Some gained experience in work of this kind in the Buffalo area and wished to profit from it; [53] others returned only for visits. Advertisements in the local Italian press encouraging men to purchase a thirty-dollar ticket for a Christmas trip home confirm the feasibility of such visits.[54] Many people returned to see their relatives, and the local Italian press reported banquets celebrating these trips. A native of Montemaggiore Belsito, for example, returned to visit his "adored mother, his dear sisters, and his affectionate brothers." At a banquet in Buffalo, *paesani* asked him to deliver greetings to their families.[55] Such rituals provided important spiritual bonds with family and friends when physical presence was not possible. The continued ties with those left abroad must have reinforced familial interaction with relatives in America:

[53] On the temporary nature of Italian immigration see Foerster, *Italian Immigration,* pp. 29ff., see comment by Joseph Lunghino quoted in Catherine McGee, "What Have the Italians Done for Buffalo?" *Sunday Times*, Sept. 4, 1927; interview with Dr. Russell Borzilleri in *IC*, Sept. 3, 1921; Hill, *Twentieth Century Buffalo*, p. 71; "Buffalo's Little Italy," *Illustrated Times*, Jan. 4, 1903.

[54] *IC*, Nov. 22, 1902. [55] *IC*, June 6, 1903.

those who helped here might some day wish to return, when their efforts would be appreciated and probably repaid.[56]

This intricate pattern of relationships should dispell many traditional notions of first-generation immigrant family life. "Disorganization" and "withdrawn nuclearity" hardly seem appropriate descriptions of the family behavior of Italian immigrants. Actually, the difficulties attending on immigration and settlement in industrial cities provided opportunities for people to use their extended family ties in new ways.

As we have seen, the new needs and conditions all fostered cohesion, dependency, and interaction.[57] Immediate family members frequently remained in Italy. Neighbors and friends might help, but blood and *comparraggio* bonds carried heavier commitments with greater stability. Perhaps these became more important because so few alternatives existed, especially in periods of crisis. The language barrier and limited occupational contacts rendered relationships with outsiders both unlikely and complicated. Charitable institutions and other middle-class organizations demanded prices for their services that most Italian immigrants were unwilling to pay.[58] Again, their shared class background and common experiences in the local job market created mutual feelings of social similarity which added another layer to family interaction. And the cash required for rent, home, and business ownership created further demands for kin support. Finally, the Italians in Buffalo had few residential options; most lived in ghetto areas, where kin were highly accessible, likely to be neighbors, and likely to know and need one another.

The presence and visibility of kin and *compari* in congested ghetto neighborhoods provided other supports for families on the move. The frequency and meaningfulness of personal contact facilitated the moral consensus and social controls sorely needed in an unsettled community. Immigrants convey the im-

[56] Anderson, pp. 158–159, discusses the possibility for reciprocation in Lancashire, where shorter distances divided relatives.

[57] See Anderson, pp. 168ff., and Elizabeth Bott, *Family and Social Network* (London, 1971), pp. 102ff., for discussion of factors encouraging family cohesion.

[58] This point is fully developed in Ch. 5.

pression that the ghetto neighborhoods provided a social stability which was very supportive and extended beyond immediate family life. "It was always friendly in my neighborhood," said Richard Ferranti, "We didn't have any trouble." "In the neighborhood I lived in," according to Frank Iannuzi "everybody knew everybody else. We were very close to one another. We were very friendly with each other. If anybody did something wrong, we'd all run. . . . You had high respect for the families."

Although some Buffalonians characterized Italians as lawbreaking and hostile, others agreed with the immigrants' assessment of their own neighborhoods. In the 1890's, insisting that Italians themselves had low crime rates, one reporter blamed outsiders for most crimes committed in the quarter. Thirteen years later, a local doctor who worked extensively among Italians claimed that these "morally . . . high" people were "fast getting control of . . . [Canal Street] . . . once famous as America's toughest thoroughfare. . . . A woman can now walk through this section of town with impunity. The same cannot be said of the lower part of Main Street which is infested with tramps and panhandlers of all nationalities." [59]

One of the difficulties with any argument connecting family stability to neighborhood cohesion is that urban historians claim to have discovered high rates of population turnover and geographic mobility within American cities. They base their arguments for high turnover upon the large proportions of individuals who cannot be traced over time from one census to another or from census to city directory. But if we trace a sample of Buffalo Italians from 1905 census to 1907 directory it would caution us against conclusions based upon record linkage of this kind. Because a large proportion of individuals could not be traced, the Buffalo sample appeared to confirm considerable movement within the same neighborhood and possibly outside the city; yet a closer look at the evidence determined that what appeared to be a high population turnover resulted from typical

[59] "Italian Colony in Buffalo," *Courier*, May 8, 1898. The doctor, Walter Goodale, makes his comments in "Children of Sunny Italy."

inaccuracies in census and directory data.[60] Obviously, if such data are suspect, we must seriously question those studies which used them as evidence for the unsettled character of urban populations.

But suppose that Italians and other inner city residents were indeed highly mobile. The question then becomes what did geographic mobility actually mean in terms of family relationships? The earlier discussion of regional intermarriage, of individual careers, and of continued communication with Italy suggests that it did not always matter very much, even when long distances were involved. Kinship and friendship networks continued to operate. In fact, geographic mobility may have rendered the family more rather than less important. Perhaps immigrants did not evolve a sense of community attached to place and neighborhood. Family, more than place or community, would have become the major focal point of their social existence, not only for the stable core of residents but also for the transients. Informal networks, after all, operated to bring immigrants into urban places, to help them settle, to find work.

[60] The group of Buffalo Italians traced consisted of a 10 percent sample of all nuclear family heads listed in NYSMC, 1905. These were checked against the *Buffalo Business Directory*, 1907. Thirty-seven percent of these family heads could be traced to the same or a new residence between 1905 and 1907; 3 percent could not be traced accurately because the directory listed too many individuals with the same name; 60 percent either left the city or were not listed by the directory, which is much too high. I would argue that a large proportion of this group did not actually leave, but were lost because of census or directory inaccuracies. Census-takers, who usually had no knowledge of Italian, spelled names inaccurately or phonetically. These names are then spelled differently in the city directory making it impossible to trace large numbers of Italians. The directories also make frequent spelling errors. Upon occasion Italians Anglicized their names—Francesco Chiesa became Frank Church or even Frank Rielly—without, however, legalizing the change. (A check of name change records in the Erie County Clerk's office showed that only legal transactions such as adoption or incorporation brought Italians to the courts to obtain *de jure* recognition of name changes.) Add to these difficulties a tendency for directories to omit laborers and the high figure of 60 percent unaccounted for over a two-year period begins to make sense. In my opinion what appears to be a high population turnover in this sample is a result of poor data. Nelli, pp. 49ff., and Thernstrom and Knights, "Men in Motion," argue for high population turnover. Nelli uses precinct lists and directories while Thernstrom and Knights rely on censuses. All of these sources are subject to the same inaccuracies.

These networks did not pass over the transients; indeed, one of their chief functions was to bring them into the city. If these suggestions are valid, historians will have to reassess their current notion that geographic mobility necessarily implies rootlessness, anonymity, lack of any possibility for developing class consciousness, and a weakening of family cohesion.

Were the Barone clan and other large families like them typical in their successful efforts to bring many relatives—both immediate and distant—to the city; and can we extend the findings of this chapter to other working-class groups? To date, one study of Italian data provides instances of successful chains from Italy to major American cities, including, incidentally, evidence of a chain from Termini Imerese, Sicily, to Buffalo.[61] American sources on Italian immigrants have provided instances of successful chains only. If census data are used, it is obvious why this is so. Families such as the Barones, those who succeeded in setting chains into motion, appear in the sources; those who failed, the most elusive ones, do not. For this reason any study which relies chiefly on American sources introduces a bias. The unsuccessful families are not accounted for, and it is not possible to estimate the frequency of successes and failures.[62] If current sociological findings are any clue, however, there is every reason to believe that, although they might differ in degree, vigor, and duration, ethnic groups of many types developed similar kinship networks in American cities.

The typicality or statistical recurrence of the Barone clan's experience is not itself the key issue; the adaptive process it illus-

[61] Briggs, "Italians in Italy and America," p. 94.

[62] Banfield, p. 88, reports, for example, that Montegrano had heavy outmigration to the United States and Argentina before 1922. Extended family ties, he argued, were not strong enough to support chains of migration. Relatives in Montegrano hoped for aid in immigration, but never received it. Were the Montegranese typical? Social life in this Italian town, according to two of Banfield's critics, was "atomistic," probably more so than in most of the Mezzogiorno. But the same scholars, noting the "precarious" nature of the multilateral kinship system in south Italy, do acknowledge cases of "broken chains" among south Italians in their own research on Australia. See MacDonald and MacDonald, "Chain Migration," p. 91. In fact, the strength of extended family ties in south Italian communities and the successful continuation of chains of migration from these towns are directly related. See letter to Edward Banfield from John MacDonald quoted in Banfield, p. 88n.

trates is. The evidence indicates that many immigrant families engaged in some part of that process; many more were touched by it. The close-knit localized networks which resulted enhance our understanding of immigrant behavior. Layer upon layer of interaction among relatives, *compari*, and *paesani* provided a security or insurance system for families; bonds between them created a personal sense of community. And this diminished need for contact with outside agencies slowed down the process of family change. Members of the close-knit, homogenous community shared values and ideologies that were reinforced by frequent interaction; and the Italian-American institutions, especially the Catholic church, added to the pressure for homogeneity. This consensus in social values acted as an effective means of social control. It also helps to explain why the nuclear family adjusted so effectively to conditions in the New World.

3 Families on the Move: The Nuclear Family and Immigration

We know that family relationships structured the Italian immigration and settlement in Buffalo. But how did these events actually affect the family? The Italian experience challenges the conventional notion that immigration disrupted primary family relationships—the nuclear family adapted readily, for example, to the immigration crisis, to new urban life styles, and to the problem of male unemployment.

If we are to understand the patterns of adjustment which occurred in Buffalo, we need first of all to understand the family relationships and traditions that immigrants had experienced before their arrival.

The Italian peasant considered marriage a sacred, liftetime bond; and the law, the Catholic church, and the community all supported this belief. Men usually made their commitment in their twenties, girls in their middle or late teens. A Sicilian proverb's advice reflected this practice: "L'uomo di ventotto; la donna diciotto" ("The man at twenty-eight, the woman at eighteen").[1] Although occasional separations occurred, the attitude toward divorce indicated the South's family orientation: the sanctity of marriage and family took precedence over individual unhappiness. Women assumed a heavy responsibility for marital success, as can be seen from the attitude toward American

[1] Interview with Rose Angelico.

divorce. The people of Milocca, Sicily, made no secret of where they thought the blame for broken marriages lay. When Columbus went to America, they said, he found "flowers without fragrance, food without flavor, and women without love." Men were also expected to contribute to marital success as diligent breadwinners and serious husbands. Italians tolerated the double standard in the premarital period: "For a man every mortal sin is venial, and for a woman every venial sin is mortal." [2] But the marriage vow carried expectations of fidelity.

Some priests complained that the long absences required of the husband by immigration and his search for work put a great strain on the marriage, but infidelity was still an exceptional occurrence.[3] Both adultery and illegitimacy, as violations of *onore di famiglia* (family honor), met with severe treatment.[4] The male family members were responsible for protecting female chastity and a woman's desirability as a future wife; [5] indeed, the family honor stood invested in a girl's virginity. Usually women did not leave their homes unchaperoned. A woman's behavior reflected both her moral character and her family's prestige—brutal vendettas followed insults to her. The strict surveillance continued through the courtship period, so that husband and wife found themselves alone for the first time on their wedding night.[6]

Cultural convention permitted husbands and fathers to dominate family affairs, and led them to expect strict obedience. The economic and family roles were strongly related, but the male head's superior status did not depend entirely upon his ability to provide. Neither seasonal unemployment and underemployment—which were, after all, normal conditions of peasant life—nor daily and sometimes longer absences from home

[2] Charlotte Gower Chapman, *Milocca: A Sicilian Village* (Cambridge, Mass., 1971), pp. 109, 41.

[3] Italy, *Inchiesta Agraria*, 13: 368ff.

[4] Leonard W. Moss and Walter H. Thomson, "The South Italian Family: Literature and Observation," *Human Organization*, 18 (Spring 1959), 37.

[5] Covello, "Italo-American School Child," p. 313.

[6] William F. Whyte, "Sicilian Peasant Society," *American Anthropologist*, 46 (Jan.–March 1944), 71; MacDonald, "Italy's Rural Social Structure," pp. 447–448; Covello, pp. 302–307.

seriously undermined his position.[7] A Sicilian study characterized the husband's expectations: his "authority in the house is final and there is no official redress to his commands." [8]

Mothers and wives performed the usual functions of childbearing and household supervision, although in fact their husband's day-long absences from home brought them additional responsibilities and decisions in these areas partly by default. Nonetheless, a wife's authority in all household affairs remained subject to her husband's, despite his absence. Yet the south Italian family was not a stereotypical partriarchy. Two anthropologists have characterized it as "father-dominated but mother-centered"—a delicate balance of wills. The women were by no means totally subservient, and they did not unquestionably submit to their husbands' desires.[9] Even the usual description of wives who are publicly submissive but privately dominant is an oversimplification. If a woman's private behavior with her husband was, according to convention, submissive and respectful, "under this guise she . . . [might be] doing things which no wife should do." [10] An Italian proverb further testifies to the mother's importance: "If the father should die, the family would suffer; if the mother should die, the family ceases to exist." [11]

Anthropologists claim that the cultural traditions of southern Italy may explain the unusually high prestige enjoyed by these peasant women. In many areas, the peasants inherited ancient Roman patterns, including matrilineal descent and female property rights. In Sicily, women enjoyed particularly high prestige and several female prerogatives. A woman's dowry and property remained her own after marriage and became her children's, not her husband's, after death. Some of the wife's responsibilities such as household management and control of her husband's earnings (while he received only an allowance) could also be popular survivals of ancient traditions.[12] Such cultural

[7] Moss and Thomson, "South Italian Family," p. 40; Covello, pp. 302–307.
[8] Cronin, *Sting of Change*, p. 104; Moss and Thomson, p. 38.
[9] Moss and Thomson, p. 38; Covello, p. 377. [10] Cronin, p. 72.
[11] Moss and Thomson, p. 38.
[12] Covello, pp. 331, 336, 349; Williams, *South Italian Folkways*, pp. 76–77.

traits expressed themselves even more clearly late in life when the male family members could not depend upon their wage-earning function as a basis for power. After retirement the men experienced a relative decline in authority and the wife's power grew proportionately.[13]

The peculiar significance which mother-son ties traditionally assumed also helps to explain the prestige of women. Instead of emancipating themselves as sons do in most western cultures, Italian sons still typically maintain close relationships with their mothers. Some authorities emphasize the "madonna complex"—strong male identification with the mother—as further support for the woman's authority,[14] while others point to the peasants' understanding of human conception as a possible limit on male domination. They believed the male's role to be one of merely "agitating the woman's capacity to induce conception." [15] Thus the combination of social values that gave priority to the family, of a work situation that necessitated male absences from home, and of extremely tenacious ties between mother and son all contributed to the woman's prestige. Luigi Barzini summed it up well: "Men run the country but women run men." [16]

In the premigration era, the people of the Mezzogiorno consistently maintained high birth rates. The average *contadino* family had six to ten children. Poverty proved to be no deterrent: the poorest families, those of the *giornalieri* or day laborers, tended to have the largest number of offspring. Since most peasants possessed little land of their own, the wish not to divide inheritances played no role in discouraging large families. And an unsophisticated knowledge of contraception is enough to explain the birth of many children.[17]

[13] Covello, pp. 303–308, 378; Moss and Thomson, p. 38.

[14] Anne Parsons, "Is the Oedipus Complex Universal," *Magic and Anomie: Essays in Psychosocial Anthropology* (Glencoe, 1969), pp. 44ff.; Cronin, pp. 77ff.

[15] Covello, p. 331. [16] Luigi Barzini quoted in Cronin, p. 83.

[17] Covello, p. 355. From 1881 to 1914 southern birth rates ranged from 40.5 to 33.4; comparable northern rates were 30.5 to 36.2. See Associazione per lo Sviluppo dell'Industria nel Mezzogiorno, pp. 61ff. On the demographic situation, see Clough and Levi, "Economic Growth in Italy," p. 350; and Hildebrand, *Modern Italy*, pp. 287ff. See also Foerster, *Italian Immigration*, p. 96; and Paul

The peasant distrust of the Catholic church meant that its influence on the family remained limited. Peasants regarded themselves as Christians, but they were not good Catholics in any ordinary sense. Few understood Church doctrine; few felt committed to the Church as an institution; and fewer still gave financial support. Because men rarely attended church services, religious influences operated most directly upon the women. A proverb emphasizes the degree to which men withdrew from such associations: "The women and the old folks are for the Church: we look after our own business." The Church did support popular family norms, and the concepts of family solidarity, male superiority, female submissiveness—even the vendetta; but most peasants looked to their own folk religion and mores for guides to behavior. These, rather than the Church's moral influence, controlled individual action and enforced "adherence to traditional folk ways governing family life." [18]

The peasant families also distrusted the South's few existing charitable institutions, and considered reliance upon them undignified. During crises, relatives might offer support; but their refusal was not censured by the community even though legal restrictions prevented those with families from entering the poorhouses. Neighbors might be more generous when deaths, funerals, or marriages occurred, but they were not motivated by any long-term sense of obligation. Sometimes villagers cooperated to protect the honor of a poor family lest a bad example should be set for others.[19]

Once in Buffalo, the immigrants conformed closely to their traditional notions of correct family behavior. The census data describe clear patterns of stability, and family migration histories show that despite the temporary break-ups often required by immigration, many Italian families were determined to reconstitute themselves in Buffalo. But what do this and other ex-

---

Campisi, "The Italian Family in the United States," *American Journal of Sociology*, 53 (1947–48), 444.

[18] Moss and Thomson, pp. 25–41; Covello, pp. 264–267; Rudolph J. Vecoli, "Prelates and Peasants: Italian Immigrants and the Catholic Church," *Journal of Social History*, 2 (Spring 1969), 217–268, discusses both folk religion and the Church.

[19] Williams, p. 73; see also Cronin, p. 62, and Covello, p. 282.

amples of family cohesion really mean? The statistical data allow us to analyze form, when ideally a discussion of both form *and* content is required. Statistics can show us that families were structurally sound without explaining their internal psychological dynamics. Families can remain or pull themselves together; this does not prove they do so free of tensions and conflict. Despite these reservations, it is important to establish that these Italian families were in fact structurally cohesive. Such evidence contravenes the conventional descriptions of immigration's disruptive impact upon the family. And, because the family is the primary socializing agent, it would be difficult to understand how Italians could have carried on their old cultural patterns or developed new ones without it.

The case for family stability and persistent traditions rests upon several critical areas: the absence of broken homes within Little Italy, a low incidence of illegitimacy, conservative migration and marriage patterns, and the negligible effects of immigration upon family size.

The commonly accepted indications of family "pathology" among the urban poor are a "casual" attitude toward marital relationships, a high male desertion rate, and the presence of many households headed by women.[20] Each of these standards is appropriate for our families because they also represent breaks with the Italian cultural norm. Family breakdowns resulting from male desertion are generally viewed as a product of irregular employment or occupational commitments that separate men from their families for long periods.[21] Despite frequent unemployment, Buffalo's Italian men performed exceedingly well as husbands and fathers. Until the 1920's brought slightly improved conditions, the majority worked in low-paying occupations, and they commonly remained without work for six or more months of the year. Frequently, construction work drew the men away from the city and their families. Immigration itself caused temporary separations for many. In cases of delayed family migration, the husbands almost always preceded their

[20] See, for example, Herbert Gans, *The Urban Villagers: Group and Class in the Life of Italian-Americans* (Glencoe, 1962), pp. 239ff.

[21] Ibid., p. 240.

wives to America and remained separated from their families for sustained periods. Yet despite these adversities, the proportion of husbandless families among Buffalo Italians remained surprisingly low.[22] Calculations based upon the 1905 New York State Manuscript Census (taken twenty years after heavy immigration into Buffalo had begun) reveal that only 4 percent of more than two thousand first-generation families had female heads with no spouse present. And some of these were widows, not deserted wives. Two groups of women, possibly unaccounted for in these figures, could swell the proportion of wives who experienced desertion: childless or pregnant wives living alone in 1905 and women who remarried after their husbands left them would appear in the census as single or married, respectively, not as husbandless wives. The surplus of Italian men in Buffalo could have encouraged a high incidence of remarriage for the deserted women, but this is unlikely because the immigrants subscribed to the Roman Catholic opposition to divorce. Although incalculables such as these may mean that the desertion rate was somewhat higher than 4 percent, collateral evidence fails to confirm this hypothesis.

Comparative data found in the published records of Buffalo's Charity Organization Society (COS) and the Bureau of Public Welfare suggest that the closely knit Italian community provided strong enough social pressures to check male desertion. Immigrant Italians were eligible for aid from both organizations. In 1908 and 1909, Italians were the ethnic group least likely to obtain welfare because of neglect or desertion by a family head; and although the percentage applying for welfare had increased by the 1920's, those giving desertion or nonsupport as their jus-

[22] It may be objected that families which eventually united in America did so because they were more stable to begin with. In cases where the father relinquished his control, or had no interest in preserving it, families never became united, and hence would not appear in the census data either. Antonio Mangano, "The Effect of Emigration upon Italy," *Charities and the Commons*, 20 (April 4, 1908), 13–25; and Victor Von Borosini, "Home-Going Italians," *Survey*, 28 (Sept. 28, 1912), 791–793, discuss families left behind in Italy. According to both authors, separations created problems, but only a minority of families were seriously disturbed.

tification actually declined from 6 percent in 1908 to 4 percent in 1926.[23]

Like any statistics concerning voluntary welfare applications, these are not thoroughly accurate indications of family pathology. There simply is no way to determine what percentage of troubled families actually requested aid. Because south Italians regarded with disapproval both desertion and acceptance of charity, many may have refrained from applying to welfare organizations. However, the percentage of families giving desertion or nonsupport as their justification for aid did actually decline, implying that desertion could not have been an increasingly important problem. Other evidence demonstrates the successful operation of social pressures against desertion. Although the census gives us no definite information about childless women, the small number of female-headed households with children present surely suggests that Italian men did not approach their marital obligations casually.

The responses to unemployment on the part of the Italian men confirm this assumption. Bitterly resenting their inability to find jobs, the unemployed struggled to support their families. One immigrant, writing to his wife in Italy and reaffirming his family ties, lamented his failure to send money. Search though he might from dawn to dusk, he found no work for an entire month:

> What disillusionment, my wife . . . we who believed we could improve our condition by coming to America. Everywhere I see injustice and inequality. I am sorry to say that this country is worse than Europe for any man with a heart who wishes to live honestly.

[23] Perhaps Italians did not admit desertion to public agencies, but other sources confirm infrequent separations and divorce. See, for example, a statement by a parish priest in "Da dove vengono nostri immigranti: come li giudica un articolista locale," *IC*, April 9, 1910; the 1908/09 figures are from *Reports of the Immigration Commission*, XXIV, *Immigrants as Charity Seekers*, I, 137. The 1926 figures were computed by the author from City of Buffalo, Department of Public Welfare, *Annual Report of the Bureau of Public Welfare for Fiscal Year Ending June 30, 1927* (Buffalo, 1927). The COS did not aid persons of the Jewish faith. There is no way to determine what percentage of all Italians were actually applying. We do know that they represented 9 percent of the total cases in 1908/09 and 18 percent in 1924/25 and 1926/27. See Table 3.

I do not wish to make you sad, but to whom can I relate my anguish if not to you?

Keep well, kiss our child, and with hope of being united as we should be and crying out strongly—death to this nation of cannibals. I kiss you.

Your Vittorio [24]

Vittorio's letter appeared in the socialist press, but other more moderate immigrants shared his frustration. Commenting on his inability to maintain steady employment, another family man complained: "See how good was this country. No work." [25]

The low desertion rates imply that Italian men and their families managed to cope with the potentially damaging effects that chronic unemployment or underemployment can inflict upon male prestige. Different expectations rooted in their old country experiences may have softened the blow. The south Italian conditions had taught these families to regard irregular male employment as the norm. Italians were accustomed to the kind of seasonal outdoor jobs with occasional opportunities for other work that Buffalo's labor market offered. These were familiar work rhythms to former peasants, who had frequently labored in mining, fishing, or agricultural industries during slack seasons. In Italy, men who could not find year-round labor were not considered delinquents; unemployment was not perceived as a breach of their family obligations, but as an expected circumstance over which they had no control. An immigrant who could not find work in America may have experienced injured pride, but the impact would have been mitigated by his deeply engrained belief that fate ultimately controlled his destiny.[26] Perhaps this viewpoint permitted the family head to maintain a positive image, without any sense of shame or individual failure, and so reducing the frustrations that lead to desertion.

Illegitimacy rates in Buffalo offer further confirmation of Italian family stability. The published census returns do not actu-

[24] *La F*, Nov. 20, 1909.

[25] Interview with Thomas Angelico; see also editorial by "X", "Miseria e morte," *La F*, July 28, 1910; editorial by "Virtus," "A chi darete il vostro voto?" *La F*, Oct. 14, 1911.

[26] See, for example, F. G. Friedman, "The World of 'La Miseria'," *Partisan Review*, 20 (March–April 1953), 218–223.

ally indicate illegitimacy rates, but the 1900 federal manuscript census showed only 1.5 percent of about a thousand Italian families with children living at home who could have been born out of wedlock. By contrast, 2 percent of a sample of a thousand Polish families had such children in their homes. Furthermore, even if the fatherless 4 percent of Italian households in 1905 were the product of illicit unions, their proportion can hardly be called pathological. A reliable source indicated that the number of Italian-American children born out of wedlock remained lower than average as late as the 1930's.[27] These figures imply that Italians consistently respected the community pressure against premarital sex.

The Italian migrants also maintained their Old World attitudes toward marriage. Two local Italian priests confirmed the infrequency of marital dissolution.[28] Immigrant newspapers rarely contained notices of divorce, separation, or desertion; perhaps immigrants simply did not report them, but this seems unlikely. When a breakup came about, news of it traveled rapidly and widely to neighbors and friends, creating a major scandal.[29] If extramarital affairs occurred, the lovers must have conducted themselves with extraordinary discretion. The Italian press reported only three violent crimes possibly linked to wifely in-

[27] The figures are from USFMC, 1900. All unbroken familes (901) living in Little Italy and reporting adequate information to census takers were included; a sample of a thousand Polish families (about one-third of the population of the major east-side Polish colony) was also taken from the same manuscript census. In both cases figures could represent an under- or an overestimation of illegitimacy. For these calculations, a child was considered illegitimate if he or she was older than the number of years his or her parents were married. The figures could represent an overestimate because some parents failed to report stepchildren as such, or an underestimate because information was given only for children living at home. The 1905 NYSMC does not provide information needed to check these estimates. Used in conjunction with the 1930's figures, the 1900 and 1905 data suggest a long-term trend of low illegitimacy. For the 1930's figures, see Buffalo Municipal Housing Authority, "Report," Pt. I, Buffalo 1935 (microfilm), p. 31, and Pt. II, p. 92. For 1930–1933, the Italian illegitimacy rate (1.4 per thousand) was slightly lower than that for the entire city (1.6). The Negro rate of 5.6 suggests a decidedly different pattern.

[28] "Da dove vengono i nostri immigranti," *IC,* April 9, 1910; interview with Dante Pellegrino, Buffalo, April 16, 1973.

[29] See for example, *IC.*, Aug. 27, 1904.

fidelities.[30] If romantic trysts were detected, either the lovers acquiesced to husbandly prerogatives or the husbands sought to protect their families from public shame. Rarely are lovers and cuckolds so consistently restrained. More probably, there were no crimes to report and few indiscretions to motivate them. If female purity does not seem a satisfactory explanation for this restraint, strong community controls and the fear of desertion in a strange land do.

The Catholic church represented another potential locus of moral and social control. Church teachings idealized the family and supported the notions of male authority and female subordination.[31] But uncongenial Old World attitudes toward the Church as an institution still limited its influence. The immigrants continued to seek moral guidance in folk and religious directives rather than in formal Church doctrine. Explaining why she and other Italians in Buffalo did not practice birth control, Mary Sansone indicated her understanding of the distinction between traditional and institutional influence. "People did not know what birth control was. . . . People had many babies; it was not the Church influence but religion" that guided their behavior.

The Church teachings may have helped to sustain male authority in the face of high unemployment, but female work patterns offer another clue to continuing male authority. Unlike other lower-class women, the Italian women in Buffalo rarely left their homes to work.[32] No evidence of any kind hints that these women sought or achieved financial independence by working. Despite male unemployment, therefore, these wives were not competing in this area with their husbands' authority. Undoubtedly this fact, along with religious and social pressures, contributed to the low desertion rates.

[30] *IC*, March 25, 1901; Dec. 9, 1901; May 9, 1914. In only one instance, a case involving a wife's attempted suicide motivated by her suspicion of her husband's infidelity, did the paper report alleged indiscretion. See, *IC*, Feb 15, 1902.

[31] See Ch. 8 for a discussion of the Catholic church and Buffalo Italian women; Raymond Firth, *Two Studies of Kinship in London* (London, 1956), pp. 91–92, discusses south Italian immigrant families and the Church.

[32] On other working-class groups, see Arthur W. Calhoun, *A Social History of the American Family*, III (New York, 1946), 160ff. Female employment patterns among Buffalo's Italians are discussed in more detail in Ch. 6 and 7.

Many of the social controls upon the immigrant family, especially those regarding female chastity and premarital sex, had their roots in the past. Upon reaching marriageable age, girls did not "mingle promiscuously" with boys as their American counterparts apparently did.[33] Parents heeded the folk proverb: "Una ragazza per bene non lascia il petto paterno prima che si sposi" ("A good girl does not leave the parental nest before she is married").[34] The immigrant Italians scorned the American practice of dating before marriage. An elderly Italian couple reminisced about their courtship:

> Mr. Angelico: I used to go to her house. She sat on one side of the table, and I on the other. They afraid I touch. You know. A few days before we were married, she was on the chair fixing curtains. As she came down, I try to kiss. "No, not yet!" she say.
>
> Mrs. Angelico: I didn't belong to him yet. That's the way we used to be then, the Sicilians.
>
> Mr. Angelico: When we go to church [with his fiancée's family] to sign the marriage register . . . three weeks before we were married, three weeks before, I say, "While we're here, let's go to the show. . . ." We came to the aisles of the theatre. My mother-in-law go first, my fiancée next, my little sister, my father-in-law. I was the last one. I had two in between [me and my fiancée]. I was next to the old man.
>
> Mrs. Angelico: No chance. No chance.

This couple's whimsical reminiscenses typify the careful supervision which relatives continued to exercise even over engaged couples. Under these circumstances, sexual indiscretions were deliberately rendered very difficult.

Arranged marriages negotiated by parents, relatives, or trusted *paesani*, another carry-over from the old country, represented additional communal efforts to ensure stable marriages. One immigrant's engagement, an event which her father and her husband's uncle oversaw, illustrates how Little Italy's informal social network contributed to such decisions:

> Next door my husband's uncle used to live. That guy, he go crazy. "I wish I had my brother here," he say to my [future] husband. He say to him, "Take this girl. She a good girl." My husband say to my dad,

[33] Goodale, "Children of Sunny Italy," 1915.

[34] Interview with Amalia Lanza, Buffalo, April 18, 1973.

"Let's have a glass of beer in the saloon." My husband's uncle say, "Take this girl. She just from Italy. Take her. Give my nephew this honor." Sure. *Cosa antica*. My father say, "I'll let you know. I'll ask the family." My father, you think he ask me? No, he ask my mother. She tell me, "This guy, he want you." I was seventeen. My mother ask me, "Do you want this fella?" I say, "Ma, I like. Nice dress. Nice personality." My mother say, "We find out." Take two weeks to get information about him. What kinda family did he come from? A good man? A good bargain? Poor Tom would ask his uncle every night: "Any answer?" Two weeks passed and my father o.k.'d the marriage. He goes out with my husband's uncle. All three came to the house. Thay's the way we introduce. Not on the street like now.[35]

Only after their families had agreed to the marriage could a suitor call upon his fiancée, and during the entire courtship, some member of the future bride's family remained present as chaperone. These practices assured the girl's chastity and male respect for it; they may also explain the low illegitimacy rates among Italians. Many immigrants married friends of their parents, distant relatives, or people from their Buffalo neighborhoods. The large number of marriages between individuals from the same provinces and towns represented an additional effort to avoid the risks inherent in less controlled American courtship practices.[36]

Other practical considerations also help to explain the prevalence of stable marital relationships. Like most immigrant communities, Buffalo had an unbalanced sex ratio. In 1905, for example, 3,140 Italian-born men and 2,040 Italian-born women lived in the city (a ratio of 153.9).[37] Even though the large figure for the men included married men with wives abroad, single Italian women found themselves far outnumbered by marriageable men. A Sicilian-born woman told how this situation influenced her life. "I married young. When Italian men came, they grabbed the girls right away. . . . Everyone wanted to marry me because there were not many Italian girls. I was married at

[35] Interview with Rose and Thomas Angelico.

[36] Goodale, "Children of Sunny Italy"; interviews with Richard Ferranti and Frank Iannuzzi. Intermarriage is discussed in Ch. 8.

[37] NYSMC, 1905.

thirteen. . . . I was fifteen when I had my first child." [38] Because women were relatively scarce, men hesitated to desert them. Also, women frequently represented an investment—thirty or forty dollars were required to bring a wife to America. Leaving a wife would mean substantial financial loss, as well as the problem of finding a new one. Immigrants struggling to make a living had to make such practical calculations. Dissatisfied husbands could have sought an outlet in Canal Street's saloons, dance halls, and brothels, but these were single men's haunts. Although lonely immigrants sought solace with dance hall women, "they were not for marrying." [39] But their tensions could have been minimized in other ways.

It is sometimes observed of working-class marriages, for example, that the couple fails to make a heavy emotional commitment in the marital relationship. The impressionistic evidence confirms this assumption. Writing of the early twentieth century, Foerster observed that the Italian husband "expects only that she [his wife] should be home-loving, industrious, and obedient to his will." In an autobiographical novel, Michael De Capite described his parents' marriage from an Italian wife's point of view. Her husband provided her with money for rent and food but, Maria mused, "There is nothing but this, being born and growing up, working and marrying and having a home and children. That is all there is. Other things come and go, but in the end that is all there is." Maria "was relieved to know that Dominic [her husband] was near, that though he said little to her, he never failed her. The hope of there ever being something else between her and Dominic was a tender dream Maria kept away locked in a corner of her mind." The point worth noting here is the wife's low expectations of fulfillment. Such expectations on the part of both husband and wife could have minimized the likelihood, need, or legitimacy of separation. [40]

The resilience of the south Italian family seems more remark-

[38] Interview with Roberta Salerno. Buffalo, April 16, 1973.

[39] Interviews with Frank Iannuzzi and Richard Ferranti. There is evidence that single men patronized saloons; see Augello, p. 41.

[40] On working-class marriage, see Herman Lantz, *The People of Coaltown* (New York, 1958), pp. 156–157; Foerster, p. 440; Michael De Capite, *Maria* (New York, 1943), pp. 30, 78.

able when we note that about half of these families did not migrate together. The average family waited three and a half to four years to reunite. A local reporter observed that ordinary Italian laborers saved for five to ten years before sending for their families. The census data give no evidence that many husbands broke their stay in Buffalo by long visits home.[41] Under these circumstances, the low rates of dissolution among Italian families seem even more exceptional since the chances of a change in family life and attitudes are increased in those communities where large proportions of individuals are living without their families. The most pronounced evidence for stress should be found among those experiencing delayed family migration; not having endured the initial crisis of immigration and adjustment to a new urban environment together, we might expect these families to be less cohesive. Yet the long separations experienced by half of them did not produce serious structural disturbances.[42]

A closer examination of those families that did not emigrate

[41] Stewart, "Rapid Fire Rises of Buffalo Italians"; NYSMC, 1905; USFMC, 1900. Mangano, p. 22, discusses temporary reunions abroad. If Buffalo men typically returned home, some indication would have appeared in the census. Among all the families in the 1905 cohort, only one case of a return home could be verified. This man stayed in Italy long enough to produce children. It is possible, of course, that those who returned to Italy were single at that time, or that fathers stayed only a very short time. In these cases, no evidence of their return—that is, Italian children conceived during their stay—would appear. Only 2 percent of husbands in the 1900 group left evidence (in the form of children conceived) that they had returned abroad. Source: USFMC, 1900.

[42] See, for example, W. Lloyd Warner, *The Social Systems of American Ethnic Groups*, Yankee City Series, II (New Haven, 1945), 107–108. The 1905 NYSMC indicates that 1,096 families left Italy together; 1,021 couples experienced separations or actually met and married after their arrival. Aside from 38 percent of these couples who had Italian-born children present in their homes in 1905, we have no way of confirming how many had actually married before the separation period. But the 1900 USFMC permits an estimate based upon that cohort: in 11 percent of families not emigrating together, a man sent for a future wife whom he married almost immediately; 36 percent men and married in the U.S.; 58 percent of the couples were married when one of the pair (usually the male) left. Extrapolating from this cohort, we can estimate that about two-thirds of those 1,021 couples in the 1905 census not emigrating together were actually married. The figure is probably higher, simply because as immigrant communities mature, entire families are more likely to emigrate. See MacDonald and MacDonald, "Chain Migration and Ethnic Neighborhood Formation."

together suggests some reasons why we find so little evidence of instability. When husbands left their wives behind, many women sought the security of their original families during the period of separation. Childless women, of which there were many, rejoined their parents' homes as dependent children, not as adults heading their own families.[43] The separation from their husbands did not involve managing a separate household—an experience that could have led to female independence inimical to continued patriarchal control. On the other side of the ocean, few husbands explored alternatives to family living. *Paesani* and relatives checked on the behavior of itinerant males; by providing homes for them, they encouraged husbands to maintain their identity as family men.

There are other explanations for this stability, among them the conservative migration patterns of families not choosing to emigrate together. Almost universally a man emigrated to this country alone, and sent for his wife later on. The Callendrucci family's experience was typical. Mrs. Callendrucci tells the story: "I was thirty when I came here. . . . That's a double life I lived. My husband was in America and called me. He was here over six years. . . . He took so long because he couldn't get [citizenship] papers. . . . There were many women [in Italy] in the same position." [44] When a man sent for his wife, she generally brought their children with her, as mothers were rarely prepared to tolerate separation from their young. In only a few instances (34), the husband apparently could not afford passage for the entire family, although in some cases the grown-up children preceded their parents to America. In the pattern of delayed family migration, wives were almost never the initiators. Some men sent for their fiancées and married them immediately, so that the couples managed to avoid a separation crisis.[45]

[43] Mangano, p. 22, discusses wives left behind in Italy. One-fifth of the women were childless when their husbands left. NYSMC, 1905 does not permit determination of the exact proportion.

[44] Interview with Marion Callendrucci, Buffalo, April 17, 1973.

[45] NYSMC, 1905. The proportion of men living in unbroken families in 1905 who preceded their families was 82 percent or more. Forty-six percent of men in unbroken families sent for a wife; 36 percent sent for a wife and child. In 5 percent of these families, children preceded both parents. This could be an un-

The determination on the part of the man to fulfill his prescribed duties must also have contributed to the family cohesion. Most families experienced separations of three to four years, certainly a long enough time to weaken a man's sense of obligation to his wife and children. There is no direct correlation between the number of children a man left behind in Italy and the number of years required to bring them to the United States; regardless of the number of children, the greatest effort for reunion occurred within the first two years after the head of the family emigrated. Men with three or more children took the most time to bring their families. But those with two children were more successful than those with only one child in bringing their families together after three years.[46] It is only possible to speculate on the reasons for this. Perhaps a woman left behind with one child could manage without her husband. Two children constituted a heavier burden, making the practical reasons for reunion more urgent.

All of the men, regardless of financial ability, anxiously sought to fulfill their obligations. The record of men who listed themselves as unskilled laborers in 1905 is particularly impressive. Despite low wages and irregular employment, almost half of the fathers in this group brought their children to the United States within a year. The shopkeepers took longer than any other group to bring their families over; only about 40 percent

derestimate, for children who left their homes by 1905 would not appear in the census with their original families. In 14 percent of these families women lived in the U.S. longer than their husbands. These females did not initiate migration for the family they lived with in 1905. They usually came with their original families and married here. In only 4 out of 546 non-unit-migration families did a married woman proceed her husband.

[46] The 1905 NYSMC provides data for 385 unbroken families who experienced separations of this kind. The following figures can only be estimates because they are based upon children still living with their families of origin in 1905. Of the family heads who left Italy with 3 or more children 19 percent took one year to bring their families to Buffalo; 22 percent took 2 years; 14 percent took 3 years; 14 percent took 4 years; 9 percent took 5 years; 21 percent took 6 or more years. Figures for men who had 2 children upon departure are: 31 percent took one year; 20 percent took 2 years; 17 percent took 3 years; 9 percent took 4 years; 7 percent took 5 years; 16 percent took 6 or more years. Figures for men who had one child upon departure are: 32 percent took one year; 18 percent took 2 years; 12 percent took 3 years; 7 percent took 4 years; 9 percent took 5 years; 20 percent took 6 or more years.

managed to do so within a year. These small entrepreneurs had not necessarily disregarded their obligations—on the contrary, they sought to fulfill them. The money they earned was earmarked for future investment; the family reunion was therefore deferred for a time, but its interests were certainly being served in the long run. Few professionals or businessmen immigrated without their families—an indication of their greater financial security upon emigration.[47] Among those who could not afford this luxury, we find no simple correlation between the success a man had achieved by 1905 and the number of years elapsing before his family was reunited. Fathers in every calling fulfilled their function as heads of families and breadwinners; separation did not weaken that sense of responsibility. And this provides another clue about immigrant family stability: these Italian men, even if they had been separated from their families or were unskilled laborers who frequently found themselves unemployed, exhibited a strong determination to maintain their families.

Such migration patterns reveal a great deal about family relationships. The peasant mores significantly shaped or adapted to delayed family migration so that even under potentially disorganizing circumstances, each member could find security in fulfilling his or her customary role. The father—the family's chief provider—left home not to avoid his obligations but to improve his family's economic position; this fact legitimized his absence. Many initially conceived of their departure as a temporary necessity, a short-term investment in the family's future. The small number of children who preceded their parents dutifully attempted to maintain family unity by sending for their parents and reestablishing households in America. Husband and wife, fulfilling parental obligations as best they could, tolerated temporary separations so that at least one could care for the children. Almost always, as we have seen, the woman stayed behind to perform this task; after all, south Italian tradition prescribed it as her primary function. Most Italian wives remained at home, rarely venturing alone either into the work world or across the ocean. This was proper behavior for a good

[47] NYSMC, 1905.

peasant woman, even if she remained temporarily husbandless. If a separation from her spouse made childbearing impossible, she quickly resumed this function after reunion. We have no way of knowing what the psychological impact of such an experience was for women of other immigrant groups who did so, but the Italian woman was maintained in a dependent position even during the initial immigration period. That experience rarely gave her the opportunity to test her personal competence. It did not wean her or her relatives from Italian familism toward an American concept of individualism.

Although these family separations do not seem to have produced any pathological effects, perhaps some more subtle long-term effects did occur. Birth rates provide one measure of change. Some scholars, assuming an "assimilationist" position, argue that women emigrating from areas characterized by high birth rates, such as the Mezzogiorno, to areas of lower birth rates, like the American city, will exhibit a decline in fertility.[48] A reduction in birth rates could indicate either that separation itself affected fertility or that the immigrants no longer viewed the prospect of a number of children positively after their arrival in Buffalo. If we are to determine the effects of delayed family migration upon the birth rate, families emigrating together must be compared to those which did not. A comparison of this kind has its perils: for a start, it assumes that all variables save one, the mode of family migration, are constant. But each group had different characteristics. When the family histories of each—their age, number of years married, and life-cycle stage attained upon leaving Italy—are studied, possible biases appear.

The family life cycle is obviously important. Many families had not begun to raise children when they left Italy. Few fami-

[48] Arnold M. Rose, "A Research Note on the Influence of Immigration on the Birth Rate," *American Journal of Sociology*, 47 (Jan. 1942), 614–621, criticizes the assimilationist position. Massimo Livi Bacci, *L'immigrazione e l'assimilazione degli Italiani negli Stati Uniti secondo le statistiche demografiche americane* (Milan, 1961), p. 51; Covello, p. 355; Campisi, p. 444, all contain observations on the large numbers of children produced by south Italians. Official birth and infant mortality rates for south Italy are in Associazione per lo Sviluppo dell'Industria nel Mezzogiorno, pp. 61ff. The Mezzogiorno had relatively high birth rates ranging from 40.5 to 33.4 per thousand from 1881 to 1914.

lies in either group had produced as many as three offspring before emigrating. The reasons for this are clear—the larger the family, the higher the costs of passage and settlement. Families not migrating together (non-unit-migration families) were less likely to have begun childrearing. We know that some couples in this group were not actually married when the husband left Italy, but half the couples who left Italy together (unit-migration families) had no children either.[49] Parental age at the time of emigration confirms beyond any doubt that the Italians in both groups conform to the widely accepted notion that young couples were the most likely to migrate. Sixty-nine percent of the husbands and 75 percent of the wives in non-unit-migration families left Italy before reaching thirty. The unit-migration families, which included a more substantial proportion of individuals who had established their families when they left Italy, were older; only 48 percent of the men and 67 percent of the women in this group were under thirty.[50]

The 1905 census fails to provide information about the number of years people had been married before leaving Italy. Data from an earlier census which includes much of the 1905 population indicate that half of all unit-migration couples had been married for seven years or less; about half (47 percent) of the non-unit-migration couples had been married for that length of time.[51] In these ways, Buffalo Italians were very typical "new immigrants." Regardless of their mode of migration, young small families, in the early stages of married life, were most eager and most suited for participation in the unsettling ordeal of immigration.

Although young married couples found their place in both groups, those separated during immigration were slightly

[49] NYSMC, 1905, permits calculations based upon Italian families who still had Italian-born children living with them in 1905. About half (927) of all these families had children at the time of emigration. Of families who emigrated together (511), 23 percent had 3 or more children, 27 percent had 2; 50 percent had 1. Of families who did not emigrate together (416) 24 percent had 3 or more children; 29 percent had 2; 47 percent had 1. Of all the 1,021 families who emigrated together, 50 percent had no children upon departure; of all the 1,096 who experienced separations, 62 percent had no Italian-born children.

[50] NYSMC, 1905. [51] USFMC, 1900.

younger, more likely to have postponed marriage until they had been united in Buffalo, and hence more likely to have deferred raising children until that time.

A significant number of women in each group (one-quarter of the unit-migration wives and one-third of the non-unit-migration wives) bore a child within a year after arrival.[52] Immigration, then, did not discourage many couples from having children. The non-unit wives, however, seem to have born their children more quickly. Some of the non-unit wives did not actually marry their husbands of 1905 until after their arrival in the United States; these women did not spend all of their first year of American residence in a marital relationship. To have born even more children than wives who immigrated with their spouses, the fertility rates of non-unit wives must have been very high during the first year of residence.

Could separation have played some part in the differing fertility patterns of the two groups of wives? A possible explanation for more immediate conceptions among wives not immigrating with their husbands is that a slightly higher proportion of them were under thirty. And it is the wives in this age group that account for most of the difference in birth rates immediately after arrival between the two groups.[53] Second, the wives not immigrating with their husbands contained a higher proportion of women who came to the United States for the purpose of marry-

[52] Eleven percent of women not emigrating with their husbands had a child before the first year's residency; 21 percent within a year; 15 percent within two years; 11 percent within three years; 14 percent within four or more years; 28 percent had no American-born children by 1905. Figures for wives who had immigrated with their husbands are 8 percent, 16 percent, 14 percent, 9 percent, 19 percent and 33 percent respectively. Figures are calculated for 1,432 women aged 15–45 upon arrival in the United States. These figures are estimates because only single surviving children living at home in 1905 in unbroken families are included. Because these families were quite young, and hence unlikely to have many children old enough to marry, the figures do not omit a significant number of surviving children. Children who died cannot, of course, be accounted for. Source: NYSMC, 1905.

[53] The age-distribution of non-unit-migration wives under 30 producing a child within a year of arrival was: 15–19, 8 percent; 20–24, 12 percent; 25–29, 16 percent. The age-distribution of unit-migration wives under 30 producing a child within a year of arrival was: 15–19, 5 percent; 20–24, 8 percent; 25–29, 9 percent, from NYSMC, 1905.

ing. As newlyweds, they were more likely to become pregnant quickly, simply because in populations not exercising effective birth control, the mean interval for first births after marriage is shorter than mean intervals between children. Or, perhaps the swelling birth rate soon after arrival for wives not traveling with their husbands resulted from an overcompensation for months of involuntary celibacy.

Married women emigrating with their husbands deferred childbearing a bit longer. The reasons for this are difficult to determine. Certainly, these women were a bit older, and their group contained fewer newlyweds. The longer delay before bearing a child could represent the longer mean interval between births. Because the group contained a higher proportion of women who had already begun their families, more of these women were able to use nursing as a means of sustaining that interval. They could, however, continue childbearing uninterrupted simply because they continued living with their husbands during and after emigration. Apparently familiarity and, more important, breast feeding put a check upon the birth rate. Many of these women bore children soon after their arrival. But these considerations could explain why they spaced their children more evenly than women temporarily separated from their husbands (Table 2.)

It cannot be argued that separation or immigration affected fertility adversely. If anything, an upward swing occurred immediately after immigration; admittedly, this upswing may have been caused by factors not directly associated with immigration itself, such as the proportion of newlyweds or a possible improvement in living standards.

In the long run each group of wives produced about the same proportion of surviving children by 1905 (Table 2). If the mode of migration had short-term effects on the way children were spaced, it did not significantly reduce the birth rates of women separated from their husbands. In fact, because this group was more likely to have left Italy without any children at all, they must have produced a greater number of surviving children once in the United States in order to approach the number produced by wives who did emigrate with spouses. Arnold

Table 2. Effects of immigration on family size: unit migration vs. non–unit migration

Number of children *	Wives emigrating with husbands (in percentages †)	Wives emigrating without husbands (in percentages)
0	18	19
1	18	17
2	17	18
3	16	17
4	11	11
5	8	7
6	6	5
7	2	3
8	2	1
9	0	1
Total number of wives	930	1,032

* Only single surviving children living in unbroken families in 1905 are included.

† Figures are rounded to the nearest percent.

Source: NYSMC, 1905.

Rose's research substantiates this position. He argued that "unknown psychological factors" associated with immigration actually increased the birth rate among Italian women.[54] However, immigration itself did not necessarily produce this change; once again, there are other possible explanations for the increase. The women who did not emigrate with their husbands were younger and more fertile—they would in any case normally produce more children than the older women. Second, although infant mortality rates remained high in congested immigrant quarters, and Buffalo's were no exception, Rose argues that the chance for survival in America probably increased by 5 or 10 percent in comparison to Italy. Hence, what appears to be an increase in birth rates among these women may actually be an increase in the survival rate. The younger women, after all, spent a greater proportion of their fertile years in America. The older group, those who immigrated with their husbands, spent

[54] Rose, p. 614.

these years in Italy where the survival rates had been lower. A long-term decline in infant mortality rates for Italians in Buffalo supports this argument. Despite high infant mortality rates in the early twentieth century, the immigrants were experiencing improved conditions by the 1930's.[55] A declining infant mortality rate also strengthens the earlier argument that nursing delayed conception for married women emigrating with their husbands. If more children survived, the mean interval between births could certainly be longer for these nursing mothers.

Cultural expectations, early marriage, and the inability or refusal to use contraception all encouraged the traditional pattern of producing large families. An Italian-American priest who grew up in Buffalo claimed that his people "never had birth control or thought of it." [56] More disinterested sources agreed. One immigrant, who witnessed the arrival of his first child nine months after marriage and eleven more in years following, accepted their arrival as a matter of fate, just as his ancestors had: "We got married and they come when they come. What could I do? I can't get rid of them." [57] In Little Italy's early days, one reporter claimed that women bore an average of 5 children. If he was referring to surviving children, the statistical data supports this observation: in 1900, Buffalo Italians had an average of 4.5 surviving children. But data for women who had completed their childbearing years give firmer proof that Italians did not practice effective birth control. The Italian women of forty-five and over had produced a startling average of 11 children, even

[55] Rose, p. 621; Rose uses a survival rate, which is not available for Buffalo. Statistics concerning infant morality for Italy and for Buffalo indicate a decline in infant mortality. For the years 1900–1902, 177.7 infants per thousand died in the first year of life in the Mezzogiorno. The only comparable statistics on infant mortality among the Buffalo Italians concern the years 1900 to 1930. At that time the chief Italian districts in the city had infant mortality rates of 102.9, 74.3, 62.0, or an average of 79.7. See, for example, COS, *Fifteenth Annual Report, 1892*, p. 36, which claims that the Italian ward had the highest infant mortality in the city. See also "Italians in Buffalo," *Express*, Aug. 27, 1901. The Italian figures mentioned above are derived from Associazione per lo Svilluppo dell'Industria nel Mezzogiorno, p. 66; Buffalo figures from Buffalo Municipal Housing Authority, "Report," Pt. I, p. 31. Livi Bacci, p. 49, also argues for a decline in infant mortality. There is no simple correlation between number of years in the U.S. and percent of women losing children.

[56] Interview with Dante Pellegrino.

[57] Interview with Richard Ferranti.

outstripping the Polish women, who gave birth to an average of 7.8 children.[58]

Child mortality, rather than birth control, put a natural check upon immigrant family size. In 1900, 60 to 89 percent of Italian women over thirty years old (grouped in intervals of five years) had at least one child die. In that same year Italian women reported that their children died at a rate of 387 for every thousand born. The comparable figures for Poles were 325 for every thousand. This means that both groups of women saw one third of their children die, a painfully high proportion.[59] The women did not report whether these children died in Europe or America, so we have no way of knowing if these traumatic events occurred before or after immigration. But the increasing survival rates suggest that immigration may have decreased, rather than increased, their frequency. In the early years after settling in Buffalo, inadequate living standards, overcrowding, protracted infant diarrhea, poor diet, cholera, tuberculosis, unsanitary conditions, and a reliance on midwives all conspired to cause frequent deaths among Italian children. Although declining somewhat, high infant mortality rates continued as late as the 1930's, when overcrowded Italian quarters averaged a death rate of 79.7 per thousand, considerably higher than the city rate of 65.4 per thousand.[60]

[58] "Italians in Buffalo," *Express*, Aug. 27, 1901. Figures are based upon USFMC, 1900. The Italian figures are based upon all Italians reporting number of children born; the Polish figures are based upon a sample of about 1,000 families, representing about a third of the major east side colony. "Our Polish Neighbors," *Express*, April 25, 1910, confirms that Italian birth rates outdid those of Poles.

[59] Figures computed from USFMC, 1900. Age breakdowns in 1900 for women with children reporting mortality of at least one child by mother's age are as follows for Italians: 15–19, 18 percent; 20–24, 32 percent; 25–29, 32 percent; 30–34, 69 percent; 35–39, 88 percent; 40–44, 89 percent; 45–49, 83 percent; 50–54, 84 percent; 55–59, 85 percent; 60 and over, 60 percent. Polish mothers reported the following: 15–19, 8 percent; 20–24, 38 percent, 25–29, 61 percent; 30–34, 65 percent; 35–39, 72 percent; 40–44, 71 percent; 45–49, 74 percent; 50–54, 82 percent; 55–59, 84 percent; 60 and over, 81 percent. Foerster, p. 388, confirms that Italians had extremely high infant mortality rates, second only to urban blacks.

[60] Specific mortality rates for Italian sections of the city between 1930 and 1933 were: 102.9, 74.3 and 62.0; comparable rates for the Negro and Polish areas were 94.1 and 74.4. See Buffalo Municipal Housing Authority, "Report,"

By the 1930's the birth rates had declined compared to those in Italy. At that time, the rate for the most heavily Italian census tract was 21 per thousand people. The Mezzogiorno rates by contrast had ranged from 40.5 per thousand, from 1881 to 1885, to 33.4 per thousand, from 1901 to 1905. This decrease may be more apparent than real because the 1930's statistics included first- and second-generation Italians, and lower birth rates among the second generation could explain the decline. Long-term residence in Buffalo did have a modifying effect; but even in the 1930's, Italians exhibited the highest relative birth rate in a city containing several immigrant groups ostensibly committed to the Roman Catholic stricture against birth control.[61]

The preceding evidence shows that immigration to the city had a minimal effect upon the actions and values of these Italian families. The Old World ways were resilient enough to adapt to periods of separation and adjustment; immigration to the city did not severely disrupt family life, even among temporarily divided families. The only marked changes were demographic: a possible increase in the birth rate immediately after immigration and an eventual long-term decline in the same rate. Neither can be characterized as symptoms of disorganization. The former merely suggests a possible improvement in living conditions, the latter an unsurprising drift from traditional attitudes over a long period. Perhaps the improved chances for child sur-

---

Pt. II, p. 31. On the frequency of and causes for childhood death, see COS *Fifteenth Annual Report, 1892*, p. 36; and Gorman, "Life and Work of Dr. Charles Borzilleri." Borzilleri used bowel washes to cure infant diarrhea and successfully cut infant mortality rates. A New York State study noted that 45 percent of all infant deaths directly involved midwives; see Elizabeth Crowell, "The Midwives of New York," *Charities and the Commons*, 18 (Jan. 12, 1907), 677. Buffalo's Italian women used midwives for many years, and the city's Italian Columbus Hospital did not establish its maternity ward until 1936; see Gorman, "Life and Work of Dr. Charles Borzilleri." Discussion of low living standards is contained in Chapter 6.

[61] Italian figures are from Associazione per lo Sviluppo dell'Industria nel Mezzogiorno, pp. 61ff.; Buffalo Municipal Housing Authority, "Report," Pt. II, pp. 29ff., gives the Buffalo figures. The most heavily Italian tract in the city had a rate of 21 per thousand in the early 1930's. Comparable figures for other census tracts by predominate ethnic group were: Poles, 16 per thousand; native white of foreign parents, 14 per thousand; Negro, 19 per thousand.

vival did increase the financial burdens, but immigrants confronted the terrible sorrow of their loss less frequently.

Infant mortality figures tell us that whether their young died in Italy or America, Italian families faced personal crisis after personal crisis. Their world was not a happy one. Their ability to deal with loss of children, along with immigration, frequent separations, unemployment, and low living standards, staggers the imagination. We cannot judge whether life in America was better for these men, women, and children than what they left behind. We know only that it was different and new, and that for these immigrants confronting the new did not mean forfeiting the old.

4 The Italian Community in Buffalo, 1880–1930

Contemporaries frequently balanced the strength of individual Italian-American families against the weakness of the Italian-American communities. Two well-known sociologists believed, for example, that the high value Italian immigrants placed on personal relationships and the "affectionate and intimate character" of their family life minimized the serious intergenerational conflicts more often experienced by Jews and Poles.[1] On the other hand, they observed that Italian leaders themselves criticized their *paesani*'s limited organizational achievements and their failure to participate in American institutions. One spokesman, a New York City priest, claimed that if his people would "unite as the Jewish people do," they would be "better off." Emphasizing the weakness and paucity of immigrant institutions, he held that "very little is done . . . for Italians by Italian organizations."[2]

This dichotomy between a faltering institutional life and a highly articulated sense of family identity, already referred to as "familism," has its roots in the Italian past. Deeply preoccupied with the family's *interesse* or interests, peasants often failed to develop simultaneous commitments to community institutions. Despite their low living standards and the high level of un-

[1] Robert E. Park and Herbert A. Miller, *Old World Traits Transplanted* (New York, 1921), p. 241.

[2] Quoted in Park and Miller, p. 239; Gans, *Urban Villagers*, pp. 36ff., documents continuing second-generation emphasis on family and peer group.

deremployment, peasants in the "typical South" made few concerted efforts to improve their situation.[3] The absence of a strong central government, combined with a long history of domination by local elites and *mafia* middlemen, deprived the Mezzogiorno's peasantry of both political experience and control over their economic fortunes. In many parts of Sicily, for example, entrepreneurial landlords working in conjunction with *mafiosi* controlled village relationships to the outside world, inhibiting the peasants' opportunities to participate in national legal and market systems. The peasants' formal participation in national political institutions was also severely limited. In the late nineteenth century, the franchise was confined to male taxpayers who met certain educational requirements. This amounted to virtual peasant disenfranchisement. Only 5 percent of Sicily's population could meet the requirements in 1882.[4]

Certain Italians—town laborers, artisans, and, less commonly, agricultural laborers—did have some experience of organizations in the Old World. Mutual aid societies founded soon after the unification of Italy provided group insurance, helped find work for the unemployed, and sometimes represented particular trades. Highly localized and limited in scope, the mutual aid societies' chief function was to provide financial assistance to troubled individuals who were trying to fulfill their family obligations.[5] And the immigrants were ultimately most successful in reestablishing exactly these kinds of organizations. Composed of kin and peers from the same villages, they devoted

[3] On the nineteenth-century situation, see Covello, "Italo-American School Child," pp. 240–241; and MacDonald and MacDonald, "Instutional Economics and Rural Development," p. 115. Lopreato, *Peasants No More*, pp. 67–67, believes Calabrian emigrants sought to escape the narrow familistic outlook. Scholars disagree concerning the underlying causes for familistic behavior. Banfield, *Moral Basis*, focuses upon an ethos, "amoral familism," as a cause. Several writers emphasize the "Southern Question," and all it implies as a major cause of the apolitical peasants' familistic behavior: see, for example, Frank Cancian, "The Southern Italian Peasant: World View and Political Behavior," *Anthropological Quarterly*, 24 (1961), 7ff.; Friedman, "World of 'La Miseria' "; Silverman, "Agricultural Organization."

[4] Blok, *Mafia*, p. 24; Blok also discusses the role of *mafiosi* as middlemen.

[5] Briggs, "Italians in Italy and America," pp. 22ff.; see also Williams, *South Italian Folkways*, pp. 187–188.

themselves to coping with family needs and emergencies. Both their goals and their structure were entirely consistent with the highly personal Italo-American community already described.

It is easy to understand why immigrant behavior in America can be viewed as a repetition of previous familistic behavior.[6] But such an interpretation relies too heavily upon Italian antecedents. While these were important, the new conditions which the immigrants faced reinforced, perpetuated, and ultimately modified them. Family-centered behavior was not just a cultural phenomenon rooted in the past; it was also a living phenomenon shaped by the present social and economic conditions in America.[7] Established Americans used an array of tactics to prevent Italians from participating in their social and political life. So excluded, immigrants fell back upon the family and a few new immigrant organizations. The move to America failed to eradicate the old ways of relating because the class and social situations in which immigrants found themselves did not encourage this change. While acknowledging the family's central role in south Italian immigrant life, this perspective nevertheless cites larger societal patterns to explain what contemporaries attributed simply to an inherent weakness of organization. Eventually the Italians did construct some institutions and integrate themselves into American society in their own fashion. We must not judge them on the basis of comparative claims implying some set notion of community organization. The important question is not whether Italians organized themselves as well and as swiftly as other groups, but how they ultimately went about doing so.

In Buffalo as in other American cities, Little Italy was a society within a larger, more complex urban community. The coexistence of these two separate cultures strongly influenced the cohesion that Italians as a group could achieve—the longer-

6 Vecoli, "*Contadini* in Chicago," and Nelli, *Italians in Chicago*, tend to take this approach.

7 Gans, pp. 229–231, discusses the low level of community organization among American working-class ethnic groups; Charles Tilly, "From Mobilization to Political Conflict" (unpublished paper, 1970), discusses the broader problem of political mobilization; I am indebted to him for his approach to this problem.

term residents reacted negatively to any concerted effort, show of power, or competence. Immigrants had, of course, experienced a similar situation in Italy, where haughty aristocrats and northern politicians severely denigrated their political capabilities. In the New World they encountered worse. Some Americans feared and despised them for their working-class status; many disdained their ethnic origins and religious affiliation.

The English-language newspapers give us a revealing glimpse into the local attitudes toward Italian immigrants.[8] Until the late 1920's, when human interest stories praised Italians who had achieved American-style financial or professional success, articles and editorials expressed either outright hostility or a patronizing curiosity toward "picturesque" Little Italy. Local journalists projected the usual ethnic stereotypes upon its residents. They described the men as card-playing brigands, lazy fellows who lived off their wives' hard labor.[9] The *Sunday Truth*'s comments suggest the fear and distaste with which some Buffalonians regarded the Mezzogiorno's children, calling them "unwashed beggards," "criminals," and "fugitives" from the *vendetta*. Italians violated the *Truth*'s sense of propriety by "seizing hold of . . . [the ladies] insisting upon them making a purchase." The journal found nothing admirable about the Italians. Unlike the Irish, Germans, and Poles, they failed to prove themselves "cheery workers." [10] Even the dead were kept at a safe distance; the obituary editors of Buffalo newspapers did not consider Little Italy's most prominent leaders newsworthy.

The Buffalo residents agreed with their journalists' low opinions. Soon after a 1907 street riot, the local police chief said: "I think that the Italians are a dangerous class for they break the law." [11] Nor did Irishmen of their own class give them a warmer

[8] Immigrants themselves observed American journalists' prejudices; see *IC*, June 15, 1906.

[9] An exception was the *Courier* article, "The Italian Colony in Buffalo," May 8, 1898, which claims that the Italians did not increase crime in the community, and that Italian women were good housekeepers; see also "Buffalo's Little Italy," *Express*, May 24, 1891.

[10] *Truth*, 1883, quoted in Samuel W. Ognibene, "Italians in Buffalo, New York," (unpublished paper, University of Buffalo, 1965).

[11] "Race Hatred is Alleged," *Express*, June 8, 1907.

reception. An interviewer reported the recollections of a second-generation Italian: "He said that his father worked as a laborer and oft-times on his return from work, as he passed along the streets, he was pounced upon by the young Irish men of the locality. Conditions became so bad that the Italians were forced to use the back streets rather than the main thoroughfares." After a series of battles between the two groups, "the Italians were left pretty much to themselves." As thrifty Italians purchased land and homes in predominantly Irish neighborhoods, the hostility of the Irish intensified. Feelings ran high, and the two groups exchanged "bottles, bricks, and fists." Incensed Irishmen dubbed a real estate dealer who sold property to his *paesani* the "wolf who chased the Irish from their homes." [12]

Politically powerless, the Italians had no way to change their public image or to improve their social position; their contemporaries meant to maintain the status quo. The local response to an unprecedented organized action by Italian laborers in May 1907 illustrates this point clearly. Soon after *Il Corriere Italiano,* Buffalo's major Italian-language newspaper, announced that a local building laborers' union had garnered a membership of two thousand to twenty-five hundred, the majority of whom were Sicilians and Calabrians, the union men decided to parade. Four hundred to one thousand Italians participated.[13]

Beginning in the Italian quarter, the men, carrying their union flag and emblem, headed straight to Main Street. Here, outside Little Italy's confines, an argument ensued between a parade marshal and a streetcar motorman who refused to relinquish the right-of-way. Smashed trolley windows and a brawl between two or three police and more than five hundred Italians resulted. More officers and several non-Italians involved themselves while thousands gathered to watch. Before police reinforcements could arrive, one officer had driven his horse-drawn patrol car zigzag through the Italian crowd, temporarily quelling and dispersing it. Four Italians were arrested for assault and incitement to riot. That night every city police station had extra men. One hundred armed officers entered the Italian quarter; al-

[12] Carpenter, p. 120. [13] *IC*, May 11, 1907.

though no outbreak occurred, the police feared that an evening religious festival might encourage one.[14]

A judge known for his judicious treatment of Italians presided over the resultant trial. Terming the disturbance a riot, he accused two union men of fomenting it.[15] The English-language newspapers agreed—reporters called it the biggest riot ever to occur in the city's history, of a "fierceness and duration" seldom seen in Buffalo's streets.[16] Not everyone agreed that anti-Italian sentiment figured in the event, but because "swarthy" Italians participated, the Buffalonians considered it a racial disturbance. *Il Corriere* attributed full responsibility for the riot to the police and anti-Italians. The defense attorney argued that the incident had resulted from "race prejudice," designed to "drive the Italians out of Buffalo." He also accused the "overzealous police" of anti-immigrant bias. The judge, who generally rejected this interpretation, nevertheless confirmed that some anti-Italian sentiment existed on the force.[17] If xenophobic feelings did not cause the outbreak, they sustained its momentum.

The confused news reports make it difficult to determine why many people took the incident so seriously. The length of the disturbance, half an hour, was not remarkable. Damages had not been extensive; the police had successfully quelled and dispersed the crowd before the violence reached overwhelming proportions, and few sustained injuries. The police and at least one non-Italian had weapons, but few actually used them. A few Italians received arms permits after they were denied official police protection for their parade, but a search of the arrested men produced only two pocketknives.[18]

[14] "Little Italy in Fete," *Courier*, May 6, 1907.

[15] "Race Hatred," *Express*, June 8, 1907.

[16] "Pitched Battle," *Courier*, May 6, 1907; "Riot Charges," *Courier*, May 7, 1907; "Race Hatred," *Express*, June 8, 1907; "Fierce Riot," *Express*, May 6, 1907.

[17] "Fierce Riot," *Express*, May 6, 1907; "Pitched Battle," *Courier*, May 6, 1907; *IC*, May 11, 1907; "Race Hatred," *Express*, June 8, 1907, *Courier*, June 8, 1907.

[18] "Pitched Battle," *Courier*, May 6, 1907; "Fierce Riot," *Express*, May 6, 1907, attributed the failure to find weapons to the fact that police had raided Canal Street the preceding winter for concealed weapons. See also *IC*, June 15, 1907.

Why, then, did this riot evoke such anxiety in the Buffalo community? First, a large number of people were involved—five hundred to one thousand Italians, a dozen or more police, and an unspecified but apparently significant number of non-Italians. Also at stake were questions of power and territoriality: the focus of the disturbance outside Litte Italy suggested that Italians might not be willing to respect ghetto boundaries. Finally, some Buffalo citizens recognized the purposeful defiance of the union men. Individuals who had been denied local political power were demanding recognition.

The English-language press and Chief of Police Regan focused on the territoriality issue. The chief insisted that he issued a permit "under the impression the parade was of a religious character," and with the understanding that it would be confined to the Italian quarter. According to the police, the paraders had been warned to stay off Main Street and away from the streetcar lines. It was perhaps "just for this reason," the *Courier* noted, that "the paraders determined to march where they were told not to." [19] The union men's careful planning of the event, their expectation of trouble, and their willingness to be pushed to violence all suggest that they had more in mind than showing their strength to fellow countrymen. They wanted to demonstrate their power to the larger community, so they planned this physical intrusion into the city's downtown political and business sanctuary. Astute Buffalonians appreciated the symbolic importance of the event. This was the first riot to take place in Buffalo's main streets, the first that police failed to confine to working-class quarters. Several organized efforts and violent incidents related to dock and railroad strikes earlier in the year had brought unprecedented unity to Little Italy's working class, and presented further cause for public concern. The Italians symbolized a double threat—working-class violence and the "foreign problem." And there lurked the possibility of future intrusions. Although later disputes eventually divided the Italian population, this disturbance represented an important step. It was the first act of unified political protest

[19] "Pitched Battle," *Courier*, May 6, 1907; *IC*, June 15, 1907; "Fierce Riot," *Express*, May 6, 1907.

against the larger community which had excluded immigrants from power and thereby reinforced their feelings of incompetence and fear.

Two impulses, one from outside Little Italy and the other from within, explain the Italian sense of political and social impotence. The riot incident suggests some of the constraints placed upon immigrants by outsiders. These included residential and social segregation, legal repression, and the denial of political power. But the security provided by the ghetto, which happened to be more deeply rooted in family and personal relationships than political ones, also discouraged full participation in American life. Both the outside constraints imposed upon Italians and the alternative social satisfactions that Little Italy offered its residents are worth examining in more detail.

Residential segregation illustrates these two impulses operating at once. On the one hand, it fostered a sense of community identity among Italians; on the other, it facilitated their exclusion from Buffalo's wider social life. For whatever reasons, the Italians were indeed residentially segregated. A recent study of several major American cities rated them higher on a residential segregation index than any other foreign-born group in 1910, 1920, and 1930. In 1910 they were more segregated than blacks in seven out of nine cities, including Buffalo.[20]

Antiforeign sentiment and restricted economic opportunities elsewhere kept Italians within their neighborhoods. One observer flatly stated that "race feeling" explained their physical isolation.[21] But why did the city's blacks have more residential options? Apparently, until large numbers of blacks entered the city in the 1930's, "swarthy" Italians represented a greater threat to the citizens of Buffalo.

Economic considerations also encouraged the formation of ghettoes. By the 1880's, southwest Buffalo, once a commercial center and hotel area, had been transformed into a region of grain elevators, rail and lumber yards, coal and ore docks.[22]

[20] Stanley Lieberson, *Ethnic Patterns in American Cities* (Glencoe, Ill., 1963), p. 127.

[21] Gillette, "Tenement Situation," p. 70.

[22] De Forest and Veiller, *Tenement House Problem*, I, 121; *Queen of the Lakes, Buffalo; Souvenir of the Tenth Convention of the National Association of*

Business moved out, real estate prices plummeted, and the Italians moved in. Some rented or purchased dilapidated homes that once belonged to suburban-bound Irish families; warehouses, stables, storage areas, and once-elegant houses were made into new homes for many others.

The substandard housing did not approach the horrors of New York City's tenement districts—the most common Buffalo tenement, a three to five story structure, housed twelve to thirty-five families.[23] But these never caused overwhelming problems because other housing options existed. Cottages built in front or in back of some businesses posed one alternative, and two-family homes—by far Buffalo's most characteristic dwelling—another.

How did Buffalo's Italians fit into this landscape? Although they fared considerably better than their countrymen in other cities, the Italian quarter had the city's highest densities. It contained the highest percentage of buildings controlled by agents or lessees who rented from an owner and then rented in turn to as many families as they could.[24] In 1905 more than one-third of over two thousand households containing Italian-born persons had six or more occupants, and almost 70 percent of all Italian families lived in dwellings housing three or more family heads.[25] Because two- or three-room apartments or homes designed for one- and two-family living were all the immigrants could afford, they had to make do with congested quarters. The Italians did not rent overcrowded apartments because, as the current stereotype had it, they loved huddling together. A settle-

---

Builders (Buffalo, 1896); "When Canal Street Saw Its Palmy Days," *Courier*, March 23, 1902.

[23] For tenement conditions in Buffalo, including Italian districts, see George Gillette, "Buffalo Tenement Houses," *Charities*, 13: 34; Gillette, "The Tenement Situation," pp. 70–73; *Immigrants in Cities*, I, 613; "Report of the Commission on Sanitary Conditions in the Homes of the Poor," COS, *Fifteenth Annual Report, 1892*, pp. 35–43; De Forest and Veiller, I, 121–128, and II, 349–464.

[24] Bernardy, "L'emigrazione delle donne," p. 82, unfortunately fails to provide exact figures for other cities, but in 1909 only fifty of Buffalo's worst tenements housed Italians. De Forest and Veiller, II, 356, claim that in 1900, 39 percent of the Italian district's buildings and only 7 percent of the Polish district's were agent controlled.

[25] NYSMC, 1905.

ment house journal noted more rationally that although they tended to be more "admirable about it [overcrowding] than other nationalities . . . they crowd together because in this way they can reduce the cost of rent which appears to be always going up." [26]

Yet economics and prejudice by themselves fail to explain residential segregation into low-income neighborhoods. The process of chain migration also helped to perpetuate it. The personal rewards reaped by living close to relatives and townsmen who shared one's own language, culture, and class experience were very meaningful. Life in the Italian quarter provided a coherence and familiarity which drew immigrants irresistibly toward it.

What kind of community was this that attracted so many immigrants? In 1930 the Buffalo Municipal Housing Authority officially pronounced the city's most populated Italian district a "slum" [27]— the standard of housing, living conditions, sanitation problems, epidemics, and general ambiance all placed it squarely in that category. The Canal Street area, "home and pleasure ground of the best thieves the world of crime had ever known," continued to be Buffalo's Bowery and sailor's quarter. Cabarets, dance halls, saloons, and brothels colored this otherwise dreary district.[28]

At that time, a feature commonly associated with slum neighborhoods, community inertia, was evident. But the failure to mobilize stemmed, once again, from both outside constraints and inner difficulties. In the first instance, outsiders effectively controlled several major institutions—schools, police, and political parties—on which Italians depended. In the second, new urban conditions generated problems within the Italian quarter. Although the Old World culture survived in Little Italy, the requirements of the city impinged upon it. Provincial divisions, ideological disagreements, a complex class structure—all products of city life—created new kinds of conflicts that the im-

[26] Welcome Hall, Buffalo, N.Y., *Annual Report, 1918*, p. 14.

[27] Buffalo Municipal Housing Authority, "Report," Pt. 1. Tracts 13 and 14, both overwhelmingly Italian, were classified as slum areas.

[28] "When Canal Street Saw its Palmy Days," *Courier*, March 23, 1902; Walter Waddell, "Development to Wipe Away Pioneer Buffalo," *Times*, Jan. 19, 1930.

migrants had not experienced before. Outside agencies and the elite Italians themselves excluded ordinary immigrants from joining in city, as well as Italian-American institutions. Most immigrants continued to be politically uneducated and powerless. Their internal divisions made effective mobilization difficult. Yet despite such divisions, Little Italy had many organizations. By the 1890's, ten years after the heavy migration had begun, the local church, an immigrant press, a political organization, and several voluntary associations had been established. By 1907 the community boasted a few parochial schools, labor unions, and a Socialist party section.

The first community-wide institution of consequence, the church of Saint Anthony of Padua, was founded in 1890. This church, along with six other Italian-American churches, offered its facilities for community activities.[29] Both voluntary societies and labor unions used church premises as meeting places. The church sponsored leisure activities, provided educational facilities, occasionally engaged in charitable efforts, and officiated at major family events—births, marriages, and deaths.[30]

The parishes could not have existed without immigrant support, and the church belonged to immigrants more than any other community institution did, but Italians rarely achieved a position of leadership or control over their local parishes. Unlike their Irish and Polish contemporaries, the Italians showed comparatively little interest in forming and supporting national parishes. One critic carped that "acquisition is the first law of . . . [Italian's] energies, and his real economies usually begin with the church." [31]

Because in Italy both Church and clergymen receive financial support from the Italian government, these immigrants, unlike

[29] *IC*, March 26, 1904; for a history of Italian churches in Buffalo, see Giovanni Schiavo, *Italian-American History*, II, *The Italian Contribution to the Catholic Church in America* (New York, 1949), 862–866.

[30] "Scuola," *IC*, Sept. 18, 1909; Beth Stewart, "Law, Business, and Medicine Can Count Buffalo Italians among their Most Brilliant Members," *Courier*, Jan. 14, 1923; "The Early History of Census Tract 12 (Ward 4)," (unpublished report, Department of Sociology of the University of Buffalo and the Buffalo Foundation, Buffalo, 1930), p. 27.

[31] *America*, (Dec. 5, 1914), 194, quoted in Vecoli, "Prelates and Peasants," p. 237.

their Irish counterparts, had no history of voluntary support. Much to the disappointment and sometimes the distaste of the Italians, Irish and Anglo-Saxon priests presided over their congregations and their diocese. Beginning in the 1890's non-Italians established and staffed most immigrant parishes—one exception was Saint Anthony's, which was developed by the Scalabrini missionary order.[32] Occasional appointments of Italian-speaking clergymen were made to win immigrant support, but Italians could not commit themselves in Buffalo any more than they had in the Mezzogiorno to an institution run by persons with whom they could not identify. Even in cases where Italian priests had been appointed, a deeply rooted anticlericalism prevented total trust. Finally, Buffalo's Italian-born priests usually belonged to a better educated class of northerners with whom the immigrants, former peasants from the South, had little in common.

From the immigrant's viewpoint, the Church was an Irish-American institution. Most Italians remained either nominal Roman Catholics or without Church ties of any kind. They continued to practice their Old World folk religion, a system of beliefs combining superstition and pagan and Christian rituals. For these reasons, one historian argues that the Church did not exercise effective social control over Italians.[33] If the Catholic Church in America itself had little control over immigrant life, deeply internalized religious attitudes did. Historical evidence tells us, for example, that the Italian women regularly attended church services and that the traditional religious attitudes toward the family and their roles within it continued to influence them in Buffalo.[34]

The immigrants had little influence over the public schools in their neighborhoods. The schools were an outside social agency with which the law required them to associate unless they sent their children to parochial schools. Residential segregation ex-

[32] Church of Saint Anthony of Padua, *Golden Jubilee, 1891–1941* (Buffalo, 1941), p. 33; and Schiavo, II, 862.

[33] For a discussion of immigrant attitudes toward priest and Church, see Vecoli, "Prelates and Peasants," p. 268.

[34] Ch. 8 discusses women and religion.

plains why the neighborhood schools were almost completely Italian, but the public school authorities seeking to maintain control of their institutions exacerbated the situation because they rarely gave Italian-Americans the opportunity to teach their own children.[35] The Italian intelligentsia protested the exclusion of Italian studies from the public schools, and some Italians understood that a public school system controlled by unsympathetic Americans would be unlikely to extoll the merits of the parental culture.[36] Although the immigrants generally avoided the parochial schools, some parents reacted by enrolling their children in them.[37] Such institutions as Saint Anthony's School performed a dual function by informing the second generation of its heritage and by keeping the young within the protective control of their ethnic group.[38]

Little Italy's first political organization, the Central Italian Republican League, was founded in 1893 to recruit Republican party members. Until that time, and well after, the Italian community, largely composed of new arrivals and transients, did not provide a strong foundation for political life. Italian voters were continually divided and crossed from one party to another as they continued to place their immediate pragmatic interests before either party discipline or political ideology.[39] *Il Corriere*'s pages reflected this confusion. Although it customarily favored Republican candidates, the paper frequently endorsed can-

[35] Erland Gjessing, "Buffalonians from Sunny Italy," *Illustrated Express*, April 5, 1908, p. 8, notes that in 1907, 95 percent of Public School Two's children had Italian parents. *Reports of the Immigration Commission*, XXX, *The Children of Immigrants in Schools*, II 402; and City of Buffalo, *Annual Report of the Superintendent of Education* (Buffalo, 1917), pp. 120, 21, indicate that the number of Italo-Americans teaching in Buffalo elementary schools ranged from 1 in 1910 to 3 in 1917.

[36] *IC*, Oct. 5, 1907; *IC*, July 9, 1904; *IC*, Dec. 5, 1903; "The Italian Colony in Buffalo," *Courier*, May 8, 1898.

[37] *IC*, Oct. 5, 1907; *IC* July 9, 1904; *IC*, Dec, 5, 1903. On the immigrant attitude to parochial education, see Vecoli, "Prelates and Peasants," pp. 249ff.

[38] Editorial, "Per una scuola italiana," *IC*, Nov. 25, 1898. For an unsurpassed detailed discussion of Italian-Americans and education, see Covello, "Italo-American School Child." For more discussion of parental attitudes toward education, see Ch. 8.

[39] Augello, "Italian Immigrants," p. 67; Ognibene, "Italians in Buffalo," pp. 15, 17; editorial by "Cigno," "L'italiano elettore," *La F*, Sept. 23, 1911.

didates of both parties. Sometimes local issues, such as Democratic support for public works construction that would provide work for Italians, won endorsement for that party; more often, opposition to the Irish-controlled Democrats, which *Il Corriere* considered the "first real sign of [Italian] political consciousness," aroused pro-Republican sentiment.[40]

Although local Italian politics received scant notice in *Il Corriere* after World War I, the prewar era was marked by continual disputes among three leaders. Horace Lanza and Joseph Lunghino, who also controlled *Il Corriere*, supported the Republicans and ran several times on that ticket; Joseph Carlino tied his fortunes to the Democrats. Because they failed to provide unified leadership, the Italian vote frequently split and all three men lost elections in immigrant districts. Even after one or the other achieved success, bitter factionalism continued to divide the immigrant polity.[41]

Dominated by an elite that failed to develop a united, positive leadership, the immigrants remained hopelessly confused, even if they chose to participate in politics.[42] Bosses' bribes lured many who did vote, hardly a sign of a burgeoning political acumen.[43] They must have been further discouraged from participation when Little Italy's most educated citizens claimed that behavior "bordering on contempt" had successfully barred Buffalo Italians from political positions.[44] Once again both the Italians' own inexperience and outside efforts to prevent any significant participation frustrated meaningful community organization.

Il Corriere Italiano, which was established in April 1898 and continued publication until after World War II, was the colony's first long-term venture in an Italian-language press. A significant accomplishment for Little Italy, *Il Corriere* was the first successful organization run by Italians designed to serve

[40] *IC*, Oct. 31, 1903; *IC*, Sept. 29, 1906; *IC*, Oct. 30, 1907; "Italian Colony in Buffalo," *Courier*, May 8, 1898.

[41] Ognibene, "Italians in Buffalo," p. 17 discusses the election of 1910; see also "La vittoria di Lanza," *IC*, Aug. 29, 1908.

[42] "Cigno," "L'italiano elettore," *La F*, Sept. 23, 1911.

[43] Editorial, "La farina del diavolo," *La F*, Nov. 5, 1910.

[44] Comment by Dr. Frank Valanti, "Italians Want Recognition," *IC*, Aug. 23, 1913.

the entire community. Little Italy's intelligentsia and its political and economic elite controlled this journal.[45] The newspaper concentrated upon news from abroad and important national events, but its editorials did attempt to unify the colony, to specify its needs, and to provide leadership. It championed efforts to eradicate provincialism—a divisive force in Little Italy. The editors favored the establishment of an Italian-language school with programs designed to inculcate cultural pride.[46] The paper called itself the representative of the working class.[47] In fact, this honor really belonged to the Italian Socialist organ *La Fiaccola* (the Torch), published from August 1909 to December 1912. One of a handful of American Italian-language Socialist journals, the paper was available on local newsstands and by August 1910 claimed more than one thousand subscribers in Buffalo and its environs.

The editors of these two major Italian-language newspapers carried on a long feud. *La Fiaccola* claimed that middle-class interests dominated *Il Corriere*, and that the paper aided in breaking up Italian workers' strikes.[48] Socialist workers found ways to retaliate: on one occasion, they disrupted a joint meeting of *Il Corriere* and the Italian-American Business Association.[49] The two organizations worked together closely, and the workers resented this. The Socialist party drew the battle lines tighter, basing much of its program on opposition to upper-class Italians who, by joining the Republican party, proved their disinterest in their underprivileged *paesani*.[50] The ill will generated by these conflicting interest groups and their petty disputes made further troubles for a community already beset with problems. Those most capable of leadership concentrated so completely upon their own ideologies and immediate needs that they neglected all community interests.

Other special interest groups frustrated the development of a

[45] Several previous efforts failed; see "Italians in Buffalo," *Express*, Aug. 27, 1901, and Augello, p. 75.

[46] Editorial, "Confederiamoci!" *IC*, Feb. 27, 1909; editorial "Per una scuola italiana," *IC*, Nov. 25, 1898.

[47] *IC*, Jan. 13, 1906.

[48] "La missione," *La F*, July 28, 1910.

[49] "Gente per bene," *La F*, Aug. 21, 1909.

[50] Editorials, "La lotta," *La F*, Oct. 9, 1909, and "Uno dei mali coloniali," Nov. 6, 1909.

strong community sense. Local *prominenti* (important business, financial, and professional men), whose education and experience qualified them for leadership roles, failed to unite Right and Left; their privileged position caused them to be the target of community resentment.[51] Both Socialists and businessmen excluded from its membership expressed hostility toward the Italian-American Business Association, Little Italy's elite organization. Jealous working men also complained that the colony's professionals too cavalierly presumed to represent Little Italy at a regional conference of Italo-Americans.[52]

Signs of conflict existed even among those community members who did organize effectively. The Italian building workers' strike of June 1910 illustrates this point. During the strike the Italian Socialists opposed union organization along craft lines, though they eventually lent their support. Had the skilled workers united with the unskilled into one union, they argued the former would not have been contract-bound to restrain from a sympathy strike with the laborers.[53] Even Little Italy's most successfully organized popular component, the building workers' union, suffered from internal divisions of the community.

The Catholic church, the labor unions, and the Socialist party found themselves in even more hopeless ideological conflict, and these conflicts between three of Little Italy's most representative and sophisticated organizations seriously damaged the prospects of mobilizing the community. The Church's opposition to unions, socialism, and radicalism, which expressed itself in the activities of priests who ministered to the Italian population, produced serious divisions.[54] During the building workers' strike of 1910, for example, after negotiations with contractors failed several times, the union asked the pastor of Saint Anthony's Church to mediate. According to the Socialist *La Fiaccola*, the clergyman then turned to his pulpit and urged the Italian

[51] Apparently, Italian colonies all over the nation faced similar problems; see Edwin Fenton, "Immigrants and Unions, a Case Study: Italians and American Labor, 1870–1920" (unpublished Ph.D. dissertation, Harvard University, 1957).

[52] Letter, *IC*, April 11, 1908. [53] "I manuali," *La F*, May 21, 1910, p. 3.

[54] Henry W. Hill, ed., *Municipality of Buffalo, New York: A History 1720–1923*, II (New York, 1923), 644.

women to persuade their husbands to return to work. "With sweet words," the journal noted, he next convinced the strikers that if they resumed work they would receive concessions. These turned out to be negligible, and the employers refused to recognize the union.[55] A few months later, an unidentified Italian priest attended a union meeting held at one of the immigrant churches. He conceded to the workers' representative that union organization was proper, but argued paradoxically that the union should not become politically involved.[56] The Socialist party had been gaining strength in Little Italy, and the priest was undoubtedly aiming his attack in that direction. But both Church and labor paid a price for constantly frustrating each other's attempts to win immigrant followers. Their altercations eventually divided the community whose united support they so badly required.

Provincial divisions added to Little Italy's problems. "*Il campanilismo*"—the sense of intense loyalty to one's village or provinces—provided security and a basis for personal relationships, but also created difficulties. By 1908 hundreds of villages and sixteen different Italian provinces were represented in Buffalo.[57] Local Italian-language newspapers were continually criticizing *il campanilismo*'s divisive effects, and one editor attributed the colony's weakness and organizational failures to it. Contrasting his own people with the local Germans and Irish, he noted their aptitude for developing more than just the usual patriotic and mutual benefit societies. They had set up viable political organizations, which the Italians had failed to do because, he argued, the Italian voter thought in personal and provincial rather than community terms.[58] The Left concurred in this condemnation. A radical editorialist stated that provincialism caused the greatest of all socialist evils: the continuing division of Buffalo's Italian working class.[59]

Efforts at civic improvement also failed to interest most Italians. It took several clubs six years to unite and collect enough

[55] Editorial, *La F,* June 18, 1910, p. 4.
[56] "Prete che fugge," *La F,* Oct. 15, 1910, p. 3.
[57] Magnani, *La città di Buffalo,* p. 30. [58] *IC,* Oct. 24, 1903.
[59] Editorial by "Virtus," "Il campanilismo," *La F,* Aug. 21, 1919.

money to present Buffalo with a monument to Giuseppi Verdi. Even attempts to establish a cemetery to provide inexpensive and dignified burial for the colony's dead failed for years. Although the Confederation of Italian Societies was finally established, indifference frustrated the effort repeatedly for ten years.[60]

The failure to prevent criminal acts against its own members indicated further organizational weakness on the part of the Italian community. Despite the local English-language newspapers' certainty that organized crime prevailed in Little Italy, impressionistic evidence offers no proof of its existence.[61] The available evidence on crime and the *mafia* in Buffalo is thin and inconclusive. Two types of criminal activity existed which were attributed either to the Black Hand or *mafia* organizations. The first concerned acts of petty blackmail carried on strictly within the Italian community. The case of Antonio Pepe, Seneca Street grocer, is one example. Pepe received a letter requesting the sum of two hundred dollars. If he refused, he was told to expect a sword through his heart, then his body would be torn into pieces like a "Bologna salami." [62] Despite the efforts of local reporters, the sketchy newspaper conclusion that a secret criminal organization performed this crime and others like it is unconvincing.

A second type of criminal action involved both Italian and non-Italian victims, and even some immigrants acknowledged the possible existence of small gangs which promoted these offenses. The authorities suspected such a group of threatening to explode the Italian quarter's Buffalo Pitts Company unless ten thousand dollars were paid. Another type of offense typically attributed to a secret criminal ring involved the financing of gambling and prostitution. Saloonkeeper Gaetano Augello, for example, received a threatening note demanding gambling and prositution concessions in his establishment.[63]

[60] *IC*, July 21, 1906; *IC*, Jan. 4, 1908, p. 3.

[61] Nelli, pp. 125–55, gives a detailed discussion of Italians and crime.

[62] *IC*, Aug. 20, 1904. Because of the Italians alleged association with crime, an analysis of crime reports located in the Erie County Clerk's Office, Buffalo, N.Y., would be interesting.

[63] "Toils Not, Yet Canal Street Gang Is Well Fixed," *Courier*, June 8, 1906, p. 6; "Did the Trap Work?" *Express*, July 17, 1907, p. 1; Augello, p. 91.

Little Italy's citizens and the police suspected that an organized criminal gang operated from a Canal Street base. *Il Corriere* claimed that Chicagoans and New Yorkers composed this slick, well dressed, English-speaking mob. Its main interest appeared to be in controlling the gambling and vice enjoyed by the longshoremen and sailors on the water front. Another source claims that one *mafia* leader, Angelo Puma, formerly a fisherman from Castellmare del Golfo near Palermo, came directly to Buffalo where he participated in blackmail, extortion, and gambling enterprises. *Il Corriere,* hoping that these men would leave the colony, claimed that local police cooperated with them.[64]

Indeed, Italians resented the police as well as the English-language press for attributing all crime in their quarter to the *mafia* or the Black Hand. Responding to what he thought unreasonable allegations, local lawyer-politician Horace O. Lanza claimed that petty blackmail was not a product of organized crime, and that it should not be treated as such. Here and elsewhere, *Il Corriere* pleaded for Italian aid to the police or for the formation of an Italian police force to eradicate local crime.[65] No such formal effort ever came to fruition.

The community's failure to protect itself from its deviants did not result entirely from its own inadequacies. It had, after all, to seek protection from a legal system and police force that were dominated by unsympathetic outsiders. The Italians' distrust of local police and unwillingness to rely upon them was not entirely unreasonable. "We are living," one journalist wrote, "in a country where we are subjected to tyranny and persecution. We go to the authorities for justice and we are persecuted." [66] Once in the courtroom, the inability to speak English and hence to defend themselves frequently posed serious problems for the immigrants. This situation lasted until 1907, when the police chief was authorized to nominate a court interpreter to the State Senate.[67] As late as 1910, when Buffalo's first- and second-

[64] Editorial, Aug. 27, 1904; Augello, pp. 90–91.

[65] *IC*, Dec. 8, 1906; editorial, *IC*, Aug. 27, 1904.

[66] Editorial by "Mi Mi," "Instancabilità e costanza," *IC,* Nov. 17, 1907, p. 4; Augello, p. 32.

[67] *IC*, June 1, 1907.

generation Italians numbered over ten thousand, the police force and the detective squad each contained only one man of Italian descent. The civil service rules barring non-citizens from the force as well as the literacy requirements partly explain this, but certainly the Italian complaint of underrepresentation was not unfounded.[68]

The efforts to organize labor were slightly more promising. Although the Socialist party and various labor organizations divided Little Italy by deliberately articulating class lines, they also represented an important if sometimes faltering step toward working-class political organization and the first serious Italian bid for community power.

Sicilian leaders dominated the Socialist party, which was unusual because the more politically experienced northerners usually led Italian-American contingents.[69] Although both northerners and southerners joined the party, the latter predominated. Perhaps the Sicilian leadership was a concession designed to overcome provincial divisions. These Socialists gained in reputation, at least, from the local party successes. By 1910, Buffalo had two Italian Socialist sections. The exact numerical membership is not clear; if large, it certainly lacked discipline and the party was not attractive to voters.[70] Even this working-class group founded by and for Little Italy's workers could not achieve wide support. A devoted hard core established and ran the party's Italian sections, but they alienated their *paesani* by, among other things, striking at what they considered to be the heart of Italian apathy—the commitment to the traditional family at the expense of all else, including politics. The party journal was anticlerical, atheist, and feminist—attitudes that alienated conservative Italians. Furthermore, while attempting to woo small shopkeepers and the intelligentsia, the party stated

[68] Gjessing, "Buffalonians from Sunny Italy;" "Poliziotto italiano," *IC,* Feb. 12, 1910; "La polizia," *IC*, Dec. 7, 1912; Augello, p. 85.

[69] Fenton, p. 21.

[70] "Cose nostre," *La F,* July 29, 1911. In 1911 the Buffalo Socialist vote climbed to almost 4,500; although a small percentage of Buffalo's 400,000 population, this was twice that garnered in Rochester or Syracuse: see "Vittorie," *La F*, Nov. 11, 1911; "Una nuova sezione," *La F*, Oct. 15, 1910; "Nuova sezione," *La F*, Nov. 1, 1912.

its determined opposition to all upper classes, including Little Italy's.[71]

La Fiaccola did not take an entirely unified stand on such issues because the local party, like the national one, contained diverse ideological commitments. The journal's directors generally allied themselves with the revolutionary camp; others favored penetrating the American Federation of Labor. *La Fiaccola* voiced its theoretical disagreement with those who joined unions, but tactical considerations led it to support "class war once it had been declared" by a local union.[72] While internal divisions and radical attitudes denied the party a significant following, *La Fiaccola* struggled nevertheless to construct unified working-class organizations. It fought against provincial divisions and formed self-help institutions within Little Italy, such as an evening school to teach English and Italian. But its most ambitious achievement was a consumer's cooperative, formed in October 1908 by sixty workers. It was modeled after the European and Italian cooperatives to "eliminate all capitalist intermediaries and pass merchandise through fewer hands." [73] Hoping to force privately owned stores to lower their prices, *La Fiaccola* urged that other types of workers' cooperatives be established. Much interest also centered upon the formation of credit cooperatives which had won notoriety in Italy.[74] Labor unions were more successful in gaining the support of working-class Italians. Until the turn of the century, many men found themselves excluded from this power center because the craft-oriented

[71] The Socialist position on the family is fully discussed in Ch. 8; editorial by "G." "Socialismo e Socialist Party," *La F*, Aug. 26, 1911, discussed the divisions within the party and its ideology; for attempts to widen membership, see *La F*, April 23, 1910.

[72] "I manuali," *La F*, May 21, 1910.

[73] Editorial, Aug. 14, 1909. See also: "Nella colonia," *La F*, Oct. 29, 1910, and April 2, 1910; "Una cooperativa di consumo," *IC*, Oct. 24, 1908; editorial, by "Virtus," "L'anniversario," *La F*, Oct. 2, 1909; "Per la cooperativa," *La F*, Nov. 27, 1909; *La F*, Aug. 7, 1909. For a discussion of Italian cooperatives see Luigi Villari, *Italian Life in Town and Country* (London, 1902), p. 59; Italian consumers' and farmers' cooperatives are discussed in Maurice Neufeld, *Italy: School for Awakening Countries, The Italian Labor Movement in its Political, Social and Economic Setting from 1800 to 1960* (Ithaca, 1961), pp. 180–181, 335.

[74] Editorial and letter, *La F*, Aug. 14, 1909.

unions denied membership to unskilled immigrants. Although the Knights of Labor had an active Buffalo organization, neither Italians nor Poles felt inclined to join a brotherhood which endorsed a restrictive immigration policy. But the difficult economic conditions encouraged union membership and increased strike activity between 1899 and 1912: Italian longshoremen, building laborers, tailors, shoemakers, and garment and tile workers joined or formed their own unions during these years.[75] These unions stressed bread-and-butter issues rather than theoretical commitments, and the immigrants who joined them were motivated by concern over immediate family needs, wages, and working conditions rather than by a sense of political consciousness.

Some might argue that the difficulties Italians experienced in forming effective political groups were typical of social disorganization in the slums generally. But from the Italians' viewpoint, such an explanation would have been inappropriate. And if the inner dynamics of this community are to be fully understood, looking at it through the prism of the immigrant's social understanding proves worth while. The informal relationships within the neighborhood and day-to-day personal contacts, not formal institutional connections, dominated immigrant life. Although differing from the larger urban community, Little Italy had a social symmetry of its own.[76] This working-class community's social organization shows, moreover, that Italians reordered their Old World ways to fit new urban conditions. Neighborhood networks woven of family and friends provide one example; mutual benefit societies, Little Italy's most successful organizations, are another case of cultural adaptation.[77] The

[75] Editorial, *La F*, Aug. 14, 1909; Horton, "Old Erie," p. 321. The following detail some of the strikes and unions in which Italians were involved: "Labor Fight on the Docks," *Express*, May 21, 1907; *IC*, May 25, 1907; "La laborer's union No. 12400," *IC*, Aug. 22, 1908; *La F*, Aug. 21, 1909; "Lo sciopero," *La F*, May 25, 1910; "Mechanics' Helpers Threaten to Strike," *Courier*, April 10, 1910; "Sciopero operaio," *IC*, May 28, 1910; "Trouble on the Docks," *Express*, Aug. 16, 1912; "Nuova organizzazione," *La F*, Aug. 5, 1911; "Associazione," *La F*, Aug 26, 1911; "Lo sciopero," *IC*, Sept. 7, 1912; "Sarti di donna," *La F*, Sept. 14, 1912; "Sciopero," *La F*, Sept. 7, 1912.

[76] See Gerald Suttles, *The Social Order of a Slum: Ethnicity and Territory in the Inner City* (Chicago, 1968), p. 155.

[77] Magnani, *La città di Buffalo*, p. 52, observes that there were 32 by 1908.

majority recruited their membership from particular towns or regions, although a few societies had wider followings. These societies were popular because they were based upon family and village ties, social relationships that the immigrants understood. Their chief function—to help the family perform its traditional duties, especially in periods of crisis—also explains their success. These urban clubs absorbed certain functions which the family had performed in the Old World, and in this way they aided adjustment. Immigrant families separated from relatives and friends needed alternative security, especially when death, sickness, or unemployment occurred. So, families came to rely upon funds from voluntary association to sustain them in needy periods.[78]

The American conditions and the Italian precedents explain Little Italy's personal, informal social life, and also its repeated failure to mobilize politically. The peasants' lack of experience with extrafamilial organizations left them ill prepared to establish such institutions in the United States. But once in Buffalo, immigrants had little reason to alter their developed set of social responses. In a number of ways, the conditions within the American city still resembled those within the south Italian village; the outside world continued to be a "source of deprivation and exploitation."[79] Although they ultimately climbed up the occupational ladder, in these early years Italians generally remained confined to certain seasonal, low-skilled or service occupations; they were underemployed, low-income laborers in America just as they had been in the Mezzogiorno. Neither the larger American society nor upper-class Italians welcomed them into their institutions or encouraged them to form their own.

American urban life did not give the former peasants more confidence in their ability to change the world than they had had in Italy. Distrusting outsiders, the Italians continued to concentrate upon the family circle. The mutual benefit societies were the only formal associations that boasted community-wide

[78] Warner, *The Social Systems of American Ethnic Groups*, pp. 254–282, discusses the functions of voluntary organizations; for an example of a Buffalo organization, see Società Italiana di Mutuo Soccorso, *Fratellanza di S. Antonio di Padova* (Buffalo, n.d. [1930?]), pp. 11, 23, 27.

[79] Gans, p. 205. Gans discusses similarities between conditions in Italy and in Boston, pp. 209–213.

support and membership. Even the decision to join a labor union initially represented a familistic rather than a political response. The south Italian peasants had been a powerless and exploited lower class in the Mezzogiorno, and the move to America caused no basic alteration in that position.

The ethnic community reduced the immigrants' need to participate in American life. A south Italian proverb emphasized the reliability of local and personal ties: "Mogli e buoi dei paesi tuoi" ("Buy cows and women from your own village"). Immigrants heeded this advice. They were able to survive outside the city's larger power structures for some time because they had their own informal social network. In some instances, the option to participate in American institutions did not exist; in others, as the next chapter on charity organizations will show, immigrants refused to pay the high price required by such participation.

5 The Immigrants and Their Helpers: The Italian Family and Charity Agencies

In a typical case history, a Buffalo doctor informed his Italian patient that she required several months' hospitalization. During her absence her husband became so anxiety-ridden that he was unable to work.[1] In south Italy people went to hospitals either to die or because they had no one to care for them. This immigrant wanted his wife at home so that he could discharge his personal obligations to her—obligations he did not think an institution could fulfill. He also wanted her home to perform her family duties and care for their young children.

This anecdote is an interesting example of the social interaction (or lack of it) between the immigrant and the American culture. The doctor was simply acting as medical expertise dictated in recommending hospitalization. The husband, on the other hand, perceived something very different. His lack of experience with modern medical practice led him to fear that he might never see his wife again; for him, normal marital relationships and his control over his family simply ceased to exist. Worse, his family's independence was threatened. As a result, he found himself incapacitated, unable to perform the masculine role of breadwinner.

Italian families had their own ways of coping with family relationships and crises. If their modes of adjusting appeared inappropriate to the middle-class staffs of American charity agen-

[1] De'Rossi, "Le donne ed i fanciulli," p. 7.

cies, they had value and meaning to the immigrants. Herbert Gans has highlighted the complexity of the transactions which occurred between second-generation Italian-Americans and the community "caretaking" agencies whose ostensible object was to serve them. Gans emphasizes that these "caretakers" were not entirely altruistic; they expected "a material or non-material return" for their services. For example, the Buffalo charity workers, whom Gans would classify as the "missionary type," expected their immigrant clients to adopt middle-class behavior and values in exchange for services rendered.[2]

The Italian immigrants were less eager to fulfill their side of the contract. Although many Italians could perhaps have benefited from Americanization programs and financial assistance, in the pre-Depression era they generally resisted even well-intentioned aid. Many viewed such efforts to help as interference. Their resistance can be explained only if we understand that once again their past experiences were coloring their perceptions of a new situation. South Italians had a cultural bias against accepting public welfare—the Mezzogiorno's peasants were not accustomed to getting "something for nothing." Because in Italy poverty was everyone's problem, peasants considered reliance upon charity even more disgraceful than destitution. If relatives failed to provide for the needy, then small donations from the community made it possible for them to get by.[3] Peasants viewed any public or institutional interference in family life unfavorably; better that they should tolerate their own ne'er-do-wells than permit upper-class institutions to control either community or private family affairs. Even the Catholic church, chiefly concerned with individual salvation, did not actively engage in philanthropic activities. The south Italian's con-

[2] Gans, *Urban Villagers*, pp. 113–114, employs Eric Lindeman's concept of "caretakers," any individual who provides services to people. Limiting Lindeman's definition to "agencies and individuals who . . . give patient care, . . . [and] other kinds of aid that they think will benefit the client, and who offer aid as an end in itself, rather than as a means to a more important end," Gans provides an excellent framework for understanding the relationships between the immigrants and the Buffalo welfare agencies.

[3] Williams, *South Italian Folkways*, pp. 65, 184–186.

tacts with organized charity or other bureaucratic agencies were, therefore, limited.[4] The peasant looked suspiciously at such charitable institutions as did exist—poorhouse, orphanage, and hospital—simply because he regarded them as places of no return. A widowed parent would do anything to avoid sending his children to an orphanage. The sick simply got well or died at home.

The peasants had never experienced any formal efforts to organize their recreation and leisure time as the American settlement later attempted to do. A highly personal, family or religious matter, recreation focused upon special ritual occasions or feasts. Women remained almost exclusively restricted to this range of activity, although the men might gamble or drink together. In cases of public entertainment such as dancing or storytelling, the sexes were either separated or closely chaperoned.[5]

If the welfare agencies failed to appreciate Italian folk culture or to incorporate it into their program, the enthusiasm with which immigrants continued to enjoy their popular customs clearly indicated where their preference lay. Despite social workers' efforts to formalize them, Little Italy's leisure activities continued to center upon family and friends. One immigrant said, "We had little time for recreation. When we wanted to relax, we were with the family." The Italians had "loud and joyous" family celebrations in their homes on "every possible occasion." At these and more formal celebrations, wine, dancing, food, and the good company of *paesani* constituted the main attractions. The immigrants' most important social events involved rituals and ceremonies connected with family life, especially baptisms, weddings, and funerals. "If somebody had a wedding," Richard Ferranti said, "the family would go out and have a good time. That would be their leisure. The holidays come like St. Joseph or St. Lucy's Day; if there was a party,

[4] Celena Baxter, "Sicilian Family Life," *The Family*, 14 (May 1933), 87, observes, for example, that charity programs did not exist in Sicily until the twentieth century. On the relative lack of Church involvement, see Covello, "Italo-American School Child," p. 227; and Banfield, *Moral Basis*, p. 19.

[5] Williams, pp. 106–113.

they'd go." [6] Religious holidays provided important occasions for family celebrations, and some festival-loving Italians incorporated such American holidays as Thanksgiving into their family calendars. Although the Church, *Il Corriere*, or some provincial organization usually sponsored picnics, these affairs also turned into family banquets or meetings of local *paesani*.

Musical instruments, radios, and victrolas were popular for home entertainment; their popularity emphasizes the family-centered nature of Italian leisure. Although some men congregated at the neighborhood saloon, card playing at home became their chief form of entertainment. One immigrant recalled how women confined themselves to activities in the house, never going out dancing or to cabarets. "The girls," he said, "never thought of that." Another confirmed this. "The women never did anything alone." As in Italy, the independent female leisure activities, sewing and talking, took place within the home.[7]

Even when they were indulging in recreation away from home, Italians preferred the company of friends and familial activity. By the 1920's the immigrants had established more than one hundred clubs and organizations, most of them formal expressions of existing kin and friendship ties between natives of particular villages. Because each town had its own patron saint, festivals celebrated with friends and relatives punctuated the year.[8] Indeed, the Italians celebrated religious and political holidays with such frequency that the Socialist press reprimanded them for wasting money on fireworks and festivities.[9] Little Italy's churches often provided community leisure activities, in-

[6] Interviews with Richard Ferranti and Marion Callendrucci. For a general description of Italian leisure in the 1920's see Weir, *Recreation Survey*, pp. 362ff. An Italian wedding is described in "Fiori d'arancio," *IC*, Oct. 31, 1908, and a baptismal party in *IC*, Aug. 31, 1901.

[7] Interviews with Frank Iannuzzi and Richard Ferranti; see also, Weir, pp. 244, 364–365; and Augello, "Italian Immigrants," p. 41. An explanation for the proper observance of Thanksgiving was provided in *IC*, Nov. 30, 1901; a picnic and an outing are described in *IC*, June 29, 1901, and *IC*, Sept. 3, 1904.

[8] Weir, pp. 244, 364–365.

[9] See, for example, editorial by "Virtus," "Alla società di mutuo soccorso," *La F*, Oct. 29, 1910.

cluding sports and outings; the immigrants formed a number of small music clubs and their passion for dancing found expression in frequent balls. Even commercial entertainment, including theater, opera, and concerts, frequently had some connection to folk culture, and many of the programs included excerpts from Italian works.[10]

The Italians in Buffalo thus created a full calendar of colorful celebrations. Almost all the events were really traditional rituals in which family members and associates from the same Italian villages participated. Excepting for the Church, no other formal institution representing the entire community played an important part in initiating and organizing these observances; all of them represented expressions of a life style to which the immigrants were accustomed. If the social welfare agencies had little appreciation of these activities or interest in promoting them, neither did the Italians relate enthusiastically to their efforts to institutionalize leisure.

Peasant distrust of welfare agencies continued to manifest itself in the New World in other ways. The immigrants commonly distrusted public medical aid, hospitals, and dispensaries. Because this lack of confidence also extended to such reform organizations as the settlement houses and the Charity Organization Society, the immigrants turned to their own countrymen or to their mutual aid societies in times of crisis.

But such cultural attitudes toward welfare agencies only partly explain the immigrant resistance to interference in their family life. The demands that American social agencies made along with their disregard of Italian culture further dicouraged amicable relationships. In exchange for their services, the evangelical reformers, middle-class amateurs, social workers, settlement workers, and ultimately also the professionals, all wanted their clients to adopt their own middle-class cultural and religious norms where family, work, and leisure were concerned. Nonprofessional charity work in particular represented an effort "to perpetuate the existing class structure" by inculcating such

[10] For notices of public entertainments, see *IC*, June 7, 1902; *IC*, July 2, 1904; *IC*, July 16, 1904; see also Weir, pp. 362–365.

values.[11] Social control of the immigrants was clearly at stake. Despite the gradual replacement of amateurs with professionals and the accompanying tendency to stress environmental and economic conditions before moral degeneration as causes for poverty,[12] the Italian response to welfare agencies did not appreciably change. The immigrant perceived all social workers as intruders into his private world, more offensive than politicians or employers whose demands, after all, did not penetrate so immediately into his intimate life.

The kinds of organizations and personnel the Buffalo charity workers used to approach their immigrant charges resembled those used in other American metropolises. But Buffalo occupied an important place in late nineteenth- and eary twentieth-century philanthropy because its citizens created a number of social experiments, including the nation's first Charity Organization Society (COS), founded in 1877. Until the second decade of the twentieth century, social work had no distinct focus. It consisted of a conglomeration of settlement work, case work, social reform, and agency administration in which anyone, paid or volunteer, could claim the title of social worker.[13] The type of relationship that the social workers in Buffalo sought to establish with the Italians varied, ranging from that of missionary and potential convert to something approaching a professional-client bond. Mary Remington's Welcome Hall, stressing temperance and evangelical morality, represented one extreme; the city's Department of Public Welfare and a few other institutions engaging in full-scale professional activities another. Between them stood a variety of organizations, including the COS (especially in its early days), the Women's Educa-

[11] Marvin E. Gettleman, "Charity and Social Class in the United States, 1874–1900," *American Journal of Sociology and Economics*, 22 (July–Oct. 1963), 419; see also Brenda K. Shelton, "Social Reform and Social Control in Buffalo, 1890–1900" (unpublished Ph.D. dissertation, State University of New York at Buffalo, June 1970), pp. 189ff.

[12] Roy Lubove, *The Professional Altruist: The Emergence of Social Work as a Career, 1880–1930* (Cambridge, 1965), p. 23.

[13] Lubove, pp. 2ff., 18, 119, provides background on the history of social work and of the COS.

tional and Industrial Union, and several settlements staffed by individuals of varying degrees of specialization from friendly visitors to medical case workers to nurses and doctors.

The agencies engaged in a host of activities among Italians and they differed both in terms of goals sought and in the degree of professional competence involved. Throughout the 1920's several organizations, including the North American Civic League for Immigrants, the Visiting Nurses Association, the city health department, and the COS, sent domestic educators—some of them professionals—into the homes of the city's poor. Some social agencies, staffed and run almost entirely by non-Italians, provided other services to Little Italy as part of city-wide programs. The COS did relief and case work for all of the city's poor. By the 1920's at least seven day nurseries and playgrounds had been founded under public and private auspices, some of them in Little Italy. The Children's Aid Society of Buffalo, another city-wide agency, provided medical care and advice for the young.[14]

Beginning in the 1890's, neighborhood and settlement houses occupied important positions in Buffalo's repertoire of charitable agencies. Generally staffed by reformers or individuals with religious goals, they represented a nonprofessional approach to social work. Welcome Hall and Remington Settlement worked chiefly with Italians in Italian neighborhoods. After the 1893 depression, the women's circle of the First Presbyterian Church decided to embark upon a relief work program and extended an invitation to Mary Remington, one of the country's most important settlement house missionaries, to help them. A reformer interested in evangelical religion and temperance, Remington left her successful settlement in New Haven, Connecticut in 1894 to establish Welcome Hall in Buffalo's Little Italy. Here she set up activities that were afterwards adopted by other settlement and neighborhood houses. These included a diet kitchen, sewing classes, a Sunday School, mothers' meetings, a nursery and

[14] J. N. Larned, *A History of Buffalo*, II (New York, 1911), 85; Bertram Ireland, *The Little Child in Our Great Cities* (New York, 1925), pp. 12–14; COS, *Thirteenth Annual Report, 1907.*

kindergarten, vocational education for boys and girls, housekeeping and cleanliness classes, and recreational programs.[15]

After a few months Remington rented two nearby tenements populated almost entirely by Italians. She initiated her temperance program by closing a saloon and dance hall located in one of them. She also hoped to keep young chidren off the streets and out of the halls of crowded buildings. Remington sought a location for her gospel meetings, hoping for "evangelization through social service." [16] In 1898 she left Welcome Hall and obtained support from wealthy Buffalonians to purchase another tenement housing about one hundred Italian families. Here in Remington House she sought to create an "object lesson of the decency of life that might be lived in such a place." [17]

By living within the neighborhoods of the urban poor, settlement workers attempted to disassociate themselves, at least physically, from the middle class, and in this way hoped to establish a close rapport with those among whom they worked. Jane Addams, the settlement movement's leader, noted this difference in approach from that of the COS friendly visitors, who, she insisted, specified "impossibly bourgeois" standards for the underprivileged.[18] Yet Buffalo settlement workers were still members of the middle class, and despite their greater insights and sympathies with the poor, they failed to overcome these associations. It is doubtful even that they wished to do so. Friendly visitors and settlement workers had distinctive personalities, techniques, and goals, but from the immigrants' viewpoint they hardly differed. Despite their physical presence in

[15] For background on these settlements, see: Hill, *Municipality of Buffalo*, II, 699; Larned, *History of Buffalo*, II, 103ff.; Welcome Hall, *First Annual Report, 1895*, p. 3; Mary Remington, *Report of the Remington Gospel Settlement* (Buffalo, 1904). Information on the ethnic origins of their clients is in: Pauline D. Wallens, "Recreation Survey of Tract 12, Ward 4" (unpublished report, Department of Sociology of the University of Buffalo and the Buffalo Foundation, 1929); Welcome Hall, *Annual Report, 1896*, p. 6; ibid., *1915*, p. 45; ibid., *1923*, p. 12.

[16] Weir, p. 282; Larned, II, 103; Anna Coushaine, "In Humanity's Name," *Courier*, March 24, 1901, p. 6; *IC*, Jan. 11, 1902.

[17] Larned, II, 105.

[18] Jane Addams, *Democracy and Social Ethics* (New York, 1911), pp. 27–28, quoted in Gettleman, p. 422.

Little Italy, the settlement workers represented a different class and culture—and the immigrants knew it.

Their class-bound outlook caused the Buffalo social workers to misunderstand the aliens and ultimately to fail in their mission. Jane Addams' pointed remarks about the attitude of the American teacher toward Italian immigrants substantiate this position. Although she was referring to a general problem, not specifically to Buffalo charity workers, her comments illustrate a typical caretaker-client interaction.

> Too often the teacher's conception of her duty is to transform him [the Italian child] into an American of a somewhat snug and comfortable type, and she insists that the boy's powers must at once be developed in an abstract direction, quite ignoring the fact that his parents have had to do only with tangible things. She has little idea of the development of Italian life. Her outlook is national and not racial, and she fails, therefore, not only in knowledge of, but also in respect for, the child and his parents. She quite honestly estimates the child upon an American basis. The contempt for the experiences and languages of their parents which foreign children sometimes exhibit, and which is most damaging to their moral as well as intellectual life, is doubtless due in part to the overestimation which the school places upon speaking and reading in English. This cutting into his family loyalty takes away one of the most conspicuous and valuable traits of the Italian child.[19]

Jane Addams' success among Italian immigrants undoubtedly stemmed from her unusual empathy. She understood that cultural differences existed between herself and the immigrants; she also understood the importance of respecting those differences. The teachers' efforts produced enormous difficulties and resentments because they tried to undercut the family and provided nothing meaningful for the immigrants in return. In contrast, Addams perceived that a stable immigrant family was the key to eventual adjustment. The social workers in Buffalo never achieved her success because they attempted to undermine Old

[19] Addams, "Foreign-Born Children in the Primary Grades," *Journal of the Proceedings and Addresses, National Educational Association* (Chicago, 1897), quoted in Sigmund Diamond, ed., *The Nation Transformed* (New York, 1963), pp. 422–423.

World culture instead of seeing its positive value. Their misunderstanding of Italians, and the immigrants' mistrust of them, also stemmed from the charity workers' identity as outsiders. On the whole, non-Italians established and controlled the social agencies. Most of the workers, and the individuals who sponsored them, had Protestant middle-class and upper-class origins. Philanthropists like J. J. Albright and George Lewis, for example, prominent in business and social affairs, clearly belonged to Buffalo's elite.[20] Frederic Almy, long-time COS secretary and local supporter of the North American Civic League, likewise had strong connections with the Protestant establishment. Finally, Protestant organizations formally sponsored some of the caretaking agencies such as Welcome Hall and the International Institute.

Until the 1920's, when the Department of Social Welfare appointed several persons of Italian birth or ancestry to the staff of Neighborhood House Number Two, not one social welfare agency formally recognized that Italians as a group had different and unique needs. Some, it is true, sought the support of prominent local Italian doctors and welcomed them as advisers.[21] And by the 1920's a few women of Italian descent had entered professional social work positions connected with public and private agencies.[22] But even in these cases, Italians did not occupy executive positions or determine agency policy. The immigrants could perhaps identify more readily with Catholic-sponsored settlements, but these organizations did not publish reports, so their relationship to immigrants and their families is unknown. Like the Protestants, Buffalo's Catholic reformers

[20] Larned, II, 105. Information concerning the background of Buffalo philanthropists was provided by Brenda Shelton in a personal letter to the author, June 27, 1969.

[21] City of Buffalo, Department of Public Affairs, *Annual Report, June 30, 1926*, p. 35. City of Buffalo, *Annual Report of the Department of Social Welfare for the Fiscal Year Ending June 30, 1929* (Buffalo, 1929), p. 39; Welcome Hall, *Annual Report, 1913*, p. 25; North American Civic League for Immigrants, New York-New Jersey Committee, *Report*, Dec. 1, 1909 to Feb. 1, 1913 (New York, n.d.), p. 2.

[22] S. P. Breckinridge, *New Homes for Old* (New York, 1921), p. 281; and Augello, pp. 82–83.

also expected a specific type of behavior in return for their services.[23]

Communication between social workers and their clients failed for other reasons. The nonprofessional Protestant workers attributed much of the Italian immigrants' problem to moral turpitude. Welcome Hall warned its domestic visitors against canting or preaching, but it required them to have "knowledge of the physical and moral causes of degeneracy," and to urge faith in God upon those they visited.[24] Remington House evangelists, who also believed that a definite moral problem existed among the immigrants, sought as their clients Socialists and anarchists who had rejected Catholicism.[25] Remington's mission and Welcome Hall even established a Sunday School and Sunday evening gospel services especially for them.

American-style sobriety, thrift, sociability, industry, cleanliness, health, patriotism, citizenship, "proper" work habits, and "proper" play—ideals familiar to the social workers but very foreign to the south Italians—won high priority in the programs of all such Protestant agencies. Welcome Hall stated the philosophy of many of these organizations succinctly when it described the purposes of its Mothers' Club: "to teach them the value of cleanliness, industry, and devotion to their homes and children and inspire them with courage to meet their daily trials." Remington's temperance interest led to the establishment of the Band of Hope Temperance Club for boys and girls. Her concern for youthful virtue provided the impetus for the Try to Do Right Club. According to Remington's own admission, the boys were not eager candidates, and evangelical morality attracted them less than the settlement's punching bag.[26]

The COS strongly urged thrift upon the Italians. It sought to educate them to follow the example of the city's Germans and Poles, who had saved enough money to purchase their own

[23] Catholic women, nuns, and priests operated these. Larned, II, 107; Hill, *Municipality of Buffalo*, II, 699; Weir, pp. 272, 365; COS, *Annual Report, 1901*, p. 58; Shelton, letter to author.

[24] Welcome Hall, *Annual Report, 1913*, p. 15.

[25] Bernardy, "L'emigrazione delle donne," p. 124.

[26] Welcome Hall, *Second Annual Report, 1896*.

homes. The COS Penny Bank program encouraged poor families to prepare for hard times or misfortune. Not to be outdone, in the 1890's Remington persuaded several Italians not to accept relief from the city's poor office. Amateur workers also emphasized the proper use of money. In order to "maintain a spirit of independence" among Italian clients at a Remington House millinery show, the Women's Association of the Congregational Church thought it prudent to charge a nominal sum for the second-hand hats it sold.[27] Even the International Institute, an organization of professional competence, endorsed the virtue of saving with its Thrift and Sociability Club. All the settlements encouraged industrious habits among their younger charges. At Welcome Hall boys and girls learned vocational skills, including shoemaking, mechanical draftsmanship, shorthand, and typewriting.[28] Meanwhile, the Women's Educational and Industrial Union attempted to discipline "restless [Italian] children," and tried to turn "into useful channels the energies and resources of these excitable" young ones.[29]

Unlike their immigrant clients, the settlement houses recognized the specialized needs of childhood. The social workers believed that play as well as work constituted a necessary part of the American upbringing. In order to provide a "wider experience" than the immigrant child was apt to receive at home, leisure activities became an important part of the settlement house programs, and the professional and public agencies soon concurred. For this reason, playgrounds and athletic events were instituted at many public neighborhood houses and the International Institute's Just for Fun Club was started.[30]

[27] "Remington Hall Millinery Show," *Express*, Nov. 17, 1905; COS, *Fifteenth Annual Report, 1892*, p. 40; *Proceedings of the Fifth Annual Meeting of the Charity Organization Society of Buffalo, Jan. 18, 1883* (Buffalo, 1883), p. 15; Remington, p. 13.

[28] Thomas Wayne Triller, "The History of the Development of the International Institute in Buffalo, New York" (unpublished Master's thesis, University of Buffalo, School of Social Work, Feb. 1952), p. 5; Welcome Hall, *Annual Report, 1895*, pp. 8–9; "Remington Hall," *Express*, May 3, 1902.

[29] Mrs. Frederick J. Shepard, "The Women's Educational and Industrial Union in Buffalo," *Buffalo Historical Society Publications*, 22 (1918), 169.

[30] Welcome Hall, *Annual Report, 1930*, pp. 14–15; Triller, p. 5; "Beneficenza," *IC*, Sept. 4, 1909.

The settlements also considered leisure, including time spent outside the home, a necessary element in women's lives. Imitating other city agencies who sponsored fresh air clubs to counter the ill effects of urban congestion, Welcome Hall provided for mothers who wished to accompany their children to its summer lake retreat. Its Mothers' Club specified relaxation for women outside the home as one of its special goals. "The value of the social element in the settlement," Welcome Hall stated, "should not be underestimated." With its recreation programs the settlement hoped to bring a "smile to faces that have forgotten how to laugh" because the pressures of poverty had become so overbearing.[31]

All the charity agencies stressed cleanliness and good health habits. Mary Remington's constant presence in her tenement house provided an example of American housekeeping customs. The International Institute and the city's neighborhood houses, staffed by professionals, took a more formal approach by conducting classes on home hygiene, but the basic goals remained the same. Day nurseries, having complete control over youngsters in the temporary absence of their parents, exerted an important infuence upon children's personal habits.[32] The North American Civic League, also an organization with professional staff members, provided still another form of propaganda: it published guidelines to domestic and public hygiene, ranging from such simple reminders as "Don't spit on the sidewalk" to advice on proper home sanitation.[33]

The professional organizations in particular encouraged patriotism and good citizenship. The International Institute established the Red, White, and Blue Club with these goals in mind.[34] Americanization classes at Neighborhood House Number Two, in the Italian area, shared these and other ends. This settlement house declared as its purpose a desire "to impart to the people of the community the true American spirit," by teaching immigrants and their children "honesty, squareness to others, and thoughtfulness for others; by teaching kindness

[31] Welcome Hall, *Annual Report, 1898–99*, p. 11.
[32] Triller, p. 5; Welcome Hall, *Annual Report, 1930*, pp. 14–15.
[33] "Norme igieniche," *IC*, July 26, 1913, p. 2. [34] Triller, p. 5.

to animals and to those who are less fortunate; and by bringing the community spirit" into the neighborhood.[35]

Both professional and amateur social workers provided their services to immigrants with varying degrees of sophistication. Yet in the words of a local critic who conducted a recreation survey of Buffalo, they lacked "appreciation of the recreational-cultural heritage" of the foreign born.[36] Although they emphasized recreation and leisure for both women and children, the Italian customs and rituals had no more place in the settlement programs than they did in those of other caretaking agencies. Such a policy would almost certainly have involved a certain amount of self-direction on the part of the clients, forcing the settlement workers to forfeit plans to control them. The social workers and reformers did not, after all, aim to preserve a peasant culture but to propagate their own ideals and to Americanize immigrants. Encouraging the Old World ways would have meant sacrificing the dependent relationship they hoped to establish with their clients.

Despite efforts to involve all immigrants, the most important activities of the neighborhood houses—play groups, mothers' clubs, and education—involved only women and young children. Adolescent boys and girls reacted well to the settlement's vocational and recreational efforts, but they responded selectively to demands made upon them. Young boys came to Mary Remington's settlement to use its athletic equipment, but they did not necessarily accept her moral preferences, and Remington herself admitted their lack of interest in her evangelical notions.

The settlements found that men and adolescent boys were the most difficult to interest. Welcome Hall established a men's debating society in the 1890's, but its activities received infrequent mention after that time. Two more men's clubs functioned in the first two decades of this century. One of these had a strictly social purpose—the facilities were used solely for banquets and amusement. The other, with a membership composed of natives of Misilmeri, in Sicily, was really an Italian

[35] City of Buffalo, Department of Public Affairs, *Annual Report, 1926,* p. 35.
[36] Weir, p. 361.

provincial organization that took advantage of the settlement house facilities.[37] The men appeared willing to exploit Welcome Hall's facilities, but like their sons they failed to accept its moral programs or to express any further interest in the settlement.

Ultimately, these neighborhood houses and settlements adopted a more realistic attitude. Because of their failure to attract men and boys, they concentrated their energies most vigorously upon women and children. With space at a premium, the city's professional welfare facilities also turned almost all of their attention to the most promising clients—women and juveniles.[38] Some agencies, such as the Young Women's Christian Association and the Women's Educational and Industrial Union, dealt with women only as a matter of policy. The settlements' almost exclusively female staffs and their concentration on attracting the women and children meant that they had little appeal even to more Americanized second-generation Italian men.[39]

The attempts on the part of the settlements to individualize women conflicted strongly with the Italian male's concept of femininity. Italian men simply did not view women as leaders. Most of them disapproved both of emancipated women and of the democratization of the family; they felt threatened by the influence of female settlement workers upon their wives and daughters. Some expressed regret that their sons chose to spend their evenings with the "bad women" who worked at the neighborhood houses.[40] Sicilian men, especially—and most Buffalo Italians were from this island—resented the settlement's intrusions into family life. Proud of their wives' domestic abilities, they ridiculed the idea that a settlement could teach a woman housekeeping.[41]

Buffalo's Italian women were more flexible, and some sought

[37] Welcome Hall, *Annual Report, 1898–99*, p. 25; and ibid., *1923*, p. 20; *IC*, Dec. 31, 1921.

[38] "Neighborhood House Reports" (unpublished report, Buffalo, New York, Jan. 1930), p. 10.

[39] William F. Whyte, Jr., *Street Corner Society: The Social Structure of an Italian Slum*, 2d ed. (Chicago, 1955), p. 103.

[40] "The Italian and the Settlement," *Survey*, 30 (April 5, 1913), 58, 60.

[41] Baxter, p. 85.

to improve themselves by attending the classes run by the settlements. Many expressed an initial enthusiasm for English classes because they hoped to teach their children the language properly, but before long they stopped attending, giving "family reasons" as their excuse. Several local charities sponsored Mothers' Clubs, but the majority of Italian women did not attend, either because of their husbands' jealousy of this outside activity, or because the men believed their wives should be at home tending the children.[42] From the male family head's point of view, the settlement constituted a threat to his control and superiority over his wife. He therefore wished her to remain at home, as she usually did.

Many Italian parents also believed that the activities and ideals of the settlement threatened their control over their children. One parent, aghast at the settlement's influence on his young ones, complained, "These are not like the children we had in Italy." [43] The settlement made little attempt to segregate male and female children—a serious violation of Italian sensibilities; furthermore, its atmosphere threatened immigrant matrimonial customs which dictated that a child should marry someone from his parents' province, and certainly someone of Italian origin. Several nationalities and provinces mixed at the settlements, and the chances of a child socializing with and marrying a stranger from outside the parents' social circle were increased. On some occasions a program—such as Welcome Hall's summer cottage or fresh air program—would temporarily separate children from their parents and even wives from their husbands, thus removing them, if only briefly, from family control.[44]

The settlement programs sabotaged parental control in more subtle ways. Welcome Hall observed proudly of the youngsters in its kitchen garden classes, for example, that in many instances the children had learned practical tasks which they could teach their mothers to do. Sometimes the children even did them better than their mothers.[45] Welcome Hall preferred to

[42] De'Rossi, "Le donne ed i fanciulli," pp. 6, 8.
[43] "The Italian and the Settlement," p. 58.
[44] Welcome Hall, *Annual Report, 1912*, p. 27; *IC*, July 6, 1907.
[45] Welcome Hall, *Annual Report, 1904*, p. 21.

work with the preadolescents when their less cooperative parents were absent. Commenting on the Lake Erie summer cottage program, the Annual Report stated: "In the case of the children, particularly when unaccompanied by their parents, there is an opportunity for training in some manners, especially at the table, regularity in rising and retiring, observance of bathing . . . and the need for personal cleanliness." [46] From the settlement's point of view, the parents interfered with the relationship they sought to establish with the children. If the parents were not about, so much the better.

In 1913 the National Federation of Settlements conducted a national survey which exposed the hostility of working-class husbands and fathers to their programs. The Federation made suggestions for involving the entire family in activities, but the presence of parents was not to become a hindrance to its work. The settlements' most serious problem, as the Federation conceived it, was the lack of permissiveness on the part of working-class men toward their families. Here its policy statement involved a direct undermining of the Italian values concerning the women of the family. "Every effort should be made," the report stated, "to appeal to his [the family head's] pride in his womenfolk and to induce him to individualize them." [47] No clearer attack upon the traditional culture of the Italian family could have been made.

The continuing domination of the family by the Italian man and his resentment of social welfare agency intrusion into family life kept the majority of Italian women from attending settlement socials and classes. One Italian social worker associated with the North American Civic League commented that the woman "remains inside the home, and that is where she will stay." [48]

The city's social agencies, including Welcome Hall, the COS, the Visiting Nurses Association, and the North American Civic League, responded to this domestic entranchment by sending

[46] Welcome Hall, *Annual Report, 1913*, p. 31.

[47] Robert A. Woods and Albert J. Kennedy, *Young Working Girls: A Summary of Evidence from Two Thousand Social Workers* (Boston and New York, 1913), p. 75. See also pp. 69, 73.

[48] De'Rossi, "Le donne ed i fanciulli," p. 8.

social workers, visiting nurses, and domestic educators out into the Italian homes. The North American Civic League began its national experiment with domestic educators in Buffalo in 1911.[49] Working with the COS, these social workers sought to give practical instruction in the home on housekeeping and personal hygiene. Welcome Hall operated a clinic and referral service to local hospitals and dispensaries, but it also sponsored classes within Italian homes in an attempt to deal with the women's unwillingness to leave them. Various city agencies, including the health and hospital departments, contributed the services of nurses who also visited the homes of the poor.[50]

One of the domestic educator's functions consisted of instructing her clients in sex hygiene. The more technical matters such as prenatal care and delivery were handled by doctors and nurses. Generally speaking, immigrant women, regardless of nationality, avoided male doctors; they preferred to rely upon midwives for delivery. Observing that she had had eleven of her thirteen children at home, Mary Sansone commented: "Most people used the midwife. It was the custom. We used to call the doctor when something was wrong."[51]

The programs established by social welfare agencies and executed by domestic educators, regardless of their professional competence, interfered in the most intimate areas of Italian family life. From the immigrants' point of view, two of their goals—the presence of male doctors at birth and sex education for women and girls—were a direct attack on the immigrant concepts of female purity and chastity. For these reasons, the Italian women as well as men regarded the domestic visitors suspiciously. According to one contemporary, although the visitors entered the immigrants' homes with the intention of teaching

[49] Welcome Hall, *Annual Report, 1912*, pp. 31f.; "Buffalo's Immigrants," *Survey*, 28 (May 18, 1912), 315; Ireland, pp. 12ff.; North American Civic League, *Report*, Dec. 1, 1909 to Feb. 1, 1913, pp. 10ff., describes the activities of these domestic social workers. See also U.S. Bureau of Education, *Education of the Immigrant* (Washington, D.C., 1913), pp. 7ff., for a more detailed description of the domestic education of immigrants.

[50] Welcome Hall, *Annual Report, 1912*, p. 31; Ireland, pp. 12–14.

[51] Interview with Mary Sansone; U.S. Bureau of Education, p. 9.

them, "they never got down to the real business of housewifery and they never got very close to the women." [52]

Despite their prejudices against charity relief, Buffalo's Italians accepted aid from public welfare agencies such as the COS and the Bureau of Public Welfare (Table 3). Indeed, the percentage of Italians receiving agency assistance seems to have increased both absolutely and relatively over time. Because no central agency coordinated the welfare figures, their significance is uncertain. Part of the increase in Italian cases, as well as the percentage difference between Italians and other groups in 1908–1909 can be attributed to the relative size of the Italian population in 1908 and 1928.[53] Nevertheless, the reasons given for welfare applications are revealing. Like the majority of cases aided, most Italian families received help because of unemployment, sickness, or insufficient income on the part of the breadwinner. Moral laxity of the father or desertion constituted less common causes for relief among the Italians than among other ethnic groups. The relatively low percentage of Italian families receiving welfare support is striking when we remember that frequently unemployed Italian men carried a heavy burden of support because they disapproved of female employment.[54] It should be stressed again that the percentage of Italian families giving desertion or nonsupport as their justification for aid actually declined during this period. As a general rule, Italian families accepted relief only when circumstances beyond their control—sickness, unemployment, or underemployment—forced them to do so.

[52] De'Rossi, "Le donne ed i fanciulli," p. 8.

[53] In Table 3, nationality refers to citizenship, except for the COS figures, which refer to the nativity of the family head. Therefore, it is not possible to determine how many first-generation Italians were contained under the heading "United States." For the 1920's the Italians were proportionately a larger percentage of cases than the Poles. However, this may be explained by the fact that the latter had been in the city for a longer period of time and many more of them had probably become Americanized and passed into the "United States" category. Italian-Americans were almost 3 percent of the total population in 1910 and almost 9 percent of the total population in 1930. See U.S. Census Bureau, *Thirteenth Census, 1910, Population,* III, *Reports by States, 216, 252; Fifteenth Census, 1930, Population,* III, Part 2, 299, 302.

[54] The Polish attitude was different. See John Daniels, "Americanizing Eight Thousand Poles," *Charities and the Commons,* 24 (June 4, 1910), 379.

Table 3. Families assisted by welfare organizations

	1908–09	1924–25	1926–27	1927–28
Nationality *				
Italian	9% †	18%	18%	19%
Polish	32%	17%	13%	14%
United States	34%	47%	55%	51%
Other	25%	18%	14%	16%
Total	2,124	1,700	2,614	3,581

* Nationality refers to citizenship, except for the COS figures, which refer to the nativity of the family head. See n. 53 in this chapter.

† The figures are rounded to the nearest percent.

Source: The figures for 1908–1909 are from the Charity Organization Society, which served the entire community except for the Jews. See U.S. Cong., Sen., *Immigrants as Charity Seekers*, I, 135; figures for later years are based upon City of Buffalo, *Annual Reports of the Bureau of Public Welfare.*

Although some Italians did accept help, it is easy to understand why the COS—the chief dispenser of public charity until the formation of a municipal welfare system—reported difficulty in obtaining them as clients. According to an Italian government investigator, Maria M. De'Rossi, several Buffalo welfare agencies that attempted to persuade women to report their husbands for lack of support had to acknowledge that they had failed. "This was not the practice in Italy," the investigator reported, "and the character of our women would not permit it." Fear of their husbands and of the negative opinions of neighbors and *paesani* discouraged these women from reporting the facts to welfare agencies. De'Rossi gave no indication of the frequency of desertion or nonsupport. But the prevailing values of the Italian community militated against the widespread occurrence of either, and, furthermore, the available census data indicated that desertion rarely occurred. When men failed to fulfill their obligations, Italian women apparently did not acknowledge the right of public interference in such matters.[55]

Once clients were obtained, the welfare agencies characteristically found it difficult to obtain full cooperation and dependence from them. De'Rossi cited her efforts under COS aus-

[55] De'Rossi, "Le donne ed i fanciulli," p. 9.

pices to deal with the wives of tubercular patients. In order to ensure rehabilitation, the agency insisted that the men rest; if the clients ignored this stipulation, the COS threatened to discontinue its aid. De'Rossi and the Society asked the wives to "swallow their false pride" and make an effort to keep their husbands at home. These cases presented serious difficulties, because both husbands and wives considered charity, as well as the husbands' relinquishment of his obligation to support his family, very humiliating. De'Rossi stated that immigrant pride interfered with other aspects of the charity program, too. Unless an Italian family found itself absolutely destitute, it made every effort to disclaim any association with welfare agencies. Of course, this effort was undermined if the social worker visited the home. On the other hand, the guidance provided by the domestic educators from the North American Civic League, who taught Italian women the cash value of American goods, was appreciated by thrifty Italian women. Realizing the value of such advice, the housewives nevertheless feared that their neighbors would think they were receiving relief, and went to great lengths to avoid this embarrassment. Some domestic educators reported that when they took Italian housewives shopping, the women insisted upon carrying the money in their own hands and paying for the goods themselves, even when they conducted their transactions far from their own neighborhoods.[56] So strong were the pressures exerted by personal ties within Little Italy that even Italians accepting aid refused to adopt a role that declared their dependency publicly.

Frequently, both professional and nonprofessional agencies did require the surrender of some of a family's independence as a precondition for aid. The type of control over clients varied from financial to psychological. In the 1890's, for example, Welcome Hall would secure work for unemployed men, but the settlement confiscated their wages for a period of time; it paid the bills, established bank accounts, and purchased provisions. The same agency encouraged its clients to discuss with its workers the "smallest details of home life." By the 1920's, when the International Institute, a professional agency, began to give advice

[56] Ibid., p. 10.

on marital problems, social agencies had penetrated the most private aspect of family life.[57]

Intrusions of this nature were unheard of in the Mezzogiorno. Undoubtedly, the well-intentioned American social workers aimed to help their clients; but had the Italians accepted their policies, some of the immigrants' most fundamental social values would have been sacrificed. The attempts to diminish the husband's control over family matters and over his wife constituted the most serious challenge to traditional ways. Not surprisingly, Italian families resisted and resented this interference and control. Accepting aid from an institution was bad enough; but permitting the institution to control the family was far worse.[58]

The men were not the only opponents of social policies that diminished their control over family affairs—the women usually stood by them. Even when professional agencies made what seemed to them unquestionably rational stipulations designed to protect the husbands' health, the Italian wives often refused to comply. Immigrant parents also bitterly resented attempts to interfere in child-rearing practices. Very few Italians, for example, made use of the city's Children's Aid Society, an agency of recognized competence. "Family ties are so strong," said one observer, that "it would be very difficult for the Society to even find cases which would concern it in the Italian community." While occasional problems arose, parents and relatives quickly took it upon themselves to reprimand or advise any children involved.[59] Insofar as parental support of and care for children was concerned, the Society had little cause to interfere in Little Italy.

Thus, the community norms, supported by personal ties among Little Italy's residents, operated strongly against Ameri-

[57] Welcome Hall, *Annual Report, 1898–1899,* p. 12; ibid., *1895,* p. 7; Triller, p. 7.

[58] Louise C. Odencrantz, *Italian Women in Industry: A Study of Conditions in New York City* (New York, 1919), p. 202, documents this attitude among New York Italians. William I. Thomas and Florian Znaniecki, *The Polish Peasant in Europe and America,* 2d ed., II, Pt. 2 (New York, 1968), 1697, make similar observations about the reactions of Polish immigrants to charitable efforts.

[59] De'Rossi, "Le donne ed i fanciulli," p. 5.

can institutional and legal interference in family life. The Italian community provided alternative solutions to accepting public charity. Despite the official agencies' efforts Buffalo's south Italians continued to organize and dispense charity among themselves in the informal, personal style to which they were accustomed. The story of chain migration illustrated how such patterns operated among relatives. If no kin resided in Buffalo, voluntary associations, most frequently composed of *paesani*, provided the necessary emergency funds in case of sickness, accident, or death. These organizations operated successfully because most Italian families regarded the poormaster's interference with horror.[60] Even charitable obligations to family and friends who had returned or were left at home were not quickly relinquished. For example, during the Sicilian and Calabrian earthquake disasters of 1905, 1908, and 1909, and for months after, *Il Corriere* printed subscription lists—usually small individual donations of less than a dollar and club donations of twenty-five or fifty dollars—from local Italians and their organizations.[61]

The immigrants turned to their own countrymen for aid in times of extreme crisis in America. In the critical winter of 1923, for example, local Italian professionals, leaders, and priests went among Little Italy's poor offering help. The Italian Ladies Relief Association performed a similar function. In these cases, destitute Italians did accept aid. Organized and staffed by friends and acquaintances of the poor, these charity campaigns were not professional, bureaucratic efforts set up by outsiders who had little knowledge of south Italy's language or culture; despite the amateur status of many, their successful operation can be attributed precisely to their personal, local style.

Most of Buffalo's social workers, even the professionals, continued to view the south Italian ways negatively well into the 1920's. They considered the Italians' failure to adopt middle-class standards and the American way of life a pathological result of social and economic deprivation or (where the least progressive among them were concerned) a result of moral infe-

60 "The Italian Colony in Buffalo," *Courier*, May 8, 1898.
61 See, for example, *IC*, Sept. 16, 1905; and *IC*, Jan. 9, 1909.

riority. They would not admit, nor could they be expected to understand, that the Italians behaved as they did because they had their own culture and their own solutions. Such an admission would have required acknowledging the existence of practical social arrangements different from the ones they championed, recognizing that change was more difficult to bring about than they assumed, and admitting that they had less control over the social order than they liked to believe.[62] They would also have had to relinquish two of their most precious ideals—the value of Americanization and the myth of the melting pot. Although the professional social workers wished to disassociate themselves from the amateurs' paternalistic, class-oriented approach, they had no desire to perpetuate Italian peasant culture.

The Buffalo social workers lived in a society characterized by anti-immigrant attitudes and serious anxiety concerning labor radicalism. They responded more positively than most by attempting to cope with and Americanize these strange foreigners. Many, especially settlement workers, sought to understand and improve social conditions among the immigrant poor in the best way they knew. From their standpoint, the best solution to immigrant problems appeared to be to try to inculcate American middle-class values, not to preserve the Italian ones. But by aiming to develop American individualists out of Italian familists, the welfare workers attacked the very basis of Italian life—the family. It is no wonder that the immigrants viewed the activities and goals of charitable organizations as threats and intrusions.

The south Italian familistic notions and patriarchal traditions triumphed over the settlements' efforts to individualize women and children, to diminish male control over the family, and to democratize family life. Husband, wife, and community cooperated in resisting all efforts to disturb these traditions. In this manner, despite the high unemployment rate among Italians, any drift toward female-controlled families was averted. Ultimately, it appeared, the Italian male would surrender his supremacy neither to his wife nor to the social workers.

[62] Gans, p. 152, makes these general points.

6 "Pasta and Beans Every Day": The Family Economy in the United States

Vincent De Bella, a Sicilian immigrant, looked back upon his successful career as a shoemaker in Buffalo and commented:

> In 1922 I came to the United States at the age of twenty-two. My master [in Italy] was a shoemaker and a bookshop owner. I was his apprentice and learned these trades. . . . [I] came to America to make a better living. . . . I didn't know English. I was able to get work without the language. You don't need the language; you need the shoes. I started out at $18 a week. Every so often I got a $1 raise. In winter I was laid off because business was slow. . . . After being in Buffalo a few years, I opened my own shop. . . . My shop to me was like a temple—shop and home. I had no bad habits. I was forty-two when I married. . . .
>
> You have to have economy. I made $30 a week and saved $20 a week. . . . I had $1,000 after two years. I earned the $30 a week in someone else's shop. These were good wages. I came at the right time—in the 1920's. Later, wages dropped. . . .
>
> The immigrants knew how to save money. One way they saved money; *pasta e fagioli tutti i giorni*—"Pasta and beans every day."

Reflecting modestly on the reasons for his rapid achievement, this sensitive craftsman reveals his positive attitudes toward work, money, and home. De Bella was more successful than the majority of Buffalo Italians, unskilled men who married earlier and raised large families in less prosperous days; but he shared their understanding of hard work, unemployment, and thrift. How did the less fortunate earn and allocate their resources in the New World?

In 1916 a Buffalo settlement report lamented that if underpaid Italians refused charity, they had to "beg, borrow . . . steal," or "live in miserable rooms, take in boarders, and send wife and children to work." [1] Since most Italians would not accept charity or stealing as solutions, their alternatives were clear. The urban poor have often met expenses by combining the wages of every member of the household. In many working-class groups, men unable to support their families without the aid of wives and children faced a possible loss of authority.[2] Yet the south Italian immigrants reacted differently to this situation. In their case, new work patterns did not strain so heavily upon family life because they successfully meshed their Old World values with their New World situation, as the statistical and phenomenological evidence show.

The south Italian work patterns set a precedent for the division of family labor in America. We have seen that the husband and father was always the family's chief breadwinner; although regional exceptions existed, most women did not work outside the home. The distance of the peasants' homes from the fields and the countryside's loneliness militated against full-time female agricultural employment.[3] If south Italian women worked, they generally did so as part of a family group, when harvest time brought a heavy demand for labor. The Mezzogiorno's agri-

[1] Welcome Hall, *Annual Report, 1916*, p. 19.

[2] Odencrantz, *Italian Women in Industry*, p. 68, discusses the family wage system. See also U.S. Cong., Sen., *Immigrants in Cities*, II, 535ff., for analyses of working members of immigrant families in several cities. Calhoun, *American Family*, III, 159ff., discusses the threat to male authority.

[3] Odencrantz, *Italian Women in Industry*, pp. 27ff. Moss and Thomson, "South Italian Family," p. 38; Sidney Sonnino, *La Sicilia nel 1876*, II, *I contadini* (Florence, 1877), 98; Chazanof, "Sicilians of Fredonia," p. 8; Odencrantz *Italian Women in Industry*, p. 373; and Campisi, "Italian Family," p. 444, describe the domestic focus of female work. Sonnino, pp. 97, 139, 195, notes, as an exception to the usual Sicilian custom, that women sometimes worked in Messina's fruit growing area. See also: Foerster, *Italian Immigration*, p. 85; *Emigration Conditions in Europe*, p. 160; Italy *Inchiesta Agraria*, 13: 17, 127. Nina J. Pane Pinto, "Post World War II Immigration to the United States: A Case Study of Italian Female Immigration" (unpublished Master's thesis, State University of New York at Buffalo, 1967), p. 49. Pane Pinto interviewed a group of Buffalo south Italians, none of whom had worked in Italy.

cultural economy has long been markedly seasonal, and women's labor became an important resource during certain periods. Wheat-growing areas demanded a heavy concentration of labor for June and July harvest; the olive season extended from September through January; fruits claimed the fall, and almonds August through October. This fluctuating, often geographically dispersed demand for workers also made seasonal migrations an established feature of south Italian life. Throughout Italy entire families migrated to harvest areas for work.[4] The mountain folk of Sicily's interior, for example, traveled to the fields below for harvesting. These rhythms provided some work throughout the year and a chance for women to increase the family resources. In the Sicilian interior, women gathered olives and hazelnuts; in Palermo's fruitgrowing areas, they harvested lemons and oranges. In each of these situations women labored, but they functioned as members of a family group, not as independent wage earners. Because their work constituted a temporary measure to help offset the family's poverty and not a year-round commitment, they did not challenge their husbands as chief providers. The public nature of the harvest also guaranteed constant surveillance by community, kin, and spouses.

Children's economic roles varied little throughout the Mezzogiorno. At the age of twelve, a male child began working; he contributed to the family economy by laboring in the fields. The boy fortunate enough to become an apprentice left home at seven. A girl's childhood terminated at ten, when her training in housewifery began. Like their mothers, girls rarely worked outside the home. Few received training in a trade. Many learned to sew as a means of minimizing the family's clothing costs.[5] Girls presented a double burden to the family: the dowry required to marry them properly represented a future debt, and the need to protect their honor prevented them from working to help pay it off. The contrasted attitudes toward male and female children were rooted in the girl's position as a family liability. A

[4] For discussion of the seasonal nature of south Italy's agriculture, see Robert E. Dickinson, *The Population Problem of Southern Italy* (Syracuse, 1955), pp. 67, 74; and Italy, *Inchiesta Agraria*, 13: 20ff. Foerster, pp. 532–533, discusses the family migrations. See also Sonnino, pp. 84, 98, 117.

[5] Williams, *South Italian Folkways*, p. 25.

Sicilian proverb quips: "My sister has six children, two boys and four burdens." [6]

Historical evidence suggests that traditional work patterns continued in the new urban-industrial setting. In the early years, clear decisions seem to have been made as to which family members could properly supplement a father's wages and which occupations were inappropriate for women and children. By the 1920's, although most of the Italian immigrants had not yet achieved financial or occupational success, many could be assured of greater job stability; the stress that unemployment had placed upon these families eventually diminished. In the interim, female and juvenile employment could be arranged in ways which minimized the threats to the men's authority.

It is difficult to reconstruct a precise picture of the living standards for Italians in Buffalo. There were fluctuations in the economy, in real wages, in employment regularity and status, family size and life cycle, each of which must be taken into consideration. A hypothetical immigrant family's economic history gives some idea of how these elements related. Let us asume that nineteen-year-old Emil Lanza arrived in Buffalo in 1882, married Amalia Iannuzzi five years later, and had eight or nine children at two-year intervals thereafter. The Lanzas suffered the loss of three or four children; poor living conditions and inadequate diet took their toll. Throughout his working life, a forty-year span, Lanza remained a laborer. He gained in real wages until 1892, but before that time the arrival of children eroded increased earnings. He did not wish his young wife Amalia, who was either pregnant or caring for her offspring, to work. The Lanzas found this period difficult. From 1893 to about 1918, when prewar unemployment had run its course, Lanza either worried about losing his job, or actually lost it. Children kept arriving. Except during 1908 and the wartime boom, however, falling prices actually helped the family along. By 1903 the Lanza's first-born son began making small contributions to the family income. The family could count upon the children's wages until 1913, when they started to leave

[6] Chapman, *Milocca*, p. 30.

home. The years 1919 and 1922 brought new waves of unemployment to Buffalo so that the postwar years were made more difficult by the loss of children's wages, frequent unemployment, and declining real wages. By the time the 1920's brought prosperity, Lanza's hard work was over, his fathering done.[7]

The Buffalo cost-of-living figures confirm the accuracy of this hypothetical family's economic history. From 1890 to 1916, an ordinary Italian laborer's wages could not support a family of five. A charity organization report described him as living on the "ragged edge."[8] Although the average family may have produced as many children as the Lanzas, in early community days it had fewer children living at home at any one time. The mean unbroken family size for all classes of Italians was 4.57 and the median size 4.[9] But age-specific figures tell a more alarming story (Table 4). In 1905, almost half of all families were entering the child-rearing stage—45 percent of Italian wives were under thirty—and an increase in family size was a real possibility for many. A glance at the wives in the thirty-five to thirty-nine age group, women approaching family completion, shows this. The median family size for these women was 6. Italian laborers continued to have relatively large families well into the 1920's when a Buffalo charity agency report indicated that the working-class families surveyed, most of them Italian, had an average of 6.3 members and too little to live on.[10] This was an

[7] This account is based upon a scheme presented in Taylor, *Distant Magnet*, pp. 208–209. Taylor uses the suggestions of R. S. Neale, "The Standard of Living, 1780–1844," *Economic History Review*, 2d ser., 19 (1966), 590–666. Buffalo cost of living data used in this chapter confirm Taylor's estimates.

[8] Welcome Hall, *Annual Report, 1916*, p. 18. This settlement dealt almost exclusively with Italians during this period. "The New York State Conference," *Charities and the Commons*, 21 (Nov. 28, 1908), 339; and "The Cost of Living in New York State," *Fourth Report, FIC*, 4 (Albany, 1915), 1688ff., 1625, estimate "normal" budget requirements at from $650 to $772 for a family of five without allowances for emergency, unemployment, or illness.

[9] NYSMC, 1905.

[10] We cannot obtain an exact notion of completed family size from 1905 census data because the census only recorded surviving children living at home. Note in Table 4 that wives aged 35 to 39 had the highest median family size of 6. This is probably a fairly accurate indication of completed family size simply because women in this age group were unlikely to have married children living away from home. Juvenile Protective Department, Buffalo, New York, "Street Traders in Buffalo," *Buffalo Foundation Forum*, No. 52 (Aug. 1926), pp. 17, 32,

old story for the urban poor: if family income increased, so did family size and expenses.

A closer look at wages and unemployment shows why Italians had difficulties making ends meet. Insufficent income was part of the problem. From 1890 to 1916 the unskilled Italian earned from $7 to $12 for a forty-eight-hour week, slightly less than the average Polish worker.[11] Skilled workers were more fortunate, even though a "superabundance" of tailors, shoemakers, and barbers—skills in which Italians had substantial representation—drove wages down in these occupations. Tailors and barbers could earn as much as $12 weekly.[12] Their chief advantage over unskilled laborers lay not so much in higher weekly incomes, but in the relative stability of their work. Wage data for higher occupations during this period do not exist. No doubt these more fortunate individuals had fewer problems.

If between 1890 and 1916 the average Italian laborer earned $7 to $12 weekly ($364 to $624 annually), some would have earned enough to meet the minimum budgetary requirements for a family of five ($650 to $772). But these yearly income figures assume year-round employment, whereas the majority of Italians remained without work for five, six, or even seven months of the year. Frequent unemployment meant that the expectation of an adequate income was in fact low. An additional problem was that the laborer's salary was not entirely his own, since labor contractors for dock and construction jobs

---

gives an average family size of 6.3 for the 1920's and this substantiates our estimate. These figures apply to surviving children only. Earlier evidence indicated that Italian women bore an average of 11 children.

[11] A dock worker earned from $7 to $9; a railroad worker $9 or less. Wage data are contained in the following sources: Welcome Hall, *Annual Report, 1916*, pp. 18, 21; *23rd Annual Report of the Charity Organization Society, 1899–1901*, p. 101; Banchetti, "Gli Italiani," p. 21; *BE*, No. 1 (1920), p. 70; editorial by "Virtus," "I manovali," *La F*, May 20, 1911; Goodale, "Children of Sunny Italy;" Lucian C. Warren, "Thrift, Labor, Mark Italian Rise Here," *Courier*, Dec. 17, 1940. Construction workers did best at $12 weekly, but they sustained long periods of unemployment; see "Mechanics Helpers Threaten to Strike," *Courier*, April 10, 1910; "Strike," *Express*, May 29, 1910; "I lavoratori," *La F*, Oct. 28, 1911; and "Operai e contrattori," *IC*, March 12, 1910. For dock laborers' and freight handlers' wages, see "Labor Fight on the Docks," *Express*, May 21, 1907; and "Central Men go Back Today," *Courier*, May 24, 1907.

[12] *BE*, No. 1 (1920), p. 70.

Table 4. Family size by age of wife, 1905

Number of children living at home	Age of wives									
	15–19	20–24	25–29	30–34	35–39	40–44	45–49	50–54	55–59	60 and over
0	52 *	26	12	10	8	12	15	18	31	47
1	38	33	20	8	10	12	10	21	19	27
2	10	24	22	17	11	16	17	16	29	15
3	0	10	23	20	16	16	22	16	4	2
4	0	4	13	16	16	14	12	16	15	2
5	0	1	8	14	15	11	7	7	2	0
6	0	1	2	9	11	8	8	4	0	2
7	0	1	1	4	8	6	4	2	0	2
8 or more	0	0	0	1	5	7	4	1	0	2
Percent of wives	6 *	18	21	15	12	10	7	6	2	2
Totals	124	365	416	296	248	215	144	122	46	41
Total wives	2,017									

* Figures are rounded to the nearest percent.
Source: NYSMC, 1905.

customarily deducted a certain proportion for themselves.[13]

Thrifty Italians used familiar Old World devices to keep their families alive. Some kept small gardens behind their homes or in outlying city districts.[14] Marion Callendrucci, who lived in the uncongested east side Abruzzese colony, told how her family got along in Buffalo: "We had our land near the house and we raised our own food. . . . At home in Italy we also used to grow things. Over here you can spend much money on food, but we manage." Other families became summer migrant workers, just as they had in Italy; they labored in the Niagara Frontier's canneries and farms, where some employers absorbed part or all of the costs of food and lodging. In 1909, for example, an Italian government representative found twelve hundred Buffalo Italians working at the establishments she visited.[15]

When an entire family of four or five worked in the canneries from April to November—longer than the customary amount of time—it could earn from $350 to $450 for the season.[16] If the father remained in the city during the summer where he could almost assuredly find an outdoor job and his wife and children worked the canneries, their combined wages provided almost enough money for the year.

Occasional or part-time work for women and children within the city itself provided another possible supplement to the male head's income. Their earning capacities varied according to season and position; but although a few women and children did engage in homework, it never paid well. Italian women and girls rarely left home to work either as domestic or factory laborers until unmarried girls began entering the labor market in the

[13] "The Italian Colony in Buffalo," *Courier*, May 8, 1898; letter, *IC*, Nov. 19, 1904; interview in Augello, "Italian Immigrants," pp. 38f. See "New York State Conference," p. 339, and "The Cost of Living," pp. 1625, 1688ff., for budget estimates.

[14] See City of Buffalo, *People of Buffalo,* p. 30; "Gli Italiani comprano molti lotti in Hillsdale," *IC,* Aug. 9, 1917.

[15] Bernardy, "L'emigrazione delle donne," pp. 85f. Immigrants did not report this part-time occupation to the census takers, so exact numbers cannot be determined.

[16] *Reports of the Immigration Commission, Immigrants in Industry*, XXII, *Recent Immigrants in Agriculture*, II, 508, 510, 494, 496. This is a high estimate. and it is based upon an Italian family with two children over 14.

1920's.[17] In that period, an unskilled woman earned from $7 to $15 weekly as a factory laborer. Because the unmarried Italian girls, unlike many other working-class women, usually lived with their families, they contributed almost all of their wages to family and dowry savings. These contributions should not be overestimated, however, because almost half of the Italian women working in eastern cities labored only part of the year in seasonal occupations. Even those who managed to find year-round employment had little chance of increasing their income because employers paid them by the piece. When women achieved proficiency at one task, thrifty managers would move them to another.[18]

The American cities, hosts to thousands of unattached men, also offered opportunities to unskilled women. Wives made an important contribution to the family income by taking roomers and boarders into their households. The women cleaned, washed, and cooked for bachelors and married men with families in Italy; in 1905, room fees alone in Buffalo's Italian section brought $3.50 weekly, a small but precious sum to a laborer's family. But even this supplement could not be counted upon—it depended upon a heavy seasonal demand for laborers which would draw unattached immigrants to the city.[19] Sons also contributed to the family income. Young men could duplicate their fathers' wages in seasonal outdoor labor. Younger boys gener-

[17] Around World War I, for example, homework wages ranged from $.17 to an unusual high of $1.50 daily during the spring clothing season. *Second Report, FIC,* II (1913), 711; *Courier*, March 11, 1911. Goodale, "Children of Sunny Italy," notes that Italian women seldom worked as housemaids or factory workers because husbands felt obliged to do the providing. Female employment patterns are discussed in greater detail in Ch. 7.

[18] Wage and cost of living information is contained in Young Women's Christian Association, Buffalo, New York, "Some Facts Concerning Women in Buffalo Industries." The wage data were obtained from a survey of 21 factories employing almost 3,000 women. In the second decade of the twentieth century, the average factory wage for women came to $5 weekly. An advertisement in *IC*, Oct. 6, 1906, offered girls $6 weekly. At this time *Preliminary Report, FIC,* II (1912), 810, claimed that a girl could not maintain a proper living standard on less than $8 weekly. On the seasonal nature of Italian women's work, see Bernardy, "L'emigrazione delle donne," p. 51.

[19] Bernardy, "L'emigrazione delle donne," pp. 16f.; for the cost of rooms, see want ads in the local papers, for example, *Courier*, May 5, 1905; COS, *23rd Annual Report, 1899–1900*, p. 106.

ally worked in street trades as newsboys or shoeshiners; they earned 22¢ daily in 1903, and $1.50 to $1.75 weekly in 1926.[20]

These various types of part-time work allowed Italian families to make ends meet despite heavy male unemployment. The 1905 manuscript census data yield a more precise specification of family work allocations. The year 1905 is a good one for our purposes—midpoint in the period covered by this study, 1905 brought neither economic crisis nor special blessings to Little Italy.[21] Family employment patterns would be more characteristic during this year than in a depression year.

The size of the family determined economic needs and potential income alike. Buffalo's Italian families were somewhat larger than average. A United States Labor Bureau survey for 1900 to 1902 reported that laborers with children (84 percent of all laborers) had an average of 2.85 juvenile dependents; unbroken Italian families with children (82 percent of unbroken families) had an average of 3.1.[22] A 1920 study of white unbroken families in Chicago reported only 30 percent with five or more members; 45 percent of a comparable group of Buffalo Italians had five or more members.[23]

[20] Adams, *Buffalo Newsboy*, p. 2; Juvenile Protective Department, Buffalo, New York, "Street Traders in Buffalo," pp. 17, 32.

[21] A word of caution: because Italian men were most likely to be employed in summer, when the census was taken, the data may exaggerate the degree of occupational security achieved by 1905.

[22] *Eighteenth Annual Report of the Commissioner of Labor* (1903), cited in Day Monroe, *Chicago Families: A Study of Unpublished Census Data* (Chicago, 1932), p. 305; more than 21,000 families were surveyed. Monroe criticizes the Bureau's biased sample. If the Bureau had included an appropriate number of families headed by older men whose children had left home, its figure for average number of children would have been smaller. Also, the Bureau's sample may have included a greater proportion of higher salaried wage-earners than Buffalo's Italians did. Income differentials between this sample and Buffalo Italians could perhaps explain the difference in family size among the two groups. The federal census also analyzed family data for the censuses of 1890 and 1900, but its conclusions are not useful for comparative purposes. It did not base its analyses upon natural families, as with Buffalo and Chicago data.

[23] Monroe, p. 88. This was so despite the slightly lower age of Buffalo wives. Forty-six percent of the Chicago wives were under thirty-five. Sixty percent of the Buffalo wives were under thirty-five. Changes in birth rates from 1905 to 1920 or class differences between the two groups could explain family size differences. The 1920 Chicago study, for example, included all white families regardless of occupation, while most Buffalo Italians were working-class. Work-

A man's occupational success seems to have influenced family size. Except for the permanently unemployed—mostly older men whose children had left home—unskilled and personal service workers had the smallest families. In the remaining occupational categories, half or more families had five or more members. Successful immigrants did not initially adopt the American middle-class preference for small families; on the contrary, the highest achievers had the largest families.[24] Class was almost certainly the determining influence here. The age differences among occupational groups or among their wives do not explain the larger size of higher-income families.[25] Either the higher-income families maintained a cultural preference for many offspring, or their children had a better chance of surviving. Higher infant mortality rates, then, may explain the smaller size of poorer families. Laborers as a group resided in the United States for a shorter period than any other category. Their wives spent more of their fertile years in Italy, where the infant survival rates were lower; the chances are that these families lost many children before emigrating. The move to America ultimately ameliorated this situation, but the ordinary laborer still could not meet the high living and health standards attained by more successful immigrants.[26]

---

ing-class groups in both cities produced roughly the same size families; at the middle range, Buffalo's Italians had larger families. Sources: Monroe, p. 92, and NYSMC, 1905.

[24] In contrast, Chicago males in 1920 tended to have fewer children as they became more successful. See Monroe, p. 92. The figures for Buffalo unbroken nuclear families are as follows: of manufacturers, wholesalers, independent contractors, and real estate men, 56 percent had 5 or more children; of officials, professionals, semi-professionals, 51 percent; of small shop owners, restaurant or saloonkeepers, service business owners, 54 percent; of clerical and sales, 55 percent; of skilled workers, 53 percent; of personal service workers, 45 percent; of unskilled laborers, 41 percent; of the unemployed, 36 percent. Source: NYSMC, 1905.

[25] The median age of wives for all save the spouses of clerical and service workers was the same—thirty to thirty-four. Differences in age structure among occupational groups do not seem to explain differences in family size. Unskilled laborers included roughly the same proportion of men under thirty-five as manufacturers, wholesalers, independent contractors, and real estate men—44 percent and 40 percent respectively. Source: NYSMC, 1905.

[26] See the author's dissertation, "Like the Fingers of the Hand," p. 32, for a breakdown of male occupations by length of residence.

Larger than average family size only begins to explain the financial stress experienced by immigrants; family life-cycle data tell us much more. As the hypothetical case of the family of Emil Lanza suggested, a family's financial needs are greatest before the children marry and leave home. A high proportion of Buffalo families were young couples just beginning married life. In 1905 almost half of the wives were still in their teens and twenties. Most women under twenty-five had just begun to have children. The experience of older wives between the ages of thirty and forty-five—those at the height of their child-bearing careers—gives some indication of their younger sisters' future prospects. About a third had five or more single children living at home.[27] By 1905, therefore, a significant number of families were already trying to support a heavy burden. Those in their teens and early twenties faced particularly dim futures; by the time they encountered the wage depressions between 1908 and 1915, most of their young ones would not be of working age. If, as some argue, the Italian birth rates and/or infant survival rates increased in the United States,[28] this group faced even more tenuous economic prospects than their elders had. Data on children under sixteen (the legal full-time working age) offer further evidence that families in 1905 were facing immediate financial stress. More than 75 percent of all unbroken families had at least one child under sixteen; and in every occupational category save the unemployed group, at least 41 percent had three or more children under sixteen.[29]

The gainful employment of other members besides the family head had much to do with the living standard an immigrant family could maintain. Like the Emil Lanzas, many of these families overcame the margin of poverty only when the children matured, went to work, and contributed to the family income.

[27] One of the difficulties census data presents, especially for our understanding of older families, is that only children living at home within a household can be studied. For present purposes, this group is less important. Fortunately, in most immigrant populations, older parents compose a relatively small group.

[28] Rose, "Research Note on the Influence of Immigration on the Birth Rate," pp. 614–621.

[29] NYSMC, 1905.

In 1905, 68 percent of Buffalo's Italian male family heads were the only earners in their families. The figure for all white Chicago families in 1920 was 61 percent. Though not large, this difference is important because the typical Buffalo Italian family produced more children than the typical white Chicago family. In 1920 Rochester had an even smaller proportion of husbands (56 percent) listed as only earners. This discrepancy resulted from the high percentage (16 percent) of Rochester housewives who took in roomers and boarders. The corresponding figures for Chicago and Buffalo were lower—10 percent and 12 percent respectively.[30] Early twentieth-century American urban families seem to have allocated their family obligations in a characteristic pattern; the figures for the number of children working and the number of families with no earners, or wife only earning, are strikingly similar. Indeed, the only difference that ethnic background appears to have made is the low percentage of Italian wives—slightly more than 13 percent—who contributed to the family income by engaging in urban occupations. The comparable figures for Chicago and Rochester were 28 percent and 34 percent respectively.[31]

This distinction may reflect the predominantly working-class

[30] The Chicago data are based upon all white families living in single-family households only; that for Rochester are for all families living in single- and multiple-family households. The Buffalo data, as already noted, are also based upon all Italian families living in single- and multiple-family households. Women who worked in the canneries part-time did not report this occupation to the census taker; therefore, they are not included in the Buffalo computation. Sources: NYSMC, 1905; Monroe, pp. 324–325; Rochester data in ibid., and extracted from Bertha Nienberg, *The Woman Homemaker in the City of Rochester, New York at the Census of 1920* (Washington, D.C., 1923), pp. 30–31.

[31] NYSMC, 1905; Monroe, pp. 324–325. The Rochester and Chicago data on percentages of wives working may be slightly inflated because of the manner in which it is presented. Nineteen percent of Rochester families and 18 percent of Chicago families are described as "husband or wife and child or children" working. To obtain the figures cited in the text, I assumed that in roughly half of these cases, wives worked.

Other family wage-earning patterns were similar. In all three cities, less than 1 percent of all families had wives as the only earner; 1 percent had children as the only earners, and 1 percent had no earners. Eleven percent of the Buffalo families had both husband and wife earning; comparable figures for Chicago and Rochester were 15 percent and 20 percent respectively. Two percent of Buffalo families had husband, wife and children earning; comparable figures for Chicago and Rochester were 3 percent and 5 percent respectively.

character of the Italian population, rather than any ethnic differences. However, a closer scrutiny of the employment patterns of the women in Buffalo suggests that cultural differences were significant. First, Italian women were more likely than any other ethnic group in Buffalo to supplement the family income by taking in boarders; 93 percent of those who worked added to family income in this manner.[32] Almost all other wives who worked went to the canneries to work part time as members of family groups. The Italian wives rejected factory and domestic work (as already noted), choosing not to labor outside the home unsupervised by relatives or friends. Their choices cannot be completely explained by demographic patterns and life cycle stage.[33]

Except for those who worked in the canneries during the summer, most of the Italian families had only one person—the male head—bringing in a salary; this was true of both lower- and upper-income males.[34] But necessity required them to show some flexibility. The larger the Italian family was, the less likely was it that the father would be the only breadwinner. He was, for example, the only person employed in 82 percent of all two-member unbroken families. But the likelihood of his being the only earner in families of three declined to 70 percent and so on.[35] The reason is obvious: the larger the family, the more mouths to feed, and the more potential wage earners.

Economically pressed families did not hesitate to use their children as a source of income. Half of all working-age children

[32] *Reports of the Immigration Commission*, XXVI, *Immigrants in Cities*, I, 640ff.; Welcome Hall, *Annual Report, 1912*, p. 12; NYSMC, 1905. Thirteen percent of Italian wives reported urban occupations; 12 percent of Italian wives reported taking in boarders.

[33] Chapter 7 contains a fuller discussion of these issues.

[34] The breakdown for percent of families with only one earner (the male head) by occupation is as follows: officials, professionals, semiprofessionals, 50 percent; manufacturers, wholesalers, etc., 75 percent; small retail shopowners, etc., 67 percent; clerical and sales, 64 percent; skilled workmen, 70 percent; personal service workers, 88 percent; laborers, 68 percent. Figures are rounded to the nearest percent. Source: NYSMC, 1905.

[35] For families of 4, 69 percent; families of 5, 70 percent; families of 6, 62 percent; families of 7, 59 percent; families of 8, 51 percent; families of 9, 34 percent; families of 10, 21 percent; families of 11 or more, 11 percent. Figures are rounded to the nearest percent. Source: NYSMC, 1905.

held jobs. The different attitudes toward male and female children determined which children would enter the work world: 67 percent of working-age sons did so compared with 29 percent of working-age daughters.[36] Family size did not consistently influence a young man's decision to work, but it played a crucial role for daughters. A young woman with two or more siblings was twice as likely to work as a girl who had none.[37]

South Italian values influenced these decisions concerning family work patterns. The majority of parents preferred to keep their working-age daughters at home, but economic necessity forced some to permit their daughters to enter the labor market. Parents had different expectations for their working-age sons. This is hardly surprising: they were merely fulfilling their traditional economic and family function; and south Italian tradition did not require such careful supervision of their activities as it did of the girls'. A boy leaving home to work did not constitute a threat to the family stability—indeed, his wages contributed to its security. In general, boys added important sums to the family income, while girls, requiring careful chaperonage and dowry savings, continued to be a liability. The child labor laws permitted children over sixteen to work full time, and more than half of all children in this age group did so.[38] Moreover, a large proportion of families (14 percent) had unmarried children over eighteen living at home.[39] Italians apparently believed that a child's obligation to the family did not cease when he or she reached adulthood.

A more detailed analysis of the employment patterns of single working-age children gives a clearer picture of their contribution to the family income and of their motivations in working. Some correlation existed between the father's occupation and the likelihood that his working-age sons would contribute to the

[36] Of 1,020 children fourteen years of age and older, 53 percent went to work, 23 percent continued in school, and 24 percent stayed at home. Source: NYSMC, 1905.

[37] Thirty percent of daughters from families with three or more children worked; 25 percent of those from families of two children worked; 16 percent of those who were only children worked. The comparable figures for sons are 65 percent, 67 percent, and 83 percent, respectively.

[38] NYSMC, 1905. [39] Ibid.

family's support. Skilled and unskilled laborers and unemployed fathers were the most likely to have employed sons; however, 70 percent of the manufacturers, wholesalers, and bankers also had working sons. The census classified most of them in the same occupational categories as their fathers or as clerical workers. Many were helping out in a family business. The hope of inheriting the family business dulled the desire to leave home. Smaller proportions of sons helped their families run small businesses, or else learned crafts from their fathers.[40] All employed sons of laborers followed in their fathers' footsteps—their aid to the family consisted of direct cash contributions. Family needs took priority over the future aspirations of these adult children who could, after all, have left the parental home to seek their own fortunes or who may have wished to attend school. Boys withdrawn from school had to pay the price of restricted job mobility, which helps to explain the Italians' slow rise up the occupational ladder. It may also explain why upwardly mobile second-generation Italians so often became printers and electricians, not doctors and lawyers.

At all occupational levels, therefore, family considerations figured in work choices, but for different reasons. Higher-income fathers sought to keep their business interests in their families, and to see that their sons inherited their economic security; the poor required their children's support in order to survive. The only consistent generalization that can be made is that, regardless of the parent's occupation, unmarried working-age daughters usually remained at home. The daughters of unemployed fathers constituted an exception, being the most likely to work. The daughters of professionals and semiprofessionals also had different prospects because they had the best chance to continue their education, at least into high school, and more than half of these girls did so. A relatively large proportion of skilled

[40] One-fifth of the sons who designated themselves as skilled workers or shopkeepers were aiding in family businesses, according to NYSMC, 1905.

Percentages of fathers with working-age sons whose sons were actually employed are: 87 percent of the skilled workers; 85 percent of the unemployed; 81 percent of the laborers; 60 percent of the shopowners; 60 percent of those in clerical and sales; 50 percent of the officials and professionals and 43 percent of the personal service workers.

workmen (65 percent) and shopkeepers (71 percent), and manufacturers and wholesalers (100 percent), listed their daughters as either at home *or* at work.[41] Instead of working outside the home, many of these daughters, like their brothers, helped in family businesses. But they had different reasons for doing so. Instead of being trained to inherit the family business, these girls contributed their labor to it. Quite a few Italians in Buffalo, for example, were tailors, and a daughter's nimble hands could be well used by them. Girls, even more than boys, sacrificed their own goals and accomplishments for the family interests. The social attitudes toward female respectability gave them little choice. But they too could expect some future satisfaction for their efforts; the family business, after all, made a wedding dowry possible, so that these young women benefited from it in the long run.

Relatives who were living with families did not make an important contribution to the household budget by way of outside employment. Many working relations were widowed men over sixty, who had passed their peak earning capacity; they could not be relied upon as a source of family income, and may, in fact, have been an added burden.[42]

The wife was the least likely to leave the home to work. Less than 2 percent found urban employment outside the home, and some of these may actually have been involved in a family business which did not require constant absence from home or give them an independent wage earner's status. The largest percentage (12 percent) of wives contributing to family income did so by caring for roomers and boarders.[43] Because families took in lodgers as a way of supplementing income, it is not surprising that in 1905 laborers headed three-quarters of all those house-

[41] NYSMC, 1905.

[42] Ibid. Less than 4 percent of all families had such relatives living with them. Only 77 families had relatives that could have contributed, 75 males and 2 females; 74 of these were 50 years or older.

[43] Actually, it is possible that this figure should be increased, because in 1900 the COS claimed that many wives did not report to them that they took boarders into their homes. See *23rd Annual Report of the Charity Organization Society*, pp. 101, 106. However, this undercount may be offset by the fact that the census was taken in summer months when Italian families, owing to the influx of seasonal Italian laborers, were most likely to have boarders.

holds with boarders and roomers. Few Italians, especially the poorer ones, owned their homes at this time, so the extra income was used for family living expenses or to make a down payment on a house. "The family with boarders," Mary Sansone reported, "could save a little bit and perhaps pay the mortgage on a house." Because over half of the family heads with lodgers had lived in the United States for more than eight years, boarders' payments were not emergency funds needed right after immigration. In some instances, boarders were taken in for business reasons; the census indicated that many worked in family-run concerns. Sixteen percent of the family heads who had boarders in their households, for example, owned stores or restaurants. Higher income families could have afforded real estate, and in such instances boarders' payments were used to discharge mortgage expenses.[44]

The prosperity of the 1920's relieved the effects of years of financial strain for Italian families. In 1927 a local banker estimated that Italian-Americans held twenty thousand bank accounts with average holdings of $700. Like Newburyport's Irish working-class families, the Italians were apparently saving money to invest in homes.[45] A local bank official's comments on Italian saving habits substantiates this position: "An Italian makes a large payment down on a piece of property, borrows additional money, and proceeds to make his payments on the loan promptly. He will go to extremes to save his property once he has an interest in it." [46]

Real estate advertisements began appearing regularly in the Italian press around 1912. Prices for two-family homes, widely

[44] NYSMC, 1905. Mary Sansone, Richard Ferranti, and Frank Iannuzzi confirmed that many families took boarders in to save for a home or to cover living costs.

[45] See Thernstrom, *Poverty and Progress,* for discussion of property mobility in Newburyport, Mass. The Italian desire to own real estate and the intense effort involved in paying for it became evident quite early. See COS, *Fifteenth Annual Report, 1892,* p. 40; Nelli, *Italians in Chicago,* pp. 34ff. observed the same tendency. Interviews with Richard Ferranti and Frank Iannuzzi confirm the eagerness to own homes.

[46] Quoted in Stewart, "Rapid Fire Rises of Buffalo Italians," *Courier,* Jan. 7, 1923; see also Catherine Mcgee, "What Have the Italians Done for Buffalo?" *Sunday Times,* Sept. 4, 1927.

available in the Italian quarter, began at $2,200. A $200 down payment and a two- or three-year renewable mortgage initiated the purchase.[47] From 1900 to the 1920's, Italian home-ownership increased significantly. A sample of about one thousand first-generation families indicated that in 1900, only 2 percent of the Italians owned homes: 16 percent of a comparable sample of Polish families owned homes.[48] The 1900 Federal Census confirmed infrequent Italian home ownership; it stated that of all Buffalonians with one or both parents born in Italy, only 94 owned their homes and two-thirds of these were mortgaged. Yet by 1925 real estate assessment rolls show that first- and second-generation families owned almost five thousand homes.[49] Some Italians had also purchased suburban tracts on which they cultivated crops, but by 1925 only a few Italians lived in middle-class neighborhoods. These were the community's wealthiest leaders.[50] Some working-class Italians lived in outlying districts, but this was in order to be near suburban-industries.

How did these financially strained families afford homes? Boarders' fees have already been mentioned as one source of income. And wives supplemented the family savings. Although Italians did not favor women's work outside the home, they did sometimes justify part-time work for women in terms of future family goals. Mary Sansone reported of the summer cannery work, for example, that "this was an acceptable way for women to work even if it was not respectable to work in a factory. . . . They used to save a little extra money and then buy a house." Other families saved by sharing living costs with relatives. Our earlier discussion of extended family cohesion suggested that the desire to own a home encouraged families to locate near and

[47] Sample real estate advertisements may be found in *IC*, 1912. John Daniels, "Buffalo's Polish Population" in Buffalo and Erie County Public Library, Scrapbook, "Buffalo's Foreign Population," I, pp. 217–219 discusses Polish home-ownership and Buffalo mortgage practices.

[48] USFMC, 1900.

[49] *Twelfth Census, 1900; Population*, II, Pt. 2, 751: City of Buffalo, City Assessment Roll, 1925. Unfortunately the real estate assessments do not distinguish between the first and second generations.

[50] NYSMC, 1905. A real estate dealer and two branches of the Onetto family, important macaroni manufacturers, had suburban homes.

live with one another so that they could cooperate in this important financial undertaking. The low standard of living also permitted cash to accumulate. Speaking of the Sicilians in particular, a Buffalo reporter commented: "If a Sicilian has $100 in the bank he can be counted on not to eat it. No matter what his deprivations and his suffering, his bank account remains untouched. That's the way he gets along in the world. It is his idea of thrift and it is immovable. Undoubtedly it results in an increased mortality among the children, for the food they get in such circumstances is not wholesome and lacks nutritive value."[51]

But Italians did not intentionally deprive their young of proper nourishment; both economic circumstances and their cultural background simply produced dietary and educational standards that were different from those considered adequate by middle-class Americans. Local banker Enrico Ortalani agreed that the average Italian would "save more than he could with comfort."[52] Reversing the reporter's judgment, he attributed the Italian parents' budgeting abilities to their love for their children and their wish to see them improve. Additional observers attributed Italian thriftiness to other motives. According to them, many Italians were determined to achieve homeownership in the United States, even if this meant sacrificing their children's educational and social interests.[53] Earlier evidence on the percentages of young men withdrawing from school as soon as they reached working age supports this contention. Frank Iannuzzi confirmed the importance of children's wages: "Most people could not afford to buy a house; you'd be lucky if you could pay the rent. When they first came, Italians could not afford a house. Only when the children grew up, and went out to work" could a family think of owning a home. Italian children took their obligations seriously. Indeed, the Juvenile Protective Department noted that these children took them more seriously than most: "To the average individual the word 'necessity' im-

[51] "Italians in Buffalo," *Express*, Aug. 27, 1901.

[52] Quoted in Stewart, "Rapid Fire Rises of Buffalo Italians."

[53] "Buffalo's Little Italy," *Times*, Jan. 4, 1903; "Italians in Buffalo," *Express*, Aug. 27, 1901. Working-class preference for property over educational mobility is widely observed in sociological literature.

plies dire or emergent need. To the boy of foreign parents, especially to the Italian and somewhat to the Polish boy, it does not have this meaning. The Italian boy is very apt to reply that it is very necessary for him to become a street trader in order to help his father pay for the house which they have bought on the installment plan. This boy's interpretation is based primarily on his sense of loyalty to his family and not on the sense of real economic necessity." [54]

The Buffalo Italians apparently believed that family interests were better served by property ownership and financial security than by children's leisure and education. The younger generation's long-term interests simply had a lower priority than the immediate family needs.[55] Besides, property conferred a kind of familiar, secure, and concrete status which immigrants appreciated. The desire to own a home can be seen as the wish of former peasants to possess—even at great sacrifice—something which had been denied to so many for generations. Land was an important symbol of wealth, security, and status in the old country. Immigrants seeking petit bourgeois status could believe they had attained it when they bought a home. The Buffalo shoemaker Vincent De Bella used an Italian proverb to explain this attitude: "L'uomo che non ha scritto un libro e che non possiede una casa è un uomo senza valore" ("The man who has not written a book and does not own a house is worthless"). "Few men," De Bella mused, "can write books, so what is left but to try to own a house? Where I came from, if a man did not own a house, he was a pariah. No property—no dignity." In fact, peasants believed that real estate was the only safe investment. Thus, the parents were not so much neglecting their children's interests, as interpreting them in terms of their own experience. Land—a tangible asset—could be proudly passed on to the younger generation.

This was the usual way of doing things in Italy. The fact that

[54] Juvenile Protective Department, Buffalo, New York, "Street Traders of Buffalo, New York," p. 19.

[55] This, of course, is the same point that Thernstrom makes in *Poverty and Progress*. On the Italian preference for property over education as a means of social mobility, see Cronin, *Sting of Change*, p. 233.

it was an impractical arrangement in the American city, where property served a different function, and where only so many children could live in a home or run a family business, did not deter the immigrants.[56] Italian-American folklore warns, and many second- and third-generation families know, the disastrous results of this practice: child fighting child for possession of the family property—property which represented years of concerted struggle, property which in concrete form symbolized both parental love and familial power. Paradoxically, that which parents hoped would hold the family together sometimes tore it apart.

In conclusion, the conditions of urban life over which Italians had no control—economic contingencies, the job market, and low-paying jobs—made it impossible for men to support their families adequately on a single wage. Cultural priorities derived from the Italian past played a part in keeping the immigrant family's living standard low. Those who could save, for example, chose to invest their money in homes rather than education, so reducing the likelihood that sons would excel their fathers. The Italians' tendency to have larger than average families, their bias against accepting charity, their tendency to place almost exclusive responsibility for support upon the father, and their unwillingness to permit married women to leave home to work all contributed to their low living standard. These immigrants could continue surviving in the urban world with such seemingly archaic responses because their wives and children could find work in a variety of part-time occupations. Certainly, those who managed to buy a home had done more than make ends meet.

An important theme runs throughout this discussion of the family economy: the adjustment of familiar attitudes to unfamiliar conditions. The continual priority of family needs over individual ones when decisions regarding employment, income allocation, social mobility, or education were made all illustrated this point. The Italians, like other working-class groups, preferred property over educational mobility. If this preference had

[56] Interview with Frank Iannuzzi, who told how all his brothers and sisters inherited the family house.

its roots in the European past, American conditions also encouraged its persistence. Social and economic discrimination isolated the immigrants and severely discouraged their participation in the American occupational struggle. The security of the ghetto as a home, or perhaps a home within the ghetto, provided a satisfying alternative.

7 Like the Fingers of the Hand: Patterns of Work and Family Organization *

"Men are like the fingers of the hand—the thumb must be the thumb, and the little finger the little finger. . . . To pull a good oar the five fingers must help one another." [1] This proverb, frequently used to define the proper relationship between an individual and his family, reflects the Mezzogiorno's familistic orientation. One Italian social worker says that her compatriots in Buffalo heeded its practical wisdom; her description of immigrant family economics recalls the old proverb's imagery and sentiment: "Dal numero delle braccia di una famiglia dipende la prosperità della medesima" ("A family's wealth depends upon the number of hands it has") [2] The immigrant families confronted urban labor market conditions which typically required individuals to enter the work world separately, not as members of a family group. Yet this apparent requirement seems to have had little influence upon how the Italians in Buffalo perceived the options available to them at work. Even as different members entered industrial America's work world, the immigrant family remained remarkably untouched.

* An earlier version of this chapter appeared as an article, "Patterns of Work and Family Organization: Buffalo's Italians" in the *Journal of Interdisciplinary History*, 2 (1971), pp. 303–312, reprinted here by permission of the *Journal of Interdisciplinary History* and the M.I.T. Press, Cambridge, Massachusetts. Some material in this chapter is reprinted from "A Flexible Tradition: Immigrant Families Confront New Work Experiences," *Journal of Social History*, June 1974, pp. 429–441, by permission of the editors.

[1] Quoted in Verga, *House by the Medlar-Tree*, p. 2.

[2] De'Rossi, "Le donne ed i fanciulli," p. 18.

The Italian experience in Buffalo contradicts a widely held assumption that technical and economic development determine the organization of the family.[3] According to this belief, economic roles within the larger society tend to structure the power arrangements within the family itself. A common assumption is that because the industrial city offers employment opportunities to women, they can achieve an independence that is potentially disruptive to patriarchal control. Another clear expression of this approach, and one we are concerned with here, suggests that "almost as a matter of definition we associate the factory system" and other industrial work patterns "with the decline of the family and social anonymity." [4] This model assumes a determinist relationship between developing material conditions and cultural values. But the south Italian culture removed to the United States did not prove so passive. In fact, immigrant behavior is better understood as a reciprocal interaction between traditional values and new social contexts. Such reciprocity implies the adaptation of an Old World culture, but certainly not its destruction.

The flexibility of the traditional culture becomes apparent as we observe immigrant families entering a new work world and struggling to meet their economic needs. In Buffalo, the peculiar occupational structure combined with job discrimination to limit their options; but they discovered alternatives for themselves. The Italians integrated themselves into this new world by choosing work that put minimal strain upon their accustomed family arrangements.[5] By interpreting their new situation in terms of past experience, they managed to adapt to it with relative ease.

If the past influenced family behavior, we must once again journey back in time to nineteenth-century southern Italy and

[3] Literature on industrialization, urbanization, and the family is plentiful. See Anderson, *Family Structure*, and Neil Smelser, *Social Change in the Industrial Revolution* (Chicago, 1959), for two important viewpoints. Handlin, *Uprooted*, p. 234, discusses the disorganizing effects of new work patterns upon the peasant family in America.

[4] Smelser, p. 193 criticizes this viewpoint, and I am indebted to his analysis.

[5] Scott and Tilly, "Woman's Work and the Family" (manuscript), p. 21, observe similar processes among European families.

examine family work experiences there in order to achieve a more empathetic understanding of the cultural prism through which immigrants perceived their new jobs.

In southern Italy, clear connections existed between an individual's economic role and his or her family role; but strong cultural traditions frequently intervened, so that to posit a correlation between the two would be hazardous. The father presided over his family and maintained its livelihood by his labors. Because he rarely owned or rented enough land to support his family, he generally hired himself out as a day laborer. The conditions of seasonal unemployment and the long absences from home required by his search for work did not seriously undermine his authority; indeed, southern cultural traditions supported it strongly.[6] But he had a competitor. We have seen that the southern peasant woman enjoyed unusually high prestige. The wife's clearly defined family and household responsibilities included obedience to her husband, family loyalty, thrift, and, most important, childbearing. She oversaw the family resources, prepared and purchased the food, mended and made the clothes, and supervised the children in household tasks. A woman's economic importance to the family also contributed to her position.

In most of the South, peasants regarded wives who left home to work disdainfully, and few did so unless poverty required it. Sicilians held very strictly to this rule. One Sicilian immigrant recalled, "It was almost a crime for women to work." [7]

Observing the persistence of this attitude even among contemporary Sicilian peasants, Blok describes how the southern women are secluded in an effort to maintain male superiority. The man who allowed his "women to work outside the home would jeopardize his honor in two ways: directly, by showing that he is not himself capable of supporting his family, and thus failing in his culturally defined role of the superior male *versus* the inferior females of the family; and indirectly, because he will be less able to control their sexual behavior." [8]

[6] Moss and Thomson, "South Italian Family," pp. 40, 38. See also, Cronin, *Sting of Change*, p. 104.

[7] Interview with Vincent De Bella.

[8] Blok, *Mafia*, pp. 49–50; Louise Tilly points out that generalizations concerning women's work roles are hazardous, because conditions varied considerably

Yet an expected part of a wife's year-round labors would include joining the family in crop harvesting. Seasonal migrations also drew entire peasant families away from their villages, but the girls and women rarely worked in nonagricultural occupations because there were few factory towns in the Mezzogiorno.[9] Women who left home to labor generally worked as members of a family unit earning a portion of the family wage. These women did not regard themselves (nor were they regarded) as independent wage earners; they did not derive their status within the family from their position as wage earners, nor did the wages they earned challenge the husband's position as chief breadwinner. The wife's function was extremely important in this peasant economy; it would be wrong to undervalue it by projecting onto it our present-day market values, which define "work" in terms of wages received for services performed individually outside the home. The important fact is, however, that the Italian peasants themselves attributed greater prestige and importance to male contributions to the family economy.

The peasants loved their children and treated them well, but the children too had responsibilities. As Covello observes, "the economic basis of married life was reflected in the evaluation of children primarily as an economic asset."[10] Their economic value as work hands shortened the period of childhood. Despite government efforts to curb child labor, in 1911 almost one-half of all children in the South aged ten to fifteen years were gain-

---

throughout Italy. But figures from the 1901 Italian census do support my generalization that southern women rarely labored outside the home in nonagricultural occupations. The figures for women 9 years of age and over engaged in work outside the home (including domestic servants) are: Abruzzi and Molise, 11 percent; Basilicata, 11 percent; Calabria, 30 percent; Campania, 19 percent; Sicily, 15 percent, computed from *Annuario Statistico, 1905*–07 (Rome, 1907), pp. 111f. These are gross figures making no allowance for urban and rural distinctions. I suspect that the figures for women working outside the home would be lower if peasants alone were considered. Even if this small percentage of women did work outside the home, we cannot assume that their behavior was socially acceptable. Blok, p. 49, supports this contention.

[9] Seasonal migrations are discussed in Dickinson, *Population Problem*, pp. 67–74, and in Italy, *Inchiesta Agraria*, 13: 20ff. Foerster, *Italian Immigration*, pp. 532–533, discusses family migrations; see also Sonnino, *Contadini*, pp. 84, 98, 117. Odencrantz, *Italian Women in Industry*, p. 27; and *Emigration Conditions in Europe*, p. 160, comment on the lack of industry in the Italian South.

[10] Covello, "Italo-American School Child," pp. 357, 359.

fully employed. Peasant parents completely ignored the child labor legislation applying to agricultural work.[11] Since they needed their children to help at home or in the fields, they often withdrew them from school. In any case, the South's meager educational facilities and inflexible public school schedules made attendance difficult. Local and governmental authorities failed to enforce the compulsory education laws, and the ruling classes viewed the peasant child's education with hostility.[12] Sometimes peasants paid to send working age children to private schools which were willing to accommodate their schedules to the long work hours and seasonal absences required at harvest times. The peasants were not necessarily opposed to education, but family needs had to take priority.[13]

Returning to the American scene, we can see how these family relationships fared in a new context. The Italians, most of them Sicilians, who journeyed from Buffalo to northwestern New York's food processing factories and the fields surrounding them are the initial basis for our discussion. Although some assume that the factory's impersonal industrial discipline and work routines prevented any possibility of continuity, these Italians had a very different experience.

Early in this century, fruit and vegetable processing companies, which were expanding rapidly, recruited employees from their local country areas and from immigrant quarters in the nearby cities. These perishable products required many hands working long hours during the busy season from June to October. Precise figures are not available, but the contemporary reports established that Italians from Buffalo commonly journeyed all over New York State to join other *paesani* engaged in this work.[14] Substantial Italian colonies existed in all the large cities near the canneries, but the upstate manufacturers still reached far west to Buffalo for their labor forces. Buffalo's peculiar eco-

[11] Ibid., p. 365.

[12] For the most comprehensive study in English on south Italians and education, see Covello, especially Ch. 8; see also Williams, *South Italian Folkways*, p. 21.

[13] Briggs, "Italians in Italy and America," pp. 65ff.

[14] Bernardy, "L'emigrazione delle donne," pp. 69, 85–87; *Recent Immigrants in Agriculture*, II, 500; *Second Report, FIC* (1913), p. 792.

nomic structure partly explains their choice. Other nearby cities such as Rochester, Syracuse, Utica, and Troy had enough homework and light industries to absorb female and child workers; Buffalo had different labor needs because heavy industry and transportation—its most rapidly expanding sectors—presented the greatest demands for male labor. Some clothing manufacture took place in Buffalo, but the canning and clothing seasons coincided. Italians got better pay working on farms and in processing sheds, mainly because they could use their children to snip beans and husk corn—in the clothing trade, they could use them only to pull bastings. Homework wages, in any case, did not promise such high returns. Although other industrial opportunities for unskilled women and children existed, and other ethnic groups took them, the Italians generally opted for summer cannery work.

While south Italians seem to have had a special preference for this type of work, the manufacturers also found it difficult to employ American-born workers, who preferred regular employment for the fathers to seasonal employment for the whole family. Each year more and more Polish women, once cannery laborers, expressed their preference for year-round domestic work in Buffalo's private homes. Because the Italian mores discouraged this, such domestic work was not a realistic alternative for unskilled women. Cannery work, on the other hand, permitted the possibility of extending community controls on the family into the factory. This explains why it seemed more respectable to Italians than any other occupation. The canneries provided a unique opportunity where laboring and living spaces existed in close proximity—manufacturers provided various types of housing located near processing plants and fields. In the living quarters, ever present parents, kin, and *paesani* could keep a watchful eye on one another. Children remained directly under parental control, and adults could work assured that their young ones were safer than they would have been left home alone or playing in the city streets.[15]

[15] *Recent Immigrants in Agriculture*, II, 491, indicates the decreasing popularity of canning work among Poles and American-born workers. Even Italian men seeking employment considered canning work more respectable than

So come summer, the south Italian women and children became migrant laborers and left their Buffalo homes—sometimes without fathers and husbands, who sought summer construction jobs in the city or wherever else they could find them. At first glance, such an arrangement seems surprising since the south Italian mores also required a husband to guard his wife and daughters jealously. But was going to the canneries really such a departure from past patterns? Seasonal migrations had not been an unusual recourse for peasant families who followed the harvests throughout the Mezzogiorno. And temporary family dissolution was no strange experience. Immediate need had justified its risks before, when many job-seeking fathers journeyed throughout the Italian South or across the sea not to escape their family responsibilities but to fulfill them. Once in America, the same kind of thinking motivated the family. And though many fathers remained in Buffalo, some could find employment with the canneries also as factory mechanics or harvesters.[16]

The removal of the family to the country had another aspect reminiscent of the Italian situation: the profitable use of children could continue without fear of reprisal for violating factory codes or child labor laws. Legislation limiting the numbers of working hours for women and children was also difficult to enforce. The canners, for their part, tended to ignore statutes limiting the weekly work hours for women and children under sixteen, on the grounds that their trade's special conditions exempted them. Although processing shed labor was industrial in character, not until 1913 did the factory legislation codes attempt to control these establishments (and then with little success). In the meantime, canners worked their employees for thirteen-and-a-half hours a day or more. Because the season lasted from mid-June to mid-October, parents also violated and avoided the compulsory school attendance laws; in the country,

---

railroad jobs. The importance immigrants assigned to control of their young is indicated in Consumers' League of New York, *Behind the Scenes at the Canneries* (New York, 1930), p. 48; and *Second Report, FIC*, II, (1913), 1297.

[16] De'Rossi, "Le donne ed i fanciulli italiani," p. 18.

school authorities could be easily circumvented.[17] The work situation, then, made it possible for the immigrant family to maximize its profits over a very short period.

Cannery wages varied according to speed and skill because employers paid by the piece for both shed and field work. In a typical cannery, no one earned less than $1.00 a day; most foreign-born men and women earned from $1.25 to $1.75. Sometimes the combined family income exceeded what a male head of household could earn in the city in railroad or industrial work,[18] and in the city the child labor laws prevented the younger children from earning. Wage supplements lowered living costs for the season—in many cases, canners provided housing, fruits, and vegetables for free or at nominal fees. Italians laboring in the New York canneries could get along on as little as $.50 to $1.00 a week. "Very thrifty" families, the Immigration Commission reported, saved "considerable sums" of money every summer, enough to get through a winter of probable unemployment for the fathers. For some who could not find work, the canneries presented the only opportunity to earn a living.[19] In short, because these immigrant families discovered and seized this opportunity to earn a supplementary cash income, they found a way to alleviate the tensions which their low urban living standard would otherwise have produced.

A situation which minimized family strain by permitting mother and child to work together attracted the Italians. Even in cases where mothers and children went alone to the canneries, they stayed away from home for only short periods, and apparently the immigrants did not perceive their absence as a serious challenge to the family's well-being. Rather, they may

[17] The labor law governing the number of hours women and children could legally work in factories was amended a number of times. The New York State Factory Investigating Commission was particularly interested in including the canneries under the factory acts and eventually succeeded in doing so. See Felt, *Hostages of Fortune*, pp. 25, 170; Bernardy, L'emigrazione delle donne," p. 66; *Second Report, FIC,* I (1913), 125; editorial by "Virtus," "La schiavitù delle donne e dei fanciulli," *La F*, July 28, 1910.

[18] *Recent Immigrants in Agriculture*, 11, 508, 494.

[19] Ibid. pp. 494, 496, 150; see also "Virtus," "La schiavitù," *La F*, July 28, 1910; *IC*, Dec. 2, 1905.

have viewed it as a chance for wife and children to return to a familiar agricultural environment.[20] It should also be remembered that in Italy the mother supervised all the household work independently of her husband. Several observers noted that south Italians tended to organize their cannery work along family lines. The labor—weeding, harvesting, and preparation for preserving—was light enough for women and children to engage in. A government investigation reported that "since the women and children can work efficiently, the laborers, particularly the south Italians, make the family the working unit. This means that the whole family engages in farm labor or berry picking and the earnings all go into the family fund." [21]

The canners' method of recruiting south Italians reflected their recognition that priority must be given to family needs. The companies usually brought migrant workers from the city in family groups. A company in Albion, New York, which employed about three hundred south Italians, instructed its *padrone* to "secure families whenever possible." "It is found," the Immigration Commission stated, "that when the family is employed as a whole on the farm all are more contented and more apt to remain for the season than when part remain in the city and part go to the country." [22]

Those who defended the recruitment of families for migrant labor and the use of child employees claimed that the foreign parents would not come to rural areas without their children. Some canners stated that they themselves did not wish juveniles to work there, but the parents insisted. Eager adults worked their children in the fields, even when the farmers, who feared that the children might damage the crops, opposed it.[23]

The general division of work among each member of the family at the canneries is a further example of south Italian adaptation. Once again, economic and family roles were closely integrated and sexes differentiated. Fathers either remained in

[20] Bernardy, "L'emigrazione delle donne," p. 88.

[21] *Recent Immigrants in Agriculture*, II, 491.

[22] Ibid., pp. 507, 492.

[23] *Second Report, FIC*, I (1913), 141; see also testimony of the plant supervisor where Italians from Buffalo were employed in ibid., III, 423. Luciano J. Iorizzo, "Italian Immigrants and the Impact of the Padrone System" (Unpublished Ph.D. dissertation, Syracuse University, 1956), p. 190.

the city or worked apart from women and children, so that the tasks of disciplining the children and of directing the work stayed in the mother's hands. If a woman had evening work, the father sometimes cared for the children, but an elder daughter or some older woman more typically assumed the responsibility. The entire family might work the bean, pea, and corn field, weeding and harvesting just as they had done in Italy. In grape-growing areas, everyone tended vines and picked fruit. Until child labor legislation was enforced in the canneries, children who once assisted their mothers in Italy now helped them prepare crops for canning or snipped and husked vegetables, while the women packaged or labeled them.[24] A comparison of the Italian conception of the child's role with that of the native-born working class, and the use each made of its offspring, points to some useful distinctions. While 90 percent of the American-born children, many of them local residents, came to the canneries as independent workers, all the Italian youngsters worked and traveled with their parents. This suggests the foreign parents' unwillingness to relinquish economic and familial control over their young.[25] A "working investigator" disguised as a laborer noted that where American help was used in snipping or husking, the work rarely began before seven in the morning. Where the Italians labored, work began at four or four-thirty A.M. during the rush season. The American children seldom did other work during the day; but Italian parents often roused their children at dawn to snip beans until daylight, when they went to the fields to pick beans. At night they went to the sheds and worked again. The investigator maintained that "cases in which American mothers force their children to work are, however, the exception and not the rule." Even when American children did work, she claimed, they eagerly awaited going to the "sheds where there are many other children and where they can earn a little spending money."[26]

A social worker observed that strong economic motives drove

[24] "Looking over the Canneries," *Express*, Aug. 16, 1912; Consumers' League of New York, *Behind the Scenes*, p. 47; *Second Report, FIC*, II (1913), 954, 775; *Recent Immigrants in Agriculture*, II, 509; George Mangold, *Migratory Child Workers* (New York, 1929), p. 4.

[25] *Second Report, FIC*, II (1913), 802.

[26] Ibid., I, 135–138.

the Italians from Buffalo who were working at the Albion company. The Italian people, she said, considered their "children as so much money value." The social workers had great difficulty convincing intractable parents, who did not agree that the children belonged in the cannery schools, not factory sheds. Throughout the summer, the social worker claimed, she and her colleagues frequently failed to keep children under ten—the legal working age for labor of this kind—out of the sheds and off the harvest fields. "You understand," she reported, "the disposition of the mothers at the beginning was to make money out of the children." [27] An Italian government agent who visited the canneries at about the same time concurred. "The canners," she said, "like the cheap labor of the Italians and their children, and the parents for their part go with pleasure because it gives them a way to earn off their children." Italian adults, she observed, were the hardest drivers. Lamenting the "precocious old age" of the Italian children, she observed that little ones "old enough to hold a bean are made to work by their parents." While the softer American parents permitted their young to leave work, the Mezzogiorno's children struggled on.[28]

To the extent that the parents controlled the organizing of shed labor, it indicated the children's subservience to the adults among all groups. Whether they wanted to or not—and these children, like most, had a proclivity for not wanting to—young ones followed their parents' orders. The adults, especially the Italians, maintained the upper hand in delegating tasks.[29] An Italian-born social worker who visited canneries where Italians from Buffalo were working had further comments to make. The mothers were "hard on the children," she said.

Although they love their children, they do not love them in the right way sometimes. They think they must bring in something and that is the Italian idea. They like to have children because they help to lift the burden.

Q. The more children the more work?

A. Yes.

[27] Testimony of Jennie Bowen, Dec. 10, 1912, in ibid., IV, 1933.

[28] Bernardy, "L'emigrazione delle donne," pp. 67, 62–64.

[29] Testimony of Mary Chamberlain, social worker disguised as laborer in *Second Report, FIC*, III (1913), 1013.

Noting that children in Italy were expected to work, she continued that she saw nothing wrong in this because it prevented them from being lazy.[30] Like the migrant laborers she commented upon, the social worker interpreted the situation in terms of her own cultural attitudes.

The styles of parental discipline of Italians and Americans varied; the former were particularly relentless, the latter more indulgent. The Italian investigator who asked children in a corn-husking shed why they continued to work so long, received the reply, "We'd get licked." [31] And testimony given to the Factory Investigating Commission relating to the situation at a cannery where many Buffalo Italians worked speaks for itself:

> The parents were constantly urging the children to work. One little boy, aged 11, was throwing some bean snippings at another little fellow and had stopped work a second. His father hit him brutally across the face and set him again at work. Everywhere parents were forcing children to work. . . . If they did not work they would shake them and sometimes hit them depending on the parent. This is not true for all parents, but the majority of the Italian parents were forcing their children to work. Most of the American parents were not forcing them to work. Take for instance, the woman, Mrs. McGaffie, the woman I have mentioned here. She had a little girl aged 10 in the factory. She did not use such stringent methods of forcing the children to work as the Italians did, but she kept the child constantly at work for 6 or 7 hours a day. But she was not so brutal about it as the Italians were, and she did let the child go home to meals, and stopped when she pleaded and pleaded with her mother that she was tired.[32]

A Factory Commission inspector's report on one such cannery tells of a twelve-year-old Italian child, little Jack, whose family woke him at three A.M. He snipped beans from four-thirty in the morning to ten P.M., with only a few minutes off for supper. After this long day's work, his only comment to the investigator was: "My fingers is broke." That day he went to sleep at mid-

[30] Testimony of Madeline De'Rossi, social worker, North American Civic League, Dec. 10, 1912, in ibid., IV, 1945.

[31] Bernardy, "L'emigrazione delle donne," p. 67.

[32] Testimony of Mary Chamberlain, Nov. 26, 1912 (taken from the diary which she kept when working under disguise at the cannery), *Second Report, FIC*, II, 1007.

night and woke up at three in the morning. He was, he said, "awful tired," but his mother made him work. Finding his hands swollen, he tried to leave work several times. His mother also constantly scolded his ten-year-old sister, who could "hardly keep her eyes open," to continue her work. Jack earned $1.40 that day. He could keep none of his wages. But, he said, labor like this was nothing compared to the pea season, when his mother and sister returned home at one and two in the morning and "they was so sick they fell down and vomited." [33]

The Factory Investigating Commission neatly summarized the differences between Italian and American attitudes toward work and child-rearing. For foreigners, the shed was "distinctly a place for work." But for the American child, the shed was more like a "playground where they play at work till they get tired and then quit." [34] The disposition of funds earned by Italians and Americans also implies different cultural attitudes toward the child's role in the family. American children, the Commission's report noted, worked to earn spending money, to buy a bike, a toy, or shoes. But Italian and Polish parents required their children to submit all their wages to the family budget.[35] Indeed, since the parents, not the children, received the wage, it is highly unlikely that the latter ever saw their earnings. An Italian government reporter put it well: "In general the child is considered as a tool and appendix of the mother, and it is she who is paid, not them." [36] As in Italy, the child did not achieve even symbolic recognition as a wage earner.

Because of this transference of family discipline into the factory, canners had few problems obtaining the highest possible output from children. As one factory investigator put it, the "severe manner of the mothers rules the house and family in largely the same manner as she controls the family in the shed or field." [37] Goaded by the need to earn a year-round income during the summer, such parents were far more effective taskmasters than the factory owners could have been. The chief factory inspector testified that so far as the canners were con-

[33] Ibid., p. 785. [34] Ibid., pp. 781, 786. [35] Ibid., pp. 786–789.
[36] Bernardy, "L'emigrazione delle donne," p. 67.
[37] *Second Report, FIC*, II (1913), 296.

cerned, children remained free to come and go; it was the parents, he claimed, and especially the foreigners, who forced the children to work. Similarly, Italian parents, not the manufacturers, sent their children running away when the canning inspector, representing the public interest in their young ones, arrived.[38] The canners felt no compulsion to keep records of the children's working hours for "they knew that the parents would keep their offspring at work, just as tenement parents, in order to increase the family's 'piece work pay.' " Or, as the Commission aptly put it: "The canners supply the materials to work on, the parents do the driving." [39]

At least one canner permitted a school on his premises for children under working age, but Italian mothers resisted allowing their children to attend; they preferred them to work just as they had in Italy. In fact, the mothers began what was described as "practically a riot . . . [though] not as bad as that," when a plant superintendent, attempting to keep children under ten out of the sheds, was besieged by angry Italian women, one of whom bit his finger "right through." [40] The Commission did not fully clarify the circumstances of this disturbance but all the witnesses agreed that many mothers, wishing their children to work rather than attend school, participated—not just the single assailant. And clearly, this "riot" resulted from the factory supervisor's interference into what the parents deemed their exclusive domain.

Most observers did not attribute the harshness of this situation to parental hard-heartedness, but to low family wages. The Factory Investigating Commission noted: "Nor are the parents alone to blame. Their parental love is often dulled by the hard grind of necessity. Manifestly a canner who pays low wages to parents cannot argue convincingly that the children should not be permitted to snip beans to increase the meager earnings of the family. If children should not be permitted to work, the can-

[38] Ibid., pp. 949, 775.

[39] Felt, p. 174; *Second Report, FIC,* I (1913), 166.

[40] De'Rossi, "Le donne ed i fanciulli," pp. 19–21; testimony of Jennie Bowen, *Second Report, FIC,* IV (1913), 1916–1923; testimony of Robert Mulree, superintendent of Olney Canning Co., Aug. 15, 1912, ibid., III, 423–424; see also De'Rossi's testimony, ibid., IV, 1943.

nery owner would still be under the necessity of obtaining the labor of their parents and unquestionably would soon have to pay the parents approximately what is now the total family income." [41] Apparently, American working-class parents could afford to be "much more careful in caring for their children" than the less fortunate foreigners, who had little choice but to count their children as economic assets and use them accordingly.[42]

Italian parents avoided, ignored, or protested against state intervention in family affairs just as they had in the Old World. Although the purposes of parents and canning manufacturers differed, the effective results of their behavior were the same. Usually, the two colluded to avoid child labor and truancy regulations. It is easy to understand the employers' motivations. Manufacturers generally knew that so long as they made no attempt to undermine Italian family organization—as, for example, in the case of family recruitment policies—they could expect to receive the optimum output from every family member. Moreover, the use of child labor usually worked to their advantage. Why, therefore—except for an occasional public demonstration of good will, such as allowing the North American Civic League to establish immigrant schools on their premises—should they resist it? As far as the parents were concerned, legal definitions of the child as a separate personality with rights more important than his family obligations made no sense to them, simply because such individualistic notions conflicted with their more familistic south Italian ones. The former peasants saw the child as a member of the family group, in which no outside influence had a right to interfere. As one scholar of child labor wrote, speaking of ninteenth-century American parents, who also brought a traditional culture with them to the factory: "The average New Yorker was as opposed to interference in the family as he was to state meddling in the market place." [43]

The same conflict between parental and legal conceptions of the child's role appeared in the city of Buffalo itself. Here parents acted entirely on their own in violation of child labor

[41] *Second Report, FIC*, I (1913), 166. [42] Ibid., II, 781.

[43] Felt, p. 9.

and truancy regulations. The Buffalo manuscript census listed few employed Italian children under fourteen, probably because parents did not report their occupations to census takers. They feared reprisal for violating the child labor and truancy regulations, which required children under that age to remain in school or to work only part time.[44] We know, however, that male dependents were the most likely to work. In 1905, for example, three-quarters of all Italian sons fifteen to nineteen years of age worked; only 5 percent remained at home. Twenty percent of all daughters in this age group worked; 62 percent remained at home. The remaining children attended school.[45]

Throughout New York State young Italian boys typically worked in candy, box, or clothing manufacturing, as messenger boys or as street traders. The Buffalo child labor reformers remained notably silent concerning Italian children in manufacturing and industries, but they frequently mentioned the newspaper trade.[46] A probable reason for this emphasis is that young boys under fourteen, the legal age for full-time work, dominated them. Street traders frequently violated truancy regulations, or reported to school fatigued from their night work. Even very young children could be affected because newsboys successfully ignored the regulations.[47] The same situation existed at the canneries, and this opportunity explains the appeal both occupations had for Italian families seeking to put their children to work.

Poverty forced many families to supplement an unemployed or underpaid father's wages. American and Polish parents also sent their children onto the streets: the American boy to get some spending money; the Polish boy to increase the family in-

[44] NYSMC, 1905, indicated few minors working. [45] NYSMC, 1905.

[46] Bernardy, "L'emigrazione delle donne," pp. 18–29; Banchetti, "Gli Italiani," p. 23; Adams, *Buffalo Newsboy;* Juvenile Protective Department, "Street Traders of Buffalo," pp. 4–33; letter to the editor, *IC*, Oct. 17, 1903 from Frederic Almy, Secretary, Charity Organization Society, Buffalo (based upon a report of the Society, "Child Labor in Buffalo," Spring, 1903).

[47] In 1903 legislation forbade boys under ten and girls under sixteen from selling papers. Boys aged ten to fourteen could not sell during school hours or after 10 at night. Boys ten to fourteen were required to get permits. The Italian newspaper expressed hope that a new bill would curb truancy among Italian children. See *IC*, Sept. 5, 1903, and Felt, p. 61.

come. But a local welfare agency claimed that some Italian parents had more ambitious goals—their boys contributed wages to help pay the family's home mortgage. In the early days of the community, sheer necessity forced the Italians to be especially harsh on their young. One critic remarked, "The boy is made to feel that he is of use only as he brings money to the home." The parents expected the child to "make certain daily returns or receive a beating." This gentleman felt scant sympathy for Italians who put children under ten to work: "The picturesque organ grinder is a veritable 'home of industry' in comparison with the fathers of some of these children. They demand the powers of parents but neglect the responsibility. The parent is chiefly interested in what he can *get out of the boy* and very rarely in what he can put into him." [48] Not surprisingly, this reformer viewed the Italian parent-child relationship from an American middle-class perspective. His opinions reflected the protective interest of American law in the child as individual; they also expressed a middle-class notion that responsible parents should focus their major energies on the child's needs. Such preferences had no place in the family-centered mentality of immigrant parents, who simply saw themselves as complying with traditional wisdom.

The same familistic mentality justified the decision to permit children to work rather than attend school, and to resist stubbornly state interference in such parental decisions. High truancy rates generally prevailed among the children of the poor; the Italians of Buffalo were no exception.[49] The canneries ag-

[48] Adams, pp. 9, 6, 7.

[49] Covello, "Italo-American School Child," discusses Italians' negative attitudes toward education. The reports of the Buffalo Children's Courts are, at best, fragmentary and inconsistent in their classifications. If anything, they show that truancy regulations could not have been well enforced. See U.S. Cong., Sen., *Children of Immigrants in Schools*, II, 297–402; and Children's Court of Buffalo, *Annual Report*, (Buffalo, 1912–1930). A New York State Tenement Commission Survey conducted in the late 1890's stated that 86 percent of all Italian children aged five to fourteen attended school, while only 43 percent of Polish children did. The Immigration Commission, about nine years later, reported that in schools with predominantly Italian and Polish attendance 59 percent of Italian children attended school nine-tenths of the term compared to 67 percent of the Polish children. Despite these discrepancies two points are clear: the children of the immigrant poor had exceptionally high truancy rates regard-

gravated the truancy situation for some. Here again, the American and Italian parents' attitudes toward education stand in sharp contrast. Because Americans regarded education favorably, their children generally worked at the canneries only after school or on Saturdays. But Buffalo's Italian children, far from their home classrooms, could not easily attend. In only three out of forty-five canning colonies investigated did Italian children attend local schools, and in most cases the local authorities ignored this situation.[50] Action would have meant tax increases and the presence of strange foreigners in their country classrooms.

The Buffalo public school truancy reports calculated that cannery children lost an average of thirty-four school days per year; some lost up to seventy-one. Half of these youngsters failed to pass on to the next grade or passed only conditionally. Public School Two, with Buffalo's largest Italian enrollment, lost almost a fifth of its 1,250 students to the canneries in one year.[51] Educators claimed that all the local schools had to fight the resistance of Italian parents who wished to send their children to the canneries. The parochial schools, experiencing similar problems, reported: "They are diligent when the canneries can't use them." [52]

Because Polish, Italian, and an earlier generation of American-born parents exhibited similar attitudes to child labor, one could argue that similarities in class and economic position, rather than cultural tradition explain their behavior here. And indeed our evidence suggests the beginnings of a lower-class subculture cutting across ethnic lines. But the cultural and class explanations are not mutually exclusive. The choice of ex-

---

less of ethnic background, and such families rejected state attempts to interfere in parental control of children. See *23rd Annual Report of the Charity Organization Society, 1899–1900*, Buffalo, pp. 101, 107. The figure cited by the Immigration Commission Report for American children attending was 63 percent, but the number in the group was small (134) and it was not representative since these were American-born children attending Polish- and Italian-dominated schools.

[50] *Second Report, FIC*, II (1913), 791, 792, 796.

[51] Truancy reports are in *Second Report, FIC*, II (1913), 794. See also "Buffalo's Little Italy," *Express*, May 4, 1902.

[52] Bernardy, "L'emigrazione delle donne," pp. 68–69.

planations depends upon what one wishes to explain. In this instance, proving that most peasant cultures adapted uniformly to industrial society is not the issue; showing how one traditional culture adapted to that society is. It is reasonable to assume that the original distinctions among traditional cultures moving into American society played some role in differentiating each group's response.

Additional evidence points to the persistence of the south Italian cultural attitudes despite the new work situation at the canneries. Extremely poor housing conditions, which certainly encouraged the deterioration of sexual controls and "moral degeneration," failed to undermine the Italian morale.[53] Housing arrangements generally allowed for little or no separation of the sexes. The facilities varied according to the cannery—tenements, barracks, or separate houses were used in different places. Not uncommonly, entire families, regardless of their size, resided in one room; worse, several families might be housed together, separated only by a canvas. Adults of both sexes slept, dressed, and washed in the same area. Often adolescents, male and female, used the same sleeping quarters. Boarders frequently intruded into a family's already limited privacy. In one colony, unmarried men and women of undetermined nationalities lived in the same barracks with only a broken partition separating them. Yet in spite of these circumstances, community pressure prevailed in the Italian quarters, where the people maintained their "good humor." [54] Other ethnic groups living under similar conditions apparently did not exercise the same degree of control. For example, Buffalo's Health Commissioner, himself of Polish origin, traced a number of illegitimate births in the Polish community to these circumstances. His failure to mention Italian illegitimacy, despite this knowledge of living conditions in Little Italy and at the canneries, implies that it was not a problem among this group.[55]

[53] Ibid., p. 88.

[54] Ibid. See also *Second Report*, *FIC*, II (1913), 884–887; and "Virtus," "La schiavitù."

[55] *Second Report*, *FIC*, II (1913), 887.

The work situation itself challenged traditional moral concepts. The manager of a cannery in Geneva, New York that employed Italians from Buffalo and Syracuse noted that despite the close association of the sexes in the dormitories and sometimes at work, moral conditions remained "excellent."[56] But there is no doubt that the work situation challenged Italian female morality. A social worker disguised as a laborer wrote in her diary of "fresh" bosses and timekeepers at the canneries, each of whom had power over the girls. "The situation," she said, "is much like that of a department store where the floorwalker has a lot of girls under him, receiving low wages and all more or less at his mercy." Male cannery superintendents apparently did not consider it beneath their dignity to offer the girls an opportunity to earn extra money, and the fact that cannery work took place at night made the situation more threatening for the women.[57] Another social worker had actually been drawn by the women into their protective community. They warned that the timekeeper was "fresh" and that she had best avoid him. Protection extended outside the immediate Italian community and the basic family group when an Italian girl warned her that "one must be careful not to get fresh with the Italian boys, because they are dangerous."[58] Sexual identification apparently triumphed over ethnic loyalty. The immigrant parent with an adolescent girl need not have feared for his daughter in this situation, for she obviously remained under the control of kin and community, which sustained and reinforced the traditional attitudes toward sex. The visible and public nature of the cannery's working and living conditions, emphasized throughout the Commission's investigations, partially explains why these controls functioned so effectively.

Another factor reinforcing community feeling among the Italians, despite the shifting nature of the migrant population, was that the work force included other hostile and competitive groups—country people living near the canneries, Poles, and

[56] *Recent Immigrants in Agriculture*, II, 502.

[57] Testimony of Mary Chamberlain, Nov. 26, 1912, *Second Report, FIC*, III, 1004.

[58] *Second Report, FIC*, III (1913), 1016.

Syrians. As one commentator has put it, "confined in a single rural factory [they] were unlikely to form much of a bond with one another." [59] Considerable conflict existed between the Syrians and Poles, who gladly accepted low salaries, and the Italian women, who wished to strike for higher pay. As for the Americans, they would side with the American employer rather than join the "Eyetalians" in a strike. Those strikes which occurred were attributed to the Italians; they provide testimony to their sense of solidarity, especially where bread and butter issues were concerned.[60] The closely knit group of Italian women frequently joined together, hoarding work under their skirts and chairs in an effort to save piecework for themselves, and so they earned the resentment of other less united but equally discontented women. The same sense of solidarity prevailed between an Italian foreman and female workers when the foreman gave the "Buffalo tables" more than their share of work.[61]

Italian immigrants sought occupational arrangements in other American cities which permitted easy adaptation of traditional practices. For example, they found homework—another semitraditional occupation—attractive. Like the canneries, this provided a transitional step for peasant groups who had recently arrived and were still attempting to cushion the full leap into industrial society. A New York State Factory Investigation Commission report on three hundred New York City families emphasized the peculiar preference Italians seemed to have for this style of work:

> The large proportion of Italians engaged in homework is significant of the fact that their home traditions lend themselves with peculiar readiness to the homework system. The Germans accept homework as a trade and adapt themselves to specific phases of it at which they may become expert. They do not do finishing, but do fine custom tailoring, making vests complete or fine hand-made button holes. . . . The Irish and Americans adopt homework only as a last resort. They do it only when they are poverty stricken and driven to it by necessity. The Ital-

[59] Felt, p. 170.

[60] Consumers' League of New York, p. 44; *Second Report*, *FIC*, I (1913), 167, and II, 872.

[61] Testimony of Mary Chamberlain, *Second Report*, *FIC*, II (1913), 1016; Consumer's League of New York, p. 45.

ians come usually from rural districts and know little about factory work and organized industry. The men become laborers and fall into seasonal trades where the wages are small and irregular and must be supplemented. As a rule they have strong home associations, they expect their girls to marry young, and they do not like them to go out into factories. Accustomed in Italy to depend upon the labor of their children in the fields, they expect them in this country to yield a financial return at the earliest possible moment and are, therefore, ready to have them adopt homework, a system that lends itself to the exploitation of women and children.[62]

In the homework and canning industries, the family continued as the basic productive unit, and its organization of the work closely resembled Italian practice. The mother's role as arbiter of household tasks and disciplinarian of children was reinforced by her economic position as work manager, be it artificial flower-making, sewing, or canning. She maintained her inferior position to her husband because she had not become the chief breadwinner. As in Italy, these families viewed the income earned by wives and children who ventured to migrant labor camps or worked at home as a supplement to the father's wages, not a replacement.

In neither case did the Italian male relinquish his obligation to support the family, nor did he forfeit his control and authority. Women and children who worked at the canneries or at home did not drift as separate individuals into the labor market. As we have seen, they were recruited, lived, and worked as family members under the close scrutiny of other Italian-Americans. Finally, like the household, the migrant labor camp permitted a close integration of living and working quarters and therefore did not separate the mother's wage-earning and child-rearing responsibilities. The Italians found such arrangements agreeable because they brought in income while minimizing sex role conflicts.

Within the city of Buffalo itself, Italian women showed a decided preference for those occupations which set the minimum stress on their traditional family roles. Other options existed,

[62] *Second Report, FIC,* II (1913), Appendix 4, "Manufacturing in the Tenements," 684–685.

and other ethnic groups took them. This suggests once again the importance of south Italian precedents in establishing family work patterns. If, as the determinist model holds, family power arrangements depended upon economic roles within the larger society, then female work patterns should give us some clues to the possible restructuring of traditional family roles. This model implies that women's work is particularly threatening in situations where male breadwinners experience high unemployment. In extreme cases, the unemployed male deserts his family altogether and female-headed households result. Because so many Italian men worked only half the year in Buffalo, they should have been susceptible to loss of authority. Yet the evidence cited earlier describing low percentages of deserted families, of households headed by women, or of applications for charity all indicated that in fact Italian men performed exceedingly well as husbands and fathers. Strong inherited traditions supporting male authority could have helped to maintain the stability enjoyed by Italian families, but it was the long-term employment patterns of the women rather than male unemployment that distinguished the Italians from other, less stable working-class families.

In 1905, less than 2 percent of more than two thousand wives reported to the census takers full-time employment that could have taken them from their domestic concerns;[63] some were involved in family enterprises which did not draw them permanently from the home or give them the status of independent wage earners. Only 1 percent of the working women had children. Italian women, then, were certainly not sacrificing their child-rearing responsibilities for work, and no trend toward female assumption of the role of chief provider existed despite the high rate of male unemployment. Evidence cited earlier indicated that most women who contributed to the family budget in this year (12 percent of all wives) did so by providing housekeeping services to roomers and boarders. Another 86 percent reported no occupation at all, but we know that many were engaged part-time in the canneries or had homework.

[63] The following data is from NYSMC, 1905.

The restrictions upon female work outside the home remained strong. Italians responded to difficult financial circumstances by removing their boys from school and sending them to work so that the women and girls could remain in a sheltered environment. The 1905 census reveals that sons and daughters under fifteen, for example, had an equal chance to remain in school. From the ages of fifteen to nineteen, they dropped out of school at the same rate—79 percent of the sons and 82 percent of the daughters left school or were not attending. But the sons entered the labor force while the daughters remained at home. Boys withdrew from school in order to contribute to family survival, but the girls' freedom and achievement were severely restricted.

As a result, Italian women almost always worked within the confines of their homes or as part of a family group, especially in the early days of the community. Most who labored did so only part time or by the season. This situation continued throughout the 1920's. If these occupational patterns are examined in detail, the way they minimized strain upon the traditional family becomes clear.

Italian women and girls rarely left their homes unsupervised by relatives or friends to work as either housekeepers or factory laborers. Because women did not report such occupations to the census representatives, we do not know the exact proportions, but literary sources unanimously confirm that Irish, German, and especially Polish women commonly sought domestic service jobs in Buffalo's middle-class homes. Mothers or married women reluctant to engage in full-time factory labor outside the home liked the flexible routines such private employment allowed.[64] But the Italian men would not permit their wives to work under another man's roof, no matter how serious the family's economic circumstances. And the efforts of various organizations in Buffalo and elsewhere to interest Italian women in

[64] John Daniels, "Polish Laborers and their Needs," *Express*, March 13, 1910; and Golab, "Impact of the Industrial Experience on the Immigrant Family," p. 29, discuss Poles in Buffalo and Philadelphia. Anderson, *Family Structure*," p. 29, observes that English wives did not report such part-time labor to census takers.

such positions failed to erode this protective attitude.[65] New York City social workers claimed that Italian women avoided domestic work "simply because the parents are so strict and jealous, and think it necessary for a girl to live with her family." [66] The women themselves preferred employment which would not separate them from their families; even the second-generation Italians failed to find service work as agreeable as did people of other ethnic groups. The Italian husbands and fathers apparently appreciated the dangers of female employment, including factory employment, outside the home. A National Federation of Settlements survey characterized Italian parents as especially hesitant to permit daughters to enter factories, citing parental concern for their children's morality as a reason. The report also stressed the sexual aspects of the factory situation, which were particularly disturbing to Italian parents: "Though the factory is morally more protected than certain other employments, conditions are far from what they should be. In many places girls work side by side with, or in the near vicinity of men. They sometimes become careless in their conduct, slack in manners and conversations, immodest in dress, and familiar to a degree that lays them open to danger." [67] When Italian women did become factory workers, many successfully internalized these parental values—the discussion of cannery workers warning of "fresh" bosses is one example.

The Italian men showed particularly negative feelings toward women working after marriage, and the women conformed. As one male immigrant noted admiringly: "They stayed at home. Work and home. Work and home." [68] One married woman cited other reasons for staying at home, indicating her cultural bond

[65] "Uncle Sam's Debt to the Italians," *Pensiero Italiano*, Utica, Sept. 26, 1914, describes an Italian baroness who attempted rather unsuccessfully to place Italian women in such positions. Italian women all over the U.S. avoided domestic work.

[66] An Italian informant quoted in "Report on Immigrant Girls," Women's Municipal League *Bulletin* (May, 1908), p. 9, cited in Karen Kearns' unpublished paper on New York City domestic workers, Fall, 1974, City University of New York Graduate Center.

[67] Woods and Kennedy, *Young Working Girls*, pp. 59, 23.

[68] Interview with Frank Iannuzzi.

to the Italian men, who also preferred their accustomed preindustrial routine: "You go to factory, you have to work just as hard as at home. Boss say, 'Hurry up! Hurry up!' At home, no one say 'Hurry up!' I figure out." [69]

Given the stringent attitude of the men, it seems strange that most women contributing to family income did so by taking roomers and boarders into their homes—a choice which kept women at home yet also exposed them to intimate contact with other men. But morality was not jeopardized for money, no matter how serious the need. The families exercised considerable discretion. Mary Sansone told how "everybody had boarders in their homes at one time or another. It would not cause problems. It was not like that in those days. The sense of family was too strong for anything like today, especially if the boarders were *paesani.*" Normally overprotective husbands allowed such men in their homes for two reasons. First, many were trusted kin or *paesani,* and the kinship and village ties which were the substructure of Little Italy's social networks could be counted upon to discourage infidelities. Second, many boarders sought only temporary residence, while seasonal work was available, or until they established their own households. The brevity of their stay limited any opportunities for indiscretion. With minimized risks, then, a family could increase its income by housing boarders.

Polish families revealed strikingly different attitudes toward women entering the work world. Very soon after they had arrived, Buffalo's Polish women eagerly sought work not only as domestics but as factory laborers.[70] Both single and married women worked as domestic servants. According to a 1910 survey of 146 Buffalo firms employing almost eleven thousand individuals of Polish background, two Polish women found employment in the city's manufacturing and industrial establishments for every eight Polish men. If *all* Italian women who worked in all occupations—excluding those in cannery work and those with boarders in their households—are considered, the ratio for

[69] Interview with Marion Callendrucci.

[70] *Recent Immigrants in Agriculture,* II, 491; John Daniels, "Polish Laborers and Their Needs."

Italians in 1905 was only one to twenty.[71] Even granting a higher proportion of Polish women to men, these differences are significant. They were not peculiar to Buffalo alone. Italians in other industrial cities behaved similarly. Butler, noting the relative unimportance of Italian women in Pittsburgh's industrial life, also emphasized the cultural differences between Italian and Polish women. "The Polish women have not the conservatism which keeps the Italian girl at home. They have not the same standard of close-knit family relations. There is a flexibility in their attitude toward life and toward their part in it." [72] In 1909, Tobenkin compared Chicago's Italian, Polish, Jewish, and Lithuanian girls and came to similar conclusions regarding the Italians' conventionality.[73]

Apparently, once in America, Italians did not perceive women's work in exactly the same way as the other groups did. True, Italian women exhibited the same preference for homework and boarders as the other immigrant women. Their shared experiences as women—childbearing and child-rearing—contributed to such mutual preferences. Yet it is also true that Italian women tended to gravitate to some occupations rather than others, that some kinds of work were more acceptable to them than others. Three criteria seem to have governed their work choices—all derivatives of their cultural past. First, work performed within the home (homework and caring for boarders) was acceptable because it did not take the women away from their children, but also because it represented a comfortable extension of the traditional household routine. Second, positions that permitted strict sexual and familial controls upon women were also favored. And third, part-time or seasonal work was acceptable because women would not be assaulting male pride by working more steadily than their frequently unemployed husbands. Homework, cannery work, and taking in boarders ful-

[71] John Daniels, "Polish Wage Earners in Buffalo," *Express*, March 6, 1910, contains information on the Polish population. The Italian data is from NYSMC, 1905.

[72] Elizabeth Beardsley Butler, "The Working Women of Pittsburgh," *Survey*, 23 (1910), 573.

[73] Elias Tobenkin, "The Immigrant Girl in Chicago," *Survey*, 23 (1909), 190.

filled many of these requirements, and this is precisely why Italians favored them.

Any discussion of the relationships between family and work must take a community's economy, work opportunities, and demographic traits into account, for these define the perimeters of behavior and the context in which cultural adaptation occurred. In a small city dominated by one industry, the relationships between family and economy should be relatively clear. In the early twentieth century, for example, Homestead, Pennsylvania, was a typical steel mill town, offering work to men on a fairly regular basis. Women could find employment only occasionally. Therefore, the possibilities for varying family occupation patterns were obviously limited. In Homestead, the overwhelming majority of working-class families adopted the attitude that men should be the breadwinners and that women should contribute to the family economy through their housekeeping skills, not by leaving home to work.[74] In a cotton mill town, another type of one-industry city, we would expect to find the women from needy families working: ethnic or cultural biases against female employment would probably be modified to meet the family's economic needs. In short, in one-industry towns, family occupational patterns would ultimately be determined by that industry regardless of cultural preferences. But in the larger, highly diversified manufacturing centers such as Buffalo, a variety of economic opportunities for both men and women existed; despite the city's emphasis on heavy industry and transportation, women could and did find work. In such cities, the relationship between occupational patterns and family organization was correspondingly much more complex. The nature of the opportunities available permitted a freer expression of cultural preferences, and Old World family values could operate easily despite the urban-industrial context.

The choices that Italian women in Buffalo made also occurred within the changing context of early twentieth-century supply and demand. Although both the proportion and the demand for

[74] Margaret F. Byington, "The Family in a Typical Mill Town," *American Journal of Sociology*, 14 (1909), 648–659.

female labor increased, married, unskilled, foreign-born women did not reap the major benefits. The greatest expansion of opportunities occurred in clerical and communications jobs—work that required a standard of literacy and a familiarity with English. Heavy immigration to American cities at the turn of the century produced a supply of women that far exceeded the demand. Moreover, two typical employers of married women, domestic industry and non-factory clothing industry, declined in importance. The demand for domestic servants and for women willing to do laundry at home remained heavy. With the exception of the Italians, many immigrant wives took such positions because each represented an extension of their traditional household routines.[75] They did not conflict with the norms assigning higher priorities to child-rearing and wifely functions than to full-time work outside the home. Before World War II, the employers' preference for young, single working women supported such priorities.[76] The second-generation daughters of immigrant women flocked to the available jobs in clothing, paper box, and soap factories; others found work in the laundry and publishing industries. Demand only partly determined their decision; the ability to speak English, a lack of child-rearing obligations, and a less receptive attitude toward traditional notions of work also explain their presence in the factories.[77]

Demographic characteristics of Italian women in Buffalo may offer further clues to their decision to forego factory work and domestic service. Earlier figures indicated that a preponderance of Italian females were young, married women. In 1905, 45 percent of married Italian women were between fifteen and thirty years of age, peak childbearing years when women were least likely to work.[78] Almost half of all women (43 percent) with

[75] Scott and Tilly, "Women's Work and the Family in Nineteenth Century Europe," p. 13 also make this point.

[76] Valerie Kincade Oppenheimer, "Demographic Influence on Female Employment and the Status of Women," *American Journal of Sociology*, 58 (1973), 949; and Robert W. Smuts, *Women and Work in America* (New York, 1959), pp. 19ff.

[77] City Business and Industrial Department, Young Women's Christian Association, "Some Facts Concerning Women in Buffalo Industries," p. 45.

[78] The following data is from NYSMC, 1905.

boarders or roomers in their households were between thirty and thirty-nine—the age at which Buffalo's Italian women were most likely to have a large number of children living at home. These figures imply that even if the women wished to work, their traditional responsibilities would have discouraged them. But age and life cycle do not fully explain why married Italians were much less likely to work than Poles. A 10 percent sample of Polish households in 1905 revealed that 36 percent of all married Polish women were under thirty. Poles, then, had only about 10 percent more married women past peak childbearing years who could engage in occupations outside the home more easily than Italians. This difference is not substantial enough to account for the different employment patterns of married Italians and Poles.

Demographic differences do explain why Buffalo factories employed larger proportions of single Polish women. The Polish population was substantially larger, and the Polish women married considerably later than the Italians. In 1905, each group had roughly the same proportion of women under thirty—50 percent for the Italians and 47 percent for the Poles. Yet only 35 percent of the Italian women under thirty remained single, compared to 59 percent of the Polish women.[79]

Free of familial obligations, a larger proportion of Polish women could seek work. But to overemphasize demography is to oversimplify. The decision to marry or to work was itself, of course, culturally informed; Italians, for example, merely continued their Old World custom of early marriage. Both groups had higher proportions of men in their communities, so abnormal sex ratios do not explain the differences in their marriage patterns.

Demographic differences between Poles and Italians—specifically, the possibility of a lower proportion of Italian women—might explain why Italian women less readily entered domestic service. Because Italian males outnumbered females

[79] NYSMC, 1905. The actual proportion of single Polish women is probably greater because the 10 percent sample was based upon Polish households only. Polish live-in servants would not be included if they worked in non-Polish households. All Italians are counted.

(a 1910 sex ratio of 144.4),[80] Italian women could eschew domestic service, finding a market for their household skills among unattached men seeking room and board. Comparable figures pertaining to the Polish sex ratio are not available, but the Polish men almost certainly predominated as males did among most "new immigrant" groups. We know, moreover, that thousands of Polish families supplemented their incomes with boarder's fees.[81] Lack of demand for their services, therefore, cannot explain why Polish wives opted for domestic service.

Because neither labor market conditions nor demographic characteristics fully explain the differences between Polish and Italian women in choosing work, the cultural basis for such decisions deserves re-emphasis. The discussion earlier indicated that Italians in industrial cities like Buffalo made similar choices.[82] When occupational structure is held constant, therefore, cultural preferences seem to play themselves out in similar ways. But the cultural argument is further sustained when one examines the Italian female employment patterns in cities with highly differentiated occupational structures. Although Philadelphia's textile factories offered opportunities to unskilled Italians, the women preferred to work at home in their own neighborhoods. The Italians in Philadelphia were more likely than any other group to engage in homework, and most of the city's homework production centered in Little Italy. A 1929 survey revealed that Italians ranked highest in percentage (70 percent) of women who had not worked since marriage.[83] The 1909 figures for working women in Passaic, New Jersey, where thousands found employment in the worsted mills, revealed that only 7 percent of a sample of south Italian women worked. The percentages for other groups were: Ruthenian, 47; Magyar, 45; and Slovak, 27.[84] Studies of other cities, including Pittsburgh and Boston, also reveal the single or married Italian

[80] *Thirteenth Census, Population*, I, 1871.

[81] See John Daniels, "Americanizing 80,000 Poles," *Charities and the Commons*, 24 (June 4, 1910), 379.

[82] See, for example, Bernardy, "L'emigrazione delle donne," pp. 8ff.

[83] Barbara Klaczynska, "Why Women Work: A Comparison of Various Ethnic Groups—Philadelphia, 1910–1930," *Labor History*, 17 (Winter 1976), 73–87.

[84] Personal communication from Michael Ebner.

woman's tendency to avoid domestic service and the married Polish woman's dependency on it.[85]

A sample of a major Italian neighborhood in New York City in 1905 indicated that almost no Italian women worked after marriage.[86] In New York, single Italian girls left domestic and personal service to other ethnic groups, but they did enter the factories. Still, they viewed factory work chiefly as an opportunity to learn a skill such as sewing which they might keep up at home after marriage.[87]

Returning to the city of Buffalo, we can arrive at a better understanding of why the Italian women chose the type of work they did. The significance of the seasonal and part-time nature of their employment patterns is that they minimized family disruption. The situation repeated the Old World experience, where a wife's occasional contributions to the household budget were appreciated but always interpreted as supplementary to the man's. Rarely did the Italian wife provide greater economic stability than her husband. For this reason, in the pre-World War I era, when Italian men were most likely to be chronically unemployed, their wives were also likely to be unemployed for at least as long. If women contributed to the family budget the year round, they generally did so by keeping boarders, which did not contribute to their social or financial independence. Cultural tradition prevented the Italian wife from taking the one suitable, readily available job for unskilled women which would have guaranteed steady employment—work as a maid or a domestic. Even if women entered factories in greater numbers, they could not have been the family's chief support. These factory laborers, like most women in industry, tended to be irregularly employed. In 1909, Odencrantz, in a study of women wage earners, found that one-half of a group of a thousand New

[85] Golab, "Impact of the Industrial Experience on the Immigrant Family," p. 29; Odencrantz, *Italian Women in Industry*, p. 33; Bernardy, "L'emigrazione delle donne," pp. 8ff.

[86] Personal communication from Herbert Gutman based on NYSMC, 1905, (for Greenwich Village, New York City). This is probably an underestimate since we know that Italian women did not always report their part-time occupations to census canvassers.

[87] Mary Van Kleeck, *Artificial Flower Makers* (New York, 1913), pp. 32, 38.

York City working girls held their jobs for less than six months, chiefly because most had seasonal occupations and their employers frequently discharged them.[88] Most of the light industries to which women flocked for employment—such as clothing, textiles, food, candy, and paper box manufacturing—responded to irregular seasonal demand. Employers in these trades could not afford to maintain a year-round labor force if they wished to maximize profits. The situation was worse in cities like Buffalo where heavy industry predominated.[89] Thus, even if the Italians there had taken a more open-minded approach, the nature of the opportunities for unskilled female labor in early twentieth-century America would have made it difficult for them to supplant their husbands as chief breadwinners. However, they could do so if, like their seasonally unemployed husbands, they were willing to alternate jobs several times annually.

During the war and pre-Depression years, when more Italian women left their homes to work, Italian men were also more likely to be steadily employed or at least more likely to be earning higher wages. Hence female employment did not represent a serious challenge to male authority at this time. Even after World War I these employment patterns had not changed radically, at least so far as first-generation wives were concerned. An analysis of fifteen densely populated blocks in the Buffalo ward most heavily settled by Italians in 1925 indicated that although the daughters had gone to work in silk factories, clothing trades, or offices, not one mother or wife in this district had left her home to work. Very few households in these blocks contained boarders or lodgers, so that the number of women contributing to family income in this way had actually declined.[90]

[88] Louise Odencrantz, "The Irregularity of Employment of Women Factory Workers," *Survey*, 22 (1909), 200.

[89] Eleanor G. Coit, "An Industrial Study, Buffalo, New York" (unpublished paper, Business and Industrial Department, Young Women's Christian Association, 1922), p. 49; YWCA, "Some Facts Concerning Women in Buffalo Industries," pp. 6–7; and H. E. Burber, *Industrial Analysis of Buffalo* (Buffalo: n.d.) each indicate some of the major companies which employed women, most of which had highly seasonal employment cycles. Triller, "International Institute in Buffalo," p. 4, quoting a report by Miss Ely (Nov. 1, 1919), notes that Buffalo's industry simply did not provide enough work for women.

[90] NYSMC, 1925.

Italian women continued to work in the canneries during the summers after the war, but we have seen that this work tended to sustain, not challenge, traditional family relationships.

Italians retained a cultural bias against female employment even among the second generation. A survey of all second-generation families in sixteen wards, once again including those most heavily populated by Italians, revealed that in 1925 only 12 percent had working wives (120 of 1,022). Moreover, these women were not forced to work because their spouses were unemployed or had deserted their families. Only one had no husband, and she may have been a widow. The remaining wives had employed husbands.[91] The evidence for 1905 and 1925 is amply substantiated by other local and national sources.[92] In some cities, expecially those with significant light industry, Italian women worked more often than they did in Buffalo; but even in these cases they tended to enter occupations which, like the canneries, ensured them the security and protection of working closely with fellow Italians or at least within Little Italy's confines.

The bias against female employment softened, but only the second generation benefitted. The majority of women entering the labor force after World War I were daughters, not wives and mothers. Although the general attitude toward women's work remained one of disapproval, rather than permit their wives to leave home, men resigned themselves "rather painfully" to daughters working in factories—a choice which minimized the potential stress upon the husband-wife relationship.[93] By contributing to the family income, daughters merely fulfilled one of

[91] NYSMC, Wards 12–27. Second-generation families were defined here as a family with an Italian name in which both spouses were born in the U.S., in which the wife was born in the U.S. and the husband in Italy, or in which the husband was born in the U.S. and the wife in Italy. In every case, a wife born in the U.S. could have been of either non-Italian or Italian descent.

[92] The following support the description of female employment: for the pre-war period, the infrequency of Italian female employment outside the home is observed in Goodale, "Children of Sunny Italy." Post-war sources on Italian female employment include: Burber, *Industrial Analysis*, n.p.; Coit, "Industrial Study," p. 44; YWCA, Business and Industrial Department, "Further Data from the Industrial Study," *Buffalo Foundation Forum* (Nov. 1922), p. 12. For a national perspective, see Bernardy, "L'emigrazione delle donne," pp. 12, 50; see also Butler, "The Working Women of Pittsburgh," pp. 571–572.

[93] Bernardy, "L'emigrazione delle donne," p. 13.

the proper functions of children and worked for the acceptable goal of dowry savings; they represented no challenge to their father's prestige and control. In any case, because daughters and sons, not wives, left home to work, the latter had little opportunity to enhance their bargaining power within the family by way of significant economic contributions.

The actual fact that women worked is perhaps less important than the immigrants' interpretation of the situation. Cultural preferences influenced not only their choices, but also what their work experiences meant to the family. A New York social worker's comments illustrate this point. Observing that Italian women did not achieve as much independence as other working women, she explained that their men saw women's work as an "inevitable evil induced by conditions of American life which did not in any way alter their dependent position. . . . In this way the women are kept in the paradoxical position of simultaneous wage-earning and dependence."[94] And the male attitude reveals further ambivalence and inconsistency rooted in attempts to comprehend new circumstances in terms of old values. Consider Richard Ferranti's comments: "My wife did not work after we were married. Why should she work?" Yet Mr. and Mrs. Ferranti initially converted their newly purchased home into a rooming house. Mr. Ferranti reported as a casual aside: "We had a lot of people. To make money . . . my wife used to take care of that. . . . I didn't pay any attention to it." Apparently in Mr. Ferranti's eyes, his wife's involvement with a boarding house was not "work." Without our understanding of how Italians perceived cannery work for women, Mary Sansone's comments would also appear inconsistent: "This was a respectable way for women to work, even if it was not respectable to work in a factory. They used to save a little extra money and then buy a house." The outside observer probably would not comprehend why cannery work was acceptable if factory work was not. But an Italian would, especially if the point of laboring at the cannery was to buy a home.

The Italian men scorned the married woman worker, but they

[94] Odencrantz, *Italian Women in Industry*, p. 176.

did not seem bothered by the apparent contradiction between this firmly held attitude and the fact that women who did cannery labor and housed boarders were, in fact, working. Several possible explanations exist for this inconsistency. Apparently, Italians did not perceive woman's work in the same way the dominant culture did. Male immigrants like Mr. Ferranti who did not see his wife as a working woman defended themselves pyschologically against female encroachment either by undervaluing the women's work or by seeing it as an extension of traditional functions. Work within a woman's traditional sphere—the home—was not recognized as work, even if the enterprise produced profits. Part-time work for some family-related goal (e.g., saving for a house) or work occurring outside the urban market place with other family members at the canneries could be rationalized in similar fashion. These immigrant attitudes to women's work appear inconsistent only if we forget that they comprehended new circumstances in terms of an Old World *gestalt*.

The conservatism of female employment patterns and the immigrants' understanding of them is clear evidence for continuing male domination, and does much to explain why female-headed families and family disorganization were so rare among Italian-Americans. The depreciation of women's work had practical importance in an immigrant community where male unemployment was extremely high. The woman's economic contributions made family survival possible, yet she apparently remained a silent partner in the marital economic relationship; Italians did not admit that their women worked, even to themselves. The wife retained the good peasant woman's acceptance of male control. Even when she did work and her husband could find no job, her sense of her own importance was not inflated. Male unemployment, furthermore, was not a new experience for immigrants any more than it was for agricultural laborers in Italy, and the Italians withstood it as well in America as they had in the old country. Their devaluation of woman's work helped to maintain the precarious balance of power between male and female.

All the occupational patterns described permitted the survival of many south Italian family traditions. Other studies suggest that the kinds of adaptations that Italians made within the city of Buffalo and at the canneries were not peculiar. They also show that employers seeking high output at cheap prices had a flexibility of their own. New Jersey silk-weaving firms, for example, frequently hired whole Italian families, probably because these employers, like the cannery owners, recognized the family's potential as a well-disciplined work unit. Smelser's study of the English Industrial Revolution observed similar phenomena in the weaving industry soon after it was mechanized, and studies of modern Japan emphasize how its economic institutions operate under traditional political and personal concepts. In Roseto, Pennsylvania, Italian factory owners often hired relatives and *paesani* as their garment workers, and labor contractors in these factories frequently assumed the "role of patriarchal leaders." [95] Finally, a study of south Italian factory laborers in Pittsburgh shows the same transference of kin control in an urban situation. In this instance, Italians did permit women and children to enter industrial occupations outside the home because their proximity to the ethnic neighborhood and the presence of other Italians in the work force provided props for expected behavior.[96]

One could argue that both the canneries and homework industries were semitraditional occupations, and that immigrant adjustment to them does not challenge conventional understanding of the relationship between family and industrialization. But such an argument does not explain the immigrants' behavior in more typical urban settings, and it obscures some important distinctions about them and the industrial society they helped to create. We tend to simplify what

[95] Clement J. Valletta, "The Settlement of Roseto: World View and Promise" in John Bodnar, ed., *The Ethnic Experience in Pennsylvania* (Lewisburg, 1973), p. 140.

[96] Foerster, p. 346 discusses the New Jersey situation; Smelser, pp. 182ff; Geertz, *Peddlers and Princes*, p. 144, mentions a Japanese study by James G. Abbegglen, *The Japanese Factory: Aspects of Its Social Organization* (Glencoe: Free Press, 1958); George H. Huganir, "The Hosiery Looper in the Twentieth Century: A Study of Family Occupational Processes and Adaptation to Factory and Community Change, 1900–1950" (unpublished Ph.D. dissertation, University of Pennsylvania, 1958), *passim*, discusses Pittsburgh Italians.

the creation of such a society means. Clifford Geertz reminds us that "economic development can take place within a context of general social and economic conservatism in which essentially traditional values and social structures are so adapted as to be capable of integration with more efficient economic practices." [97]

Sometimes with their employers' cooperation and sometimes without it, the Italian immigrants transformed the canning factories into communities where Old World social attitudes and behavior could continue, maintained by kinship ties. The way these families fitted themselves into their new context confirms that despite the necessity for efficiency and rationality the modern economic institutions were quite capable of incorporating such traditional needs. In the case of female work patterns within the city, the demands of employers and working-class cultural priorities coincided. The seasonal, part-time, sporadic work patterns of wage-earning women stemmed partly from their condition as women, for most dropped out of the labor market during childbearing and child-rearing years. A developing capitalist industrial economy's need for a cheap labor force that could be discharged periodically with the minimum of difficulty also explains their position. The traditional, conservative character of this era's working-class culture advocated keeping women at home in order to avoid family tensions, and in this way provided the part-time labor force that employers needed.

There was ample room in industrial America for immigrants wishing to avoid a head-on collision with a new way of life. But the immigrant preference for fringe occupations shows how tradition influenced both their perception and their use of work options. In short, immigrants once more constructed and interpreted their social reality in terms of past experience. Without taking their perceptions into account, we cannot properly understand either them or their history.

[97] Geertz, *Peddlers and Princes*, p. 144.

8 "Sacrifice Is Her Most Becoming Ornament": Family Attitudes and Behavior

In 1907, Mr. A. Pappalardo addressed *Il Corriere*'s readers on an issue of much concern to Italian immigrants—"Woman's Honor." The true woman, he said, understands that "sacrifice is her most becoming ornament."[1] Exactly how many "true women" existed in Buffalo's Little Italy is difficult to determine. Was Mr. Pappalardo merely confirming what every respectable woman already knew? Or was he trying to reassure himself and convince his audience of the continuing efficacy of tradition? We will probably never know or understand Mr. Pappalardo's personal reasons for editorializing upon woman's honor, and they need not detain us any longer. But many other Italian-Americans also feared the decay of the family and morality as they understood them. The Italian press, moderate and leftist, focused to a remarkable extent on family affairs. That the public news media became a forum for discussion of intimate personal relationships indicates the extent of the community interest and concern.

The preoccupations and attitudes of elite immigrant journalists are one thing; the actual behavior of the ordinary immigrant quite another. Evidence concerning child-rearing, intermarriage, education, and political and community activity tells us that most working-class Italian families avoided the changes and disruptions that *Il Corriere*'s writers in particular feared. In-

[1] Editorial, "Woman's Honor," *IC*, Nov. 9, 1907.

deed, the Italian leftist editorials imply that immigrants retained many conventional attitudes and practices—too many in their view.

What, then, does literary evidence indicating an elite concern about family life mean? The leftist journalists lamented family conventionality because they believed it obstructed social change. Their motivations are easy to understand. But how should statements by *Il Corriere*'s more moderate writers be evaluated, especially when they imply real departures from family tradition? In fact, the apparent contradictions between such elite attitudes and working-class family behavior are not so problematic as they seem. Ordinary Italians ultimately did assimilate many American ways, but such changes occurred over two or three generations. *Il Corriere*'s writers were reacting to their own more immediate problems. While leftists actively sought a revolution in social values, *Il Corriere*'s journalists, an elite group whose power and prestige derived from their superior position within Little Italy, had much to lose if the character of that community changed. And, if these journalists' attitudes did not mirror those of the ordinary immigrant, it was because they had easier and earlier access to American society and ideas. Aspiring toward Americanization, higher-class status, and local power, these educated few were the first to confront and record the new social pressures.

Early twentieth-century Americans experienced major cultural changes, which effected everyone, not just immigrants. The feminist movement, World War I, the "crisis of civilized morality," and the popularization of Freudian psychology—including new ways of perceiving and treating children and adolescents—had some indeterminate but perceptible effect upon urban dwellers everywhere.[2] All Americans, native and foreign born, faced the task of integrating such new ideas into their established family patterns.

Even the immigrant press recognized that pressures experienced by newcomers were being felt elsewhere. Observing that women in America and Europe enjoyed new life styles in the

[2] See Nathan Hale, *Freud and the Americans* (New York, 1971), especially Chapters 10 and 17 on "civilized morality."

1920's, *Il Corriere's* woman's column emphasized World War I as a major cause: "This war has taught us many things, among them woman's valor. She, with strong spirit and great sacrifice, offers her country not only her sons, her spouse, and her brothers, but also herself." Journalists hypothesized that the women's assumption of responsibilities outside the home—opportunities created by a shortage of men and the wartime economic crisis—initiated the change. Women, *Il Corriere* stated, labored heroically on the front helping the wounded. They worked in offices, munitions plants, and air plane factories. They reponded to the country's needs, "discharging their new obligations with ability and exactness." [3]

Even if feminist efforts and the wartime demand for female labor produced no permanent radical change in the American woman's status,[4] they succeeded in making her a public issue. The progressive reformers' increasingly popular concern for health focused public interest upon women and children too. When women were subjects of political interest, their inferior family status was sure to be scrutinized. Italian writers responded by questioning or reaffirming the value of tradition.

Family tradition met with a further test as women and children increasingly involved themselves in urban institutions outside the home. As Caroline F. Ware suggested in her fine analysis of New York City Italians, American institutions were "normally . . . designed to deal with people as individuals rather than in family . . . groups. Democracy, community participation, and public school education" all rested upon "individualist assumptions." Such American institutions severely "wrenched" the immigrant family's internal dynamics, because whatever individualized women and children tended to "upset their subordination to the group as a whole and to the man who was its dominant head." The most fundamental of all Italian institutions "suffered constant erosion," and, Ware argued, "the breakdown of Italian culture" could be traced to the changing

[3] Women's column, "La lingua inglese è necessaria alle donne," *IC,* June 18, 1921; article by "D.C.," "Il voto e la donna," *IC,* Oct. 11, 1917.

[4] William H. Chafe, *The American Woman: Her Changing Social, Economic and Political Roles, 1920–1970* (New York, 1972), takes this position.

position of women and children.[5] Our earlier discussion of social welfare organizations supports this characterization of the American agencies; but Italian familial culture proved less immediately susceptible to their intrusion than Ware believed. Information about other aspects of family life indicates that despite pressures toward liberalization, change occurred only gradually.

The immigrants of all cultures and classes regarded the possibility of family disruption anxiously; and their circumstances made them keenly aware of its dangers. Many experienced temporary separations from their loved ones, which caused hardship and personal conflict, no matter how much support community and kin provided. In an Italian town of five to six thousand inhabitants, about a thousand male family heads might be away for as long as two or three years at a time. Because human beings are only human, strain, illegitimacy, and adultery sometimes occurred in these situations.[6] Men who came to American cities unaccompanied by their families found themselves directly affected, or feared they might be. *Il Corriere* warned its readers with a fable, hoping to stimulate male consciousness of the problem. An immigrant, the story went, sent money regularly to his wife and children. Upon his return to Italy, his spouse welcomed him joyfully, declaring how wretched she had been without him. Yet shortly after this glorious reunion, the man's friends reported her inconstancy. *Il Corriere* concluded with a warning: "Woman's fidelity, an apparatus as changeable as a barometer, must be carefully guarded in the new atmosphere produced by immigration." [7] Significantly, the paper issued no such caveat to the wives of male itinerants. Most remained abroad outside its audience; perhaps reluctance to offend its virtuous readers also played a part.

Letters written by immigrants indicate that in this case ordinary Italians shared the concern of the journalists. The inability to support families left in Italy worried the immigrants, who

[5] *Greenwich Village: 1920–1930* (New York, 1965), p. 175.

[6] See Antonio Mangano, "The Effect of Emigration upon Italy," *Charities and the Commons,* 20 (April 4, 1908), 13–25; and Victor Von Borosini, "Home-going Italians," *Survey,* 28 (Sept. 28, 1912), 391–393.

[7] Guido Celli, "Emigrazione e fedeltà," *IC,* June 5, 1909.

feared the possible effects of poverty on their loved ones. In their letters, several immigrants indicated their sorrow at living apart from their families, and angry disappointment that they had little money to send to wives or parents. A certain Armando complained that "although America looks like a remarkable land from Italy, one is treated like a blockhead here. In this land of plenty, nothing exists but work, maltreatment, and privations." Armando was a Socialist, and perhaps this explains his acidity; but his awareness of the responsibilities he should have performed in person and his fears that his absence threatened a family left abroad were typical. Armando's letters to his sister in Italy revealed both preoccupation with and feelings of responsibility for maintaining his family's welfare. "Comfort mother," he wrote, "respect your husband, because it is with reciprocal respect that we are able to keep peace in the family." [8]

Immigrant concern usually focused less upon the disruptive effects of temporary separation than upon the permanent challenge of liberal morality. The looser American attitudes toward marriage, women, and sex aroused particular anxiety. Divorce, separation, and desertion received frequent mention in *Il Corriere*'s weekly woman's column soon after its initial appearance in the early 1900's. One writer stated his position strongly but succinctly: "The goal of marriage is creation of a family." He still considered marriage a permanent, personal, sacred institution in which the state should not interfere: "If a couple wants happiness, they should not have to resort to the law to obtain it." [9] Another critic of American family ethics concurred. "Spouses," he claimed, "derived their character from their function as parents" —that is, family members. Anyone who viewed an individual as "freed" by divorce had, therefore, been duped by "false liberalism." [10] Catholic doctrine and Old World custom obviously influenced this immigrant's thought. The infrequency of separations and divorces among Italians suggests that the average Italian shared his opinions.

American practices had some impact, for *Il Corriere*'s image

[8] *La F*, Sept. 4, 1909; see also *La F*, Oct. 3, 1909; *La F*, Nov. 20, 1909; *La F*, Nov. 27, 1909.

[9] "Il problema matrimoniale," *IC*, June 19, 1909. See also *IC*, July 8, 1905.

[10] Alfredo Oriani, "Il divorzio," *IC*, Jan. 24, 1914.

of the ideal marital alliance showed that its writers modified some traditional concepts. One editorial emphasized that husband and wife should be sympathetic and understanding friends to one another. Accepting the value of companionship in marriage did not imply any acceptance of other American ideas and habits, especially the decline of "pure moral love" and its replacement by "vanity, glory, and sentimentality." American marriage, *Il Corriere* claimed, had become a "superficial relationship." Infidelity and indifference burdened entire families with unhappiness. *Il Corriere*'s writers feared that parental amorality would be imitated by the young. When husband and wife set a poor example, children would also give "free expression to their desires." How else explain the young American male's disregard for feminine virtue? In America all was "moral chaos." What need could immigrants have for this new morality? [11]

The paternalistic notions of proper marital responsibility had great tenacity, even for Little Italy's middle-class journalists. According to *Il Corriere*, a good husband should be both family head and "gentle adviser." A moral man brought honor, not disgrace, to his home. He received psychological gratification from his major obligation—the support of his wife and children. In his old age, he could expect the education with which he had provided his children to benefit him. Wives and children, still considered inferior, owed service and respect to their family head. From his position of authority, the husband was advised to act as a "father to his wife," but also as her "brother," protecting her from both physical and moral danger. A good wife deserved a proper husband, a man who regarded her with "sacred reverence." [12]

The "home" and home traditions never had the place in Italian culture that they held in America. But in Buffalo, the ideal of the home developed, as a haven from the rest of society, a place where the "world's troubles and sorrows fade away." [13]

[11] A. Pappalardo, *IC*, Nov. 16, 1907.

[12] Editorial, A. Pappalardo, "La moralità paragonata con l'utilità," *IC*, Jan. 11, 1908; editorial, "Un buon marito," *IC*, May 11, 1912.

[13] "Un buon marito," *IC*, May 11, 1912. Villari, *Italian Life*, p. 79, contrasts the English idea of home to the Italian.

Observing this new phenomenon, one outsider characterized Italians as "home loving" people who valued cleanliness and good housekeeping, so difficult to achieve in overcrowded apartments.[14] *La Fiaccola*, a working-class newspaper not characteristically seduced by sentimentality, referred to home as the family's "nest," a man's "kingdom." The enterprising journal could not resist an opporunity to propagandize on the concept. Unfortunately, it claimed, among the poor, home was often a man's "hell," not his castle. If the man sure of an adequate income had a serene and peaceful abode, the laborer who returned to hungry children with no promise of work the next day "suffers in desperation." Were things more equal, the journal ruefully mused, each family would have its own little domicile, clean, healthy, sunny, well ventilated, decorated with flowers, and perhaps even boasting a pet. The children would be well fed, healthy, and robust.[15]

The most important confirmations of continuing family conventionality can be found in the political arena. Fortunately for us, the socialist writers, frustrated by working-class conservatism, have documented it in their writings. Radicals seeking Italian support had a difficult assignment. They faced immigrants who had little positive prior experience with modern political institutions. And there were even more serious barriers. Popular mythology claimed that orthodox Marxism favored the family's eventual dissolution, a result family-oriented Italians could hardly accept enthusiastically. Perceiving that political participation itself conflicted with peasant family attitudes, many immigrants regarded radicalism suspiciously. Any female involvement in public life seriously threatened the Italian husbands who feared that liberation might follow. And any commitment on the part of the men to socialist politics frightened uneasy Italian wives, who foresaw family problems. Although socialists everywhere debated socialism's possible effects upon the family, in Buffalo's Italian socialist circle it became *the*

[14] Goodale, "Children of Sunny Italy"; see also "The Italian Colony in Buffalo," *Courier*, May 8, 1898, in which attention is given the housekeeping habits of Italian women.

[15] Z. Traldi, "La casa è un nido," *La F*, March 4, 1911.

major issue, exceeded in importance only by conflicts over tactics and political ideology.

An important debate between the local Catholic clergy and the Socialist party's Italian section during the first two decades of the twentieth century confirms the persistence of traditional family attitudes among working-class Italians. Disputes over the nature and responsibilities of family life marked only one phase of an animosity already firmly established by the time of *La Fiaccola*'s initial publication in the early 1900's.

Parish priests obeyed hierarchical directives when they admonished against socialism's evils; and their technique for reaching immigrants was telling. The women, the community's churchgoers, remained well within their sphere of influence; but the men did not. Family religious functions presented one of the rare instances when clerics could be assured of a mixed audience. On one such occasion a wedding service—hardly an appropriate forum for a sermon on religion and politics—a priest delivered a tirade against socialism. He asked his wayward flock to return to religion and the Church. Then, fully aware of the presence of wives, mothers, and daughters, whom he expected to uphold his position, he insisted that the men abandon the party or their families would surely suffer some horrible fate.[16]

Buffalo's Catholic church had good reasons to oppose radicalism. *La Fiaccola* featured fiercely anticlerical attacks both in its editorials and in the letters to the editor. One correspondent called the priest "one of the most dangerous men in the world, a liar and a thief." "I hope," wrote a blasphemous immigrant to his sister, "your child will not be contaminated by priestly waters."[17] Reflecting upon the "injustice and infamy" inflicted upon workers, one sardonic sage found no consolation in clergymen's promises that suffering in this world brings joy in the next. Writing to his mother and father, this immigrant stated angrily, "Ask the priest if it is right that I must leave you. Ask him if it is right that your sons are so many miles away, working

[16] Letter from Domenico Nurzia, *La F*, July 9, 1910.

[17] Anita Albertini, Vermont correspondent, *La F*, Nov. 12, 1910; letter from Armando, "Propaganda famigliare," *La F*, Sept. 4, 1909.

to exhaustion, yet still unable to help their parents." [18] Such anticlericalism typified Italian-American sentiment. Although Church teachings reinforced many Italian family ideals, including male superiority, strict parental authority, and the idealization of the family, many Italians still distrusted clergymen and the Church as an institution.[19]

Ample evidence indicates that if the Italian men remained anticlerical or as indifferent as they had been in Italy, priests continued to influence the women of the family. *La Fiaccola* urged its male readers to convince the women, who were perceived as a reactionary influence, that their anticlericalism was serious. "You ought to be ashamed," claimed one editorialist addressing the community's men, "to walk into a church, even for family matters such as marriages and baptism." [20] Apparently, Socialist men attended such occasions out of familial respect, but hard-core radicals aimed to discourage them even from this minimal religious contact.

Several Socialist doctrines overtly opposed Catholic orthodoxy. Among these was birth control; the Socialists advocated rational family planning so that a father could sufficiently provide for his children. *La Fiaccola* presented anecdotes to make its point. A Polish woman, one story goes, had eleven children. Certainly the priest would approve. But *La Fiaccola* noted, we would ask her, "How do you feed them?" [21]

Radicals propagandized parents in an effort to keep Italian children out of parochial schools and removed from religious influences. This campaign obviously threatened local clerical control. Shortly before a new Catholic school opened in Little Italy, *La Fiaccola* warned of the priests' incompetence as teachers, and their tendency to stress superstition before knowledge. The journal presented statistics allegedly compiled by a juvenile court judge demonstrating that Catholic children had the highest juvenile delinquency rate in the city. These statistics incontestably demonstrated the shortcomings of Catholic schools, the

[18] Letter from G. Valvo, "Propaganda famigliare," *La F*, July 16, 1910.

[19] On anticlericalism, see Vecoli, "Prelates and Peasants." On the Italian family and the Church see Firth, *Kinship*, pp. 91–92.

[20] "All'anticlericale," *La F*, Sept. 18, 1909.

[21] "Per fare onore alla prosperità," *La F*, July 30, 1910.

newspaper argued. Many Italian parents agreed with Socialist opinion. In 1909, for example, several parents protested that Principal Charles Ryan of School Two, the public institution with the largest Italian enrollment, required students to attend religious training and ceremonies at Saint Anthony's Church. Like most of their countrymen, the Italians in Buffalo had an aversion to parochial education.[22]

As their debate moved to discussion of family life, the clergy, as might be expected, espoused conservative ideals. The Socialists—sometime feminists and family planning advocates—attacked orthodoxy vehemently, but ultimately conceded to tradition. Despite intense mutual hostility, both priests and Socialists referred to the family's disintegration as a frightful possibility. The clerical insistence that all Socialists opposed the family, or that a socialist utopia required its dissolution, had no factual basis, but the clergy commonly used such claims to discredit their adversaries. They understood the family's centrality in immigrant culture. Recognizing the force of clerical claims, Italian Socialists stressed that no such dissolution need occur. *La Fiaccola*'s editors were realistic revolutionaries. They recognized the family's significance to working-class Italians as well as the clergy did. Some acknowledged that socialism could bring family discord in the form of personal disagreements, but they claimed that this resulted from the fervor which often moved those committed to socialist theory.[23] Usually they argued that socialism's efforts to eradicate poverty would ultimately strengthen the family, not disrupt it. Because some believed the family perpetuated inequalities in capitalist society, they favored its eventual dissoluton. But in all of *La Fiaccola*'s articles on family matters, such radical concepts received mention precisely once, and then the journal emphasized only that there *might* be no need for the family when the world's miseries were totally alleviated.[24]

This debate gives us further clues about Italian family life.

[22] "Italiani di Buffalo," *La F*, Jan. 13, 1912; "Scuola laica e religione," *La F*, July 30, 1910; "Per un maestro-sagrestano," *La F*, Oct. 16, 1909.

[23] "Il solitario," "Per la pace in famiglia," *La F*, Jan. 14, 1911.

[24] Editorial, "Il socialismo dissolve la famiglia?" *La F*, May 21, 1910.

The Socialists placed a high priority upon propagandizing the women, a good indication of female conservatism. In their battle with orthodoxy, astute Socialists exploited the women's strong family sympathies by pronouncing family interests and church demands incompatible. The articulate Armando wrote to his sister in Italy: "Put your duties to your husband and your mother before religion."[25] And *La Fiaccola*'s Vermont correspondent warned Buffalo's Italian women that religious piety would necessarily conflict with their positions as women and wives: "Who inculcates lies in the soul of a woman? The priest with the pretext of confession attracts her to lies. . . . The woman who has the priest's confidence is not a good woman nor can she succeed in being a good mother and wife. She must be kept from the priest and from the confessional, for the priest will make her his tool. . . . The woman who is a friend of a priest is an eternal slave."[26] The same correspondent cleverly appealed to the conservatism of Italian women in one phrase and in the next encouraged them to fight for social justice on the basis of this conservatism: "A woman's place is in the family, and in the fight to improve it." She again claimed that the aims of the family and of religion were opposed: "The woman who is the priest's confidant cannot be a model family woman."[27]

Canny radicals, like prudent priests, used familism for their own ends. As organizers, the Socialists' primary interest was in permanently settled individuals, who might involve themselves in sustained action, and the particular audience to which they addressed themselves indicated this. Despite the presence of large numbers of unattached immigrants in Little Italy, Socialists continually appealed to family men and women. They recognized the family as the basic social unit. Instead of phrasing their propaganda in terms of individual decisions to join the movement or individual rights and responsibilities, they emphasized family roles and obligations. This strategy placed them on a firm footing in their competition with the Church, and en-

[25] "Propaganda famigliare," *La F*, Sept. 4, 1919.
[26] Anita Albertini, "La donna e la [*sic*] prete," *La F*, Nov. 12, 1910.
[27] Quoted in Albertini, "Bugia pretesca," *La F*, July 29, 1911.

abled them to avoid a head-on collision with Italian cultural attitudes.

The Socialists urged working-class Italians to join a building laborers' union, not only in order to ensure worker solidarity, but also "for the dignity of your family." [28] Radicals appealed directly to Little Italy's men as fathers. Socialism, they argued, could provide the bare necessities they currently lacked. "Socialists," one writing laborer assured his readers, "are greatly preoccupied with the interests of the family, of all society, and they wish to satisfy with their own labor the needs of life for themselves and their children, for the handicapped and the aged." [29] For those who wished to join the party but feared they might fail in their roles as fathers, husbands, sons, or brothers as a result, one radical offered assurance, in an outburst of sentiment, that the Socialists perceived the passionate ties and feelings of devotion that bound men to their families as a sweet refuge from life's bitter suffering.[30] Not to be outdone by the clergy, the Socialists also conducted their own morals campaign. The vices they attacked most vigorously were those commonly recognized as detrimental to family life: they urged men and women not to become slaves to their senses or to patronize saloons and houses of prostitution.[31]

The Socialists also used motherhood, that sacred Italian institution, to touch the hearts of Buffalo's immigrant women. *La Fiaccola* chided dutiful mothers by reminding them that while they could scarcely afford milk for their children, others lived ostentatiously.[32] For the working mother, one writer claimed, maternity is often a sorrow, not a joy. From the first day she realizes she is carrying a child, the working-class woman suffers "profound anguish." In hours stolen from rest, she lifts tired hands to sew infant clothing. Some cannot afford materials for hand-made garments. This woman welcomes her child into

[28] Editorial, *La F*, Oct. 15, 1910.

[29] "Un lavoratore," "Le idee dei Socialisti," *La F,* Sept. 11, 1909.

[30] F. Cicotti, "Come dev'essere il buon socialista nella famiglia?" *La F,* Oct. 29, 1910.

[31] J. Nicolini, "La moralità," *La F*, Jan. 15, 1910.

[32] Editorial, "Leggete mamme!" *La F*, Oct. 15, 1910.

the world with mixed feelings of love and sorrow; he suffers from lack of food and proper clothing. His mother sees him grow, enter the work force, and exhaust his young body. And then the anguished mother wonders, would it have been better had she never borne him? "Bourgeois society closes its eyes to this tragic rendering of a mother's heart," *La Fiaccola* continued, "while the church makes some vague promise of future happiness." The Socialists, on the other hand, wished "to redeem motherhood, to return it to the healthy joys and happiness of fertility. We do not wish mothers to weep because they cannot provide for their children. We want justice and bread for all." [33] *La Fiaccola* reminded Italian mothers of death's partiality; it tended to prefer the children of the poor—their children. "Your offspring," a writer warned them, "are weakened by your suffering." By working until the last minute before delivery, laboring mothers lost their strength. Finally, women were reminded of their inability to provide food and medical care for their young as the rich were able to do.[34]

The attempts to involve women in politics also appealed to the traditional sense of parental responsibility. "It is woman," *La Fiaccola* stated, "who raises our sons, who must be able to educate the new generation. She must be a teacher. How can she do all this if she herself never learned to express herself politically?" [35] Women, no less than men, the paper stressed, struggled to provide for their families. One female propagandist argued that landlords and foodstore owners hoped women would remain in their homes uninvolved in politics. And, she continued, those women who did stay home or who worked to aid the family, were defenseless, maltreated, exploited, and poorly paid. She exhorted Italian women to fight such exploitation by entering political life or at least by joining a union. And she evoked the responsibilities of motherhood: "It is in the interest of your family to become a Socialist, to become involved in politics." [36] Another article, addressed to both male and female

[33] "Mammina," "Il pensiero dei figli," *La F*, July 29, 1911.
[34] Maria Riccardo Goia, "Nemmeno la morte," *La F*, Nov. 13, 1909.
[35] "Virtus," "La donna è politica," *La F*, June 22, 1912.
[36] "Mammina," "Non è per la donna la politica?" *La F*, Nov. 5, 1910.

workers as parents, asked: "Do you want happy, healthy, educated, adequately clothed children? . . . Do you wish the elderly in your family to live in comfort? . . . Do you wish your sons to be kept from fighting wars?" If readers desired all of this plus the opportunity to earn a decent living—as any devoted parent would—then socialism provided the only solution.[37]

The radicals also clothed their opposition to child labor in a veil of family sentiment. In one editorial, "Virtus" attacked the cruelties of child labor. Capitalists, who sought only to save money for themselves, profited from child and female toil. This, "Virtus" claimed, challenged the family's well-being. Exactly how "Virtus" thought family life was endangered is telling. Not surprisingly, he believed that women and children were overworked. But he expressed even greater concern that children and mothers worked while husbands and fathers remained unemployed. His anxiety suggests a haunting fear of declining male control. Although he did not specify the mechanics of the situation, "Virtus" concluded that out of this situation of "the working-class family," crime, suicide, and prostitution resulted.[38]

Those women who kept their husbands from joining the Socialist party received a guilt-inducing reminder: throughout history conservative wives have hindered the growth of great ideas. The Socialist husband would become a "more content man for having heeded his conscience . . . with a mind and heart more disposed to tender affection because the company he keeps will open him to the life of the spirit and thought, and will teach him respect for women." The woman married to such a man should give faith and strength to her husband, then she would be "once again, his wife."[39]

On one occasion *La Fiaccola* confronted the problem raised by clergyman directly, asking bluntly: Does socialism dissolve the family? No, the blame lay elsewhere. When the home was "reduced to a stinking hovel," with parents and children

[37] "Lavoratori, lavoratrici, che cosa volete voi?" *La F*, April 13, 1912.

[38] "La legge sul lavoro dei fanciulli," *La F*, April 6, 1912; "Wanted . . . wanted . . . wanted," *La F*, July 8, 1911.

[39] E. De Amicis, "Alla moglie del lavoratore," *La F*, Nov. 27, 1909.

crowded into it, when the "frustrated" father left home to seek his amusement in a tavern, when hardship provoked husband and wife to arguments, "the family offers a very sad spectacle." Children were left alone, given little attention and no education, while impoverished parents left home searching for work or a piece of bread. These circumstances, *La Fiaccola* argued, cause "the dissolution of the best of family sentiments." Husband and wife, aggravated by their misery, began fighting with each other. Children followed their parents' poor example; many suffered maltreatment. Some became ashamed of home and family; ties of blood lost their meaning. "Look at two families," an editorial requested, "one with a decent living standard and another without. You will see real differences in their behavior. In the poor family, moral and physical maladies easily take root. When people have enough to eat, on the other hand, they have a better attitude toward life." Socialism urges workers to improve their condition, to achieve a better society, and to eliminate conditions destructive to the family. Poverty, Socialists believed, destroys the family; "socialism redeems it." [40]

The intensity of the dispute between the Socialist party and the Catholic church and the importance which a private social institution—the family—assumed in this political controversy is unusual. Both parties to the controversy claimed that they, and not the other, favored its preservation. Their positions amount to a clear recognition of the deeply rooted traditionalism of Italian immigrant family life. This particular conflict also explains why at least one segment of the immigrant working class found radicalism so difficult to embrace. The Italian immigrant's attitude toward his family was conservative, and understandably so, because much of his life focused intensely upon it. Socialism threatened to undermine the very core of his social existence, or so the priests warned him and his wife. In the face of this potential disaster, abstract political goals had little appeal.

Another family matter was of obvious public concern. Immigrants of all classes and political persuasions were deeply concerned about the negative effect which American life-styles

[40] Editorial, "Il socialismo dissolve la famiglia?" *La F*, May 21, 1910.

could have upon the female character. Although they approached the problem differently, the "woman question" troubled both *La Fiaccola* and *Il Corriere,* especially in the pre-World War I days of feminism. The former, of course, sought the working-class woman's attentions; *Il Corriere* courted a broader audience. But editorial ambivalence is apparent in the dual messages both journals gave to readers. On the one hand, *Il Corriere* introduced Italian women to American ways of thinking and living; on the other, it balked at total assimilation of these customs. Even *Il Corriere*'s editors ultimately preferred Italian to American attitudes. These men believed that the "true woman" understood that "sacrifice is her most becoming ornament." They portrayed American women as parasites and libertines; "insatiable" in their desire for clothing, leisure, and dining out, they passed most of their time at bazaars, candy stores, fashion shows, and theatres. American cutlure, *Il Corriere* continued, suffered from a "cult of woman." "The American woman," so "G.C." claimed, "is undoubtedly the chief exponent of that immense liberty which guides and influences American social life." The lady was not being complemented, for "G.C." sardonically offered her character to psychologists as "good material . . . to reflect upon." American women dominated their homes. They stole the reins of authority from their men; fathers, husbands, and brothers knelt submissively at their feet. To satisfy their trivial needs, they turned their men into money seekers, offering little in return.[41]

Another early editorial disapprovingly attributed female "aggressiveness" to American child-rearing practices, and urged that Italian ways be preserved. From childhood, the American girl occupied the center of attention. Most disturbing of all, the family considered her "even superior to her brothers."[42] Because she received an education, she entertained an "exaggerated idea of her own importance." And the editors chafed at other American customs which concerned women. Childless

[41] Editorial by "Licurgo," *IC*, Jan. 27, 1906; also by "Licurgo," Feb. 3, 1906, and Feb. 10, 1906; editorial on American women by "G.C.," "La donna in America," *IC*, July 20, 1912.

[42] "Licurgo," *IC*, Jan. 27, 1906.

marriages were incomprehensible to them; mothers who hired nurses to care for their young, even more so. Because the "feminist idea" included reduction of work, *Il Corriere* noted, many American women chose to live in boarding houses and so deprived their husbands of even the comforts of home.[43]

But it was the American woman's independence, especially when it involved competition with men over jobs, that disturbed the moderate male writers most. They considered the working woman and the independent woman one and the same. In Europe, "G.C." wrote, one frequently encountered ladies engaged in work "properly considered women's work." Here, however, one could be "overcome with repugnance" at the sight of women holding men's job in post offices, financial establishments, and restaurants. American women emphasized their independence from their husbands to the point of being "ostentatious about the most trivial acts." They left home alone and remained out until all hours. "You have the outward appearance of domestic peace when beneath the surface inner trouble brewed." "G.C." believed that such "excessive liberalism" contradicted the American Puritan ethic, and that the nation's cultural fabric stood imperiled. Threatened by female emancipation and a possible change in status of the women in his ethnic group, he sought to establish a necessary connection between emancipation on the one hand, and prostitution, divorce, and declining birth rate on the other.[44]

Most immigrant journalists, then, had clear notions of the ideal woman. In this case it is likely that they articulated the views of ordinary immigrants. The strong Sicilian traditions about women, and especially the cult of motherhood, are entirely consistent with the respected (although idealized) position they assigned to them. Such notions were, of course, reinforced by the Victorian attitudes that many Americans still held. *Il Corriere*'s pages make it clear that elite Italians continued to endow their women with a madonna-like aura. As one editorialist put it: "Woman should not be thought of as a thing of luxury, for she was created as a comfort to aid man in life, and to moan for

[43] "Licurgo," *IC*, Feb. 3, 1906.

[44] "G.C.," "La donna in America."

his sorrows. When a woman rules her family, we can live secure and certain that under her noble and elevated domain we can live in harmony until death, and then die satisfied. The force of woman's virtue satisfied us." A child was not to be permitted so much as an angry glance at his mother. Nor should a husband abuse his rights over his wife but honor her above all creatures. Such a paragon is the woman of the family that one should "respect her, venerate her, adore her." [45]

On certain occasions even *La Fiaccola*'s Socialist writers, who might have been expected to hold more liberal views, emphasized the woman's traditional roles as mother and wife. Like many Socialist writers, they recognized woman's subordination as a problem. If formal doctrine pushed toward radical feminism, ordinary practitioners usually ducked the issue by subordinating the "woman question" to the class struggle.[46] Italian Socialists in Buffalo found themselves caught in the middle with something to gain from either position: Italian women certainly needed enough liberating to be politicized; yet any suggestions in this direction could be perceived as downright indecent and threatening by the women, their husbands, or both. The Socialist emphasis upon motherly and wifely roles indicates both an insensitivity to the "woman question" and a political concession to immigrant conservatism.

The writings of one radical, more sympathetic than most, illustrate this Socialist dilemma. He called the assumption that woman's place is in the home a "dangerous prejudice to all humanity and an idea we ought to combat. . . . Not all women become mothers nor are all absorbed by maternal duties for all of their lives." He offered his ideal—the activist woman laborer—as an example for all. "She is not a doll in a doll house but a complete worker who struggles and lives the life of this world." Women, he believed, owe a debt to society just as men do. To fulfill it, they must develop their minds. Nonetheless, even this radical ultimately paid his respects to tradition. A

[45] Editorial, A. Pappalardo, *IC*, Nov. 9, 1907.

[46] Juliet Mitchell, *Women's Estate* (New York, 1971), p. 76, refers specifically to mid–twentieth-century views, but they apply to the early twentieth century as well.

woman's primary role still consisted of educating her children; but in order to do so effectively she must become better acquainted with the world outside their home.[47] Even a writer who challenged tradition, then, took the circuitous route of offering its preservation as an ultimate goal. If the Socialists themselves rejected convention, immigrant conservatism required such tactics.

Socialists approached the "woman question" almost as ambivalently as *Il Corriere*'s more moderate editors did. Radicals viewed Italian women as the weaker sex, especially susceptible to archaic religious influences. Mothers, wives, and sisters could become "religious bigots under the influence of the clergy and priestly superstitions because they are forced to seek in the Church the comfort of which woman has more need than man." [48]

One of the first steps taken in a propaganda campaign addressed to women in 1910 was an invitation to Anita Delich-Albertini, a Socialist and feminist from Vermont, to attend a conference in Buffalo. Radicals considered this campaign an "absolute necessity," suggesting that the chasm between their views on women and the ordinary immigrant's views was a wide one. Albertini's articles on working-class women, their rights and obligations, appeared frequently in *La Fiaccola*, and Italian women had their own column in the paper by 1910.[49] Here the radicals, using as their lure news of various social activities and bazaars, presented the arguments for women's equality and political involvement.[50]

The Socialist party had sound political reasons for wishing to attract women. So long as they were required by custom to focus their attention upon the home, women remained politi-

[47] *IC*, March 5, 1904. This is a rare instance of a liberal viewpoint being presented in *IC*. Perhaps the writer demanded space to counter the usual conservative positions presented.

[48] Editorial by F. Cicotti," "Come dev'essere il buon socialists [*sic*] nella famiglia," *La F*, Oct. 29, 1910.

[49] "Alle sezioni socialiste," *La F*, June 4, 1910. An early example of the woman's column is in *La F*, Feb. 5, 1910.

[50] See, for example, "Il bazaar delle donne socialiste," *La F*, Dec. 2, 1911.

cally apathetic. Concrete proof of the urgent need to convert Italian women to the cause was demonstrated in 1910, when, according to *La Fiaccola*, local priests influenced wives to persuade their husbands to end a building workers' strike.[51] And shortly thereafter, the Socialist press responded: "Educate woman. If she is not the worker's enemy, then she is still a highly conservative force. Woman must be made to fight the worker's battle with men. If not, she is the militant worker's first and most intimate enemy. It is she who holds back the fight. She is invited to evening meetings, but does not want to leave the home." *La Fiaccola* further encouraged the men to transform women into companions, friends, and comrades; with female support, their force in the movement would increase a hundredfold.[52]

Socialists cast men in the role of redeemers of these "intimate enemies." The revolution in woman's status, they believed, must begin within the family itself. Men should not maltreat or dominate their wives, but love them "strongly, confidently, and respectfully." [53] Socialists counseled against treating a woman like "a trinket for pleasure or display." Instead, men should sympathize with them as exploited persons. Superstitious, prejudiced attitudes must be replaced with "love, fraternity and peace." Then women would not feel inferior. It was man's obligation to free woman from moral and material slavery, "not because he alone was creative enough" to do so, but because he was "solely responsible for female silliness and backwardness." [54]

Occasionally Socialists addressed women as though they were fully capable of liberating themselves. The radicals' woman's column assumed that its readers were capable of independent thinking when it asked them to evaluate for themselves both

[51] "Lo sciopero dei manovali," *La F*, June 18, 1910. Italian female conservatism seems to have begun eroding elsewhere around 1910, about the time that Buffalo Italian Socialists began their women's campaign. See Fenton, "Immigrants and Unions," p. 46.

[52] Anna Kuliscioff, "Educate la donna!" *La F*, July 30, 1910.

[53] Cicotti, "Come dev'essere il buon socialista."

[54] "Maria," "La donna," *La F*, April 9, 1910.

the capitalist exploitation of women and the Italian conception of a woman's place. One writer asked Little Italy's women: "Do you wish to be a slave forever?" He continued: "Today surely woman is a slave. She is a slave in the factory. The peasant woman is everybody's slave. The domestic servant is a slave to her employer. The wife is a slave to her husband even if he is not a rogue. The sister is a slave to her brother who can humiliate and fight her. The aged mother is a slave to her male children who make her their servant." [55]

Still another article reprinted from a Venetian Socialist women's publication emphasized inequalities within the family as well as outside it: "Men are no one's servants. We are slaves of our own husbands, of our own sons. . . . Why? Because of the social inequities, shrewdness and violence of rulers that enslave us. Woman was not always a slave. She should not continue to be." [56]

Radicals proposed a progressive female psychology: women who considered themselves inferior to men had simply been misinformed. *La Fiaccola* attacked those who believed that women had smaller brains than men (a common argument against recognition of female capabilities), that they were giddy and jabbered on "like chickens," and that they therefore should have no rights. Priests who cried out with "the air of a Torquemada" against women interfering in politics were pronounced reactionaries. "Virtus" compared them to corrupt bosses and capitalists who, knowing that they stood to lose from such involvement, opposed the entry of women into political battles over social injustice.[57]

Socialist doctrine, *La Fiaccola* explained, required women to be treated on a par with men and to have the same rights—including the vote, legal protection, participation in lawmaking, and influence in the administration of public funds. In a society based upon the rights and work of all, no one would be a slave or a dependent. But a Socialist woman also had obligations

[55] "Dovrà essere sempre schiava?" *La F*, June 11, 1910.

[56] "La causa della nostra schiavitù: alle donne," *La F*, Sept. 16, 1911.

[57] "Virtus," "La donna è politica," *La F*, June 22, 1912.

which drew her from her home and, incidentally, further away from Italian tradition, "to fight at the side of her husband and father because so long as they are slaves, she is also, so long as they remain oppressed, she will also." [58]

The radical position on women was far from typical, but the woman's movement did have some impact upon Little Italy's elite. Newly appreciative of female abilities, *Il Corriere*'s journalists made more specific and more liberal demands for emancipation. *La Fiaccola*'s institution of a separate woman's column is not surprising; the appearance of a similar section in *Il Corriere* had different significance. Occasionally, this column set out to instill conventional moral and sexual ideologies; immigrant women read of "The First Duties of Woman," "Daily Family Meals," "Woman and Grace," and "The Good Wife." [59] But the column also addressed its audience as intelligent human beings, capable of making decisions concerning their own and their family's welfare—a modest advance, yet a genuine one. The woman's column also provided an occasional outlet for liberal demands. *Il Corriere*, for example, specifically connected women's accomplishments outside the home to suffrage. Initially, female political involvement was a highly controversial issue, but by 1918 *Il Corriere* was urging women to seek political power. The paper did not endorse wholesale radicalism; it could not approve "the ridiculous image of the suffragate." [60] And far from advocating female activism, *Il Corriere* urged its readers only to encourage the men in their families to approve the Nineteenth Amendment. While avoiding a hasty departure from tradition, *Il Corriere* did urge women to discard their prejudices toward political involvement. The moderate immigrant press approved some feminist demands, but we should not exaggerate the importance of its position. This support was tempered by concessions to tradition and by the apparent unwillingness of many ordinary women to endorse them, proving, by the way, that south Italian women as well as their husbands

[58] "Virtus," La donna è politica."

[59] *IC*, June 25, 1925; *IC* July 16, 1925; *IC*, Feb. 21, 1918; *IC*, July 13, 1912.

[60] *IC*, May 9, 1918.

continued to find security in established values. If conservatism subsided at all, it was a slow and painful business, even among Little Italy's educated elite.

One example offers an illustration. A woman's column article published in 1921 exhorted females to learn English so that they could participate in the world outside the home. Work, civic responsibilities, and social life—activities which belonged strictly to the husband in Italy—awaited those who understood the language. But this new demand was made rather late—in the 1920's—and a conservative reminder accompanied it. *Il Corriere* assured timid traditionalists that knowledge of the language would help women perform their maternal and wifely duties such as speaking to teachers and shopping at American stores. The journal's final rationale was a pragmatic one: English was necessary for women in case of an accident or some danger.[61]

By the 1920's *Il Corriere*'s woman's column assumed it quite proper for young Italian women to be educated. American laws requiring male and female school attendance had enforced this departure from Old World practice, so that this particular change in attitude was not entirely a product of choice. The woman's column also approved the employment of "sensible" females in appropriate occupations—office work, sales positions, or telephone company jobs. But again, conservative reminders anxiously accompanied the new departures. A young lady, the journal warned, should not "abandon her good sense," for "her first duty is to her family and to her home, and the most profound pleasures are those deriving from the modest obligation of housewife." *Il Corriere* argued that housekeeping and all of its "refinements" were, as they had been in Italy, a woman's appropriate domain. The paper still encouraged Italian women not to imitate Americans who shirked such tasks. One of the worst violations of Italian sensibilities was the American habit of reducing the preparations for a meal to "opening a series of tin cans." Weary of such culinary crassness, American husbands

[61] "La lingua inglese," *IC*, June 18, 1921.

frequently took their families out to dine on "good food prepared by an Italian or French chef." [62]

Other conventional attitudes found confirmation in the immigrant press. Certain "female virtues" such as grace and gentility remained highly regarded. In 1918 at the suffrage movement's height, *Il Corriere*'s woman's column complained that "today's women act like amazons . . . [but] female grace is virtue composed of mighty strength and the perfume of a flower." [63] Although they could now be friends to their husbands, women still remained subservient to them. Woman's "noble humility," one editorial claimed, permitted her "to ask pardon knowing that her husband was at fault. The good wife is a fountain of affection and unlimited patience even when her husband is harsh, unjust, or ungenteel." The higher standard of living achieved by at least some Italian immigrants added to a wife's obligations. She should create "attractive meals" in "simple but peaceful settings," she should see that even for daily meals "the rules of etiquette not be broken," and she should "keep a clean and comfortable home without neglecting her person." To sustain her husband's interest, she should cultivate her good looks. The wife who wanted to look attractive could do so despite her household duties. The best wife was neither capricious nor jealous. One writer's attitudes show that emotional preferences need no logic. "The best woman," he said, "is one who, without being a slave, does all her husband wishes." [64]

By the 1920's the feminine image had undergone an improvement in the immigrant press. Paradoxically, anxiety concerning her changing status abated at the same time. *Il Corriere*'s concern over women's changing position, aroused chiefly by the threat of their possible financial independence, was inversely related to the reality of the threat. In earlier days, when Italian women were unlikely to be employed and when they rarely took part in any activities outside the home and family, the greatest

[62] "Il primo dovere della donna," *IC*, June 25, 1925; "La donna americana," *IC*, Dec. 25, 1924.

[63] "La donna e la grazia," *IC*, Feb. 21, 1918.

[64] "Pranzi giornalieri in famiglia," *IC*, July 16, 1925; "La buona moglie," *IC*, July 13, 1912.

number of articles appeared on woman's changing status. Later on, when more women actually had some work and community experience, the journal's articles indicated considerable acceptance of the "new woman," and less fear that she was challenging Italian masculinity. This suggests more than passive resignation on the part of the Italian men to changes beyond their control. We have seen that male unemployment seriously affected many families early in the twentieth century. By the twenties, the situation had considerably improved. Female employment alone, therefore, did not arouse male anxiety. Rather, male unemployment and consequent inability to perform the masculine breadwinning function created fears that Italian women, like their American counterparts, might became an equal or dominating family force. During the more prosperous 1920's, a working wife or daughter did not present so great a threat because men found themselves in more secure positions.

In the 1920's girdle and nylon stocking advertisements and admonitions to lose weight appeared in *Il Corriere*, signaling an increase in female readership. It is best, the woman's column advised, to be neither too fat nor too thin. But thin women, women who looked "elegant, spiritual, sensitive, delicate and vibrant," were the kind men prefer.[65] Advocates of dieting and constricting undergarments frequently placed a higher priority on fashions designed to please men, or on selling a product, than on women's comfort. But encouragment to lose weight for medical reasons and advice on exercise, posture, and ventilation operated to improve women's health—a consideration for which peasant culture had provided inadequately. Women readers were encouraged to discard harmful or useless health practices and superstitions. They received counsel on how to live in their new urban homes. "The woman who is on her feet all day, or the woman factory worker needs physical exercise and fresh air. If she works in the city, she should use city playgrounds and beaches and try to get country fresh air." To be a healthy and beautiful woman, the paper advised, "eat well, exercise, bathe, wash your hair often, watch your diet and avoid a lot of sweets.

[65] See, for example, "Fra i due estremi," *IC*, Aug. 17, 1912.

Care for your posture and your health, and observe precautions against tuberculosis."[66] Even if the woman's column sought only to improve beauty, health, and cooking, its implicit assumptions were more important. The articles which discussed such issues addressed women as potential decision makers. And while it is true that the decisions to be made usually concerned woman's traditional estate, important issues were at stake—child-rearing, morality, and a woman's right to control her own body.

In the twenties, for example, *Il Corriere* began to instruct Italian women on procedures for safe, sanitary pregnancy and childbirth. The journal encouraged expectant mothers to attend professionally staffed maternity clinics.[67] Believing in many taboos and superstitions regarding pregnancy, Italian women frequently refused. To protect their unborn children from the *mal'occhio* (evil eye),[68] they chose to keep their condition secret. A public clinic simply would not do. Columbus Hospital, an important medical agency serving Italians, did not open its maternity section until 1936.[69] The Italian women of Buffalo preferred midwives, most of them Italian-educated, to male doctors. Adding its influence to welfare agency efforts, *Il Corriere* campaigned for stringent controls on their practices.[70] Although the weekly advertisements of one Professor Collins claimed a cure for "any malady" or kidney ailment, Italian newspapers did not have any drug advertisements obscurely promising successful self-induced abortions. Perhaps local midwives were consulted for this purpose. Women could have used folk remedies to deal with unwanted children, but this conjecture is not substantiated by historical evidence.

The 1920's health campaign also focused on infants and young children, encouraging mothers to disregard another

[66] "Che fare del tempo," *IC*, July 9, 1921; see also "La donna sana e la donna bella," *IC*, May 19, 1927.

[67] "Per salvaguardare la madre," *IC,* April 30, 1921 and "Leggi necessarie alla salute dei bambini," *IC,* May 7, 1921.

[68] Williams, *South Italian Folkways*, p. 102.

[69] Gorman, "Life and Work of Dr. Charles R. Borzilleri."

[70] "Leggi necessarie alla salute dei bambini"; see also advertisements in *IC* for midwives' services specifying their education, for example, July 2, 1904.

group of south Italian superstitions. Peasants believed, for example, that weighing a child stunted its growth, while wet diapers facilitated it.[71] Such beliefs obviously frustrated doctors' efforts to improve children's health. *Il Corriere* assured Italian mothers that it would be perfectly proper for them to leave their homes to attend infant feeding and child care clinics. Diet preoccupied the woman's column contributors, who instructed mothers to feed milk, oatmeal, and farina to infants and to send children to school with a sandwich, fruit, and milk in their lunch boxes.[72]

Such are the ideas which immigrant journalists expressed about family affairs. To what extent did their ideas reflect actual behavior? The kinds of responsibility and independence which women assumed outside the home and family are useful indicators of change. We have already seen that women's work did not always bring women's independence. What about other activities performed by women outside the home? The establishment of voluntary associations by and for women, a practice unknown in the Mezzogiorno except among the very rich, suggests that some Italian women were beginning to assume greater independence. Five types of voluntary associations for women were founded about the time of World War I—religious, nationalistic, charitable, political, and labor. The religious organizations hardly embodied a break with tradition: the stated purpose of Young Ladies of Saint Anthony's Parish, established in 1913, was "to cultivate virtue of the mind and heart, moral and religious progress of members and material aid to the parish."[73] Other religious clubs for women devoted themselves to quite proper female functions.[74] So did women's patriotic groups. The Veronica Gambra Lodge, female counterpart of the Sons of Italy established in 1917, functioned chiefly as a mutual aid society designed to help and maintain the family. Moreover, women's involvement in the organization remained limited. In 1922, for

[71] Williams, p. 104.
[72] *IC,* Aug. 6, 1921; "Per la 'lunch box,' " *IC,* Oct. 6, 1927.
[73] "Il primo ballo," *IC*, Nov. 8, 1913.
[74] "La riuscitissima," *IC*, May 30, 1918, and *IC*, Dec. 21, 1918.

example, there was one lodge for women and six for men in the city.[75] Scanty female labor union membership is another indication of conservatism among the women. Although labor organizations commanded increasing enrollments, the Italian press never acknowledged female participation.[76]

The first indication that Italian women were making some effort to involve themselves outside the home appeared in 1918, when a group of women formed the Italian Woman's Organization of the Twenty-seventh Ward. *Il Corriere* approved, stating that since women had the vote they should take a political role in the community. Two officers of the club, the president, Mrs. Oddo, and her daughter, belonged to the immediate family of one of Little Italy's most important politicians.[77] These women probably gained entry into politics with their husbands' encouragement. The organization's life seems to have been short, for it never achieved prominent mention in the press again. Perhaps politically inspired office-seeking husbands hoped to use it to gain female votes. If so, even these women were acting in their familial role rather than as individuals. Nevertheless, such political participation by respected Italian women suggested the propriety of public roles for women.

The most successful organizations founded by Italian women were not political clubs but charity societies. These tended to be church-related; like the religious and voluntary organizations, they devoted themselves to proper womanly goals. The Aid Society of Saint Anthony's Church assisted the city's poor.[78] The Italian Ladies Relief Association, an offshoot of Buffalo's Charity Organization Society, gradually established its own autonomy and competence. It originally aimed to aid needy Italian-Americans, "especially in bad seasons," and many in the community benefited from it. Another of its activities concerned the establishment in 1924 of a child-care nursery for working

[75] *IC*, July 26, 1917; Laris Meloy, "Italians Much Given to Clubs," *Courier*, Jan. 15, 1922.

[76] See, for example, "Lo sciopero," *IC*, Sept. 7, 1912.

[77] "L'organizzazione femminile," *IC*, March 21, 1918.

[78] "Per i poveri," *IC*, Dec. 25, 1915.

parents. Supporting a city-wide movement, its founder hoped to aid one-parent families.[79]

The careers of the officers and members of the Ladies Relief Association indicate their middle-class status.[80] Adelina Milani was a bookkeeper. Mrs. Michael Strozzi was a member of one of Buffalo's oldest Italian families and the wife of a pharmacist and drug-store owner. Her daughter Madeline, also active in the group, taught school. The Oddos, related to the political leader, have already been mentioned. Louise Latona's husband was a chef, she herself a schoolteacher. Two other Association members were social workers connected to professional organizations devoted to work among the foreign-born. Further indication of the middle-class character of this and other women's organizations is that they frequently held their functions in the Italian Business Club, Little Italy's most socially restricted organization. Finally, the small size of the Ladies Relief Association, only fifty members, underlines its exclusiveness.[81]

Far from presenting a feminist or radical front, these organizations were usually church-affiliated and concerned themselves with middle-class, "lady bountiful" reforms—charity, education, health, and sanitation.[82] Although none directly threatened family equilibrium, the mere fact that such organizations existed signaled a departure from the home-orientation of Italian women. The prestigious character of their membership implies community approval of participation by respectable women in activities outside the family. The Relief Association's success in particular improved the image of women, if not their status. The aims and activities of many of these organizations show that Italian women took their cues from respectable Buffalo groups such as the Charity Organization Society and at-

[79] "Charitas," *IC*, May 1, 1909, and *IC*, Jan. 31, 1913. See also "La Italian Ladies Relief Association," *IC*, Feb. 25, 1922; *IC*, March 20, 1924.

[80] *The Buffalo Business Directory, 1911, 1915* (Buffalo, 1911, 1915) was used to identify the individuals concerned and provided information on the occupations of these women and their husbands. See "Per i poveri," *IC*, Dec. 25, 1915; officers of the Italian Ladies Relief Association are listed in *IC*, June 22, 1912.

[81] Augello, "Italian Immigrants in Buffalo," pp. 80, 82; and Beth Stewart, "Soul of Italian Race," *Courier*, Jan. 21, 1923.

[82] "L'organizzazione femminile," *IC*, March 21, 1918.

tempted to imitate prominent American women. And the character of these groups indicates that the liberation of Italian immigrant women was led, as it has been among more established Americans, by the better educated, more privileged among them—the wives and daughters of Little Italy's intellectuals, politicians, and successful businessmen.

Even if they read the Italian press, most immigrants did not seem impressed with the arguments for female emancipation. Few Italian girls, for example, attended institutions of higher learning. In 1910, 1911, 1912, and 1915 for example, five men graduated from business and vocational school, but only one woman graduated from normal school. Twenty-six men graduated from college, six from medical school, six from law school, and one each from dentistry, pharmacy, and engineering schools. Not one woman received a college or professional degree during these years. The low proportion of women who received an education may be attributed to the relative youth of Buffalo's Italian community. Yet, by the early twenties, when the Italian-American community numbered more than thirty-five thousand, it boasted only twenty-nine professional and business women: three medical doctors, four pharmacists, three social workers, seventeen teachers, and two businesswomen.[83] The continued reluctance to educate women explains this small proportion.

Most immigrants saw little utility in educating soon-to-be-married daughters. Amalia Lanza's father, a well-educated Sicilian, nevertheless had a conventional attitude toward her college education. "She's more interested in boys," he said. "It's not worth the money if she is going to turn around and get mar-

[83] Biographies: Frederic Strozzi, *IC*, May 10, 1910; Angelo Scalzo, *IC*, June 4, 1910; "Il progresso degli Italiani," June 25, 1910; biographies of Phillip Catalano, *IC*, June 24, 1910; Victor Valanti, *IC*, June 24, 1911; "Fine dell'anno," *IC*, June 24, 1911; "I nuovi professionisti," *IC*, June 31, 1911; Sebastiano Lunghino, *IC*, June 8, 1912; Joseph Lojacono, *IC*, June 8, 1912; Louis La Duce, *IC*, June 15, 1912; "Fine dell'anno," June 22, 1912; "La fine delle scuole," *IC*, June 29, 1912. See also, *IC*, June 5, 1915; June 12, 1915; June 19, 1915; and June 25, 1915, for lists of graduates. On the women see Stewart, "Soul of Italian Race." In the early 1920's the Italian community numbered 35,000. If we assume that roughly half of these were women, the number of Italian women achieving professional success was certainly low.

ried." The children sometimes paid a price for rigid parental attitudes. Caught in the clash of different cultural expectations, one plucky young girl wrote her school principal: "Please send a letter to my pa telling him that he'll be arrested if he doesn't let me come to school." [84] Even as late as the 1920's, Italian women rarely attended college. The majority of parents preferred to keep their adolescent daughters at home. Immigrant parents were not indifferent to education; it was simply that fulfilling family needs and maintaining customary sex roles seemed more important to them.[85]

Apparently most Italian women conformed to *Il Corriere*'s high moral expectations. The newspaper described them in dulcet tones: they "have one thousand talents superior to the other women around them," and are seen as paradigms of virtue, thrift, and chastity. Excellent mothers, they lived for their children and loved them with "great strength." We have seen that there is little evidence of infidelity,[86] another confirmation of female constancy. American observers apparently agreed with *Il Corriere*'s high evaluation. As one noted, if a woman's tasks were to stay home, keep a clean abode, and pass her time in housework's joys and tribulations, Italian women managed to do them well, despite poverty and overcrowding. And, in Buffalo's Little Italy, one would never come upon the "shocking sight" of a drunken woman, "one of the most serious disrupters of family peace." Except for a few, forced by abject poverty to wander about selling wood and rummaging for garbage, women remained cloistered at home involved in household tasks, never straying far away, "never . . . seen on the streets at night." [87]

The impulse for domestic entrenchment did not emanate entirely from the women themselves. We have seen that husbandly protectiveness and family obligations led Italian women to work in canneries and to do homework, where they were not

[84] Quoted in Goodale, "Children of Sunny Italy."

[85] See Fred Strodtbeck, "Family Interaction, Values and Achievement" in David McClelland, *et al.*, eds. *Talent and Society* (Princeton, 1958), pp. 151, 155, on attitudes to children.

[86] See also, editorial, *IC*, Dec. 23, 1905.

[87] "Italian Colony in Buffalo," *Courier*, May 8, 1898; see also *IC*, Dec. 23, 1905.

separated from their families. Working-class Italian women entered the world of community affairs with even more faltering stride. They involved themselves in politics and labor disputes only when they felt that their traditional roles as wives and mothers were being infringed upon. Two incidents associated with the 1910 Italian building workers' strike illustrate this conservatism.

After three weeks of strike activity, the building contractors began to use police-protected Polish scabs. Two Italian men who had allegedly abused scabs were arrested. An undetermined number of Italian women, joining their husbands, gallantly marched to the strike scene. The news media failed to specify the women's motives for marching to the site with their husbands, but the cause for the arrest of one of their number is clear. The Italians chased about twelve guarded scabs from the area. One officer fired a gun, and although no one was injured, the women accompanying their husbands became agitated. The gunshot could have wounded their children who played in a nearby park; apparently, this enraged one woman who, after being grasped by a policeman, boxed his ears.[88]

A woman's delegation decided to visit the mayor and the police station in protest. They marched, with babes in arms, to City Hall to request the mayor's intervention. The unresponsive city executive asked the police to remove them. The same women's delegation, about two hundred strong, then headed for the police station to present themselves to the chief of police, whereupon two or three of them were arrested for disorderly conduct. One of those arrested had torn a picket off of a fence and pummeled a policeman on the head with it; another scratched an officer's face.[89]

At one point during the strike negotiations, the women, for some unknown reason, ended up cursing the pastor of Saint Anthony's Church, who had been called in to aid in settlement. But *La Fiaccola* claimed that they really constituted a reaction-

[88] "I lavoranti in sommossa," *IC*, June 11, 1910; "L'incidente di giovedì," *La F*, June 11, 1910.

[89] "L'incidente di giovedì," *La F*, June 11, 1910; and "Laborers," *Express*, June 10, 1910.

ary force in the strike, largely responsible for the partial defeat of the workers, who obtained a pay increase but no closed shop. The Socialist paper insisted that clergymen had ultimately seduced the women into convincing their husbands to return to work, when holding out longer could have meant total victory.[90]

These incidents and acts of violence can be interpreted as signs of female politicization, but the women's goal was bread, not power. They mobilized because of their interest in immediate practical issues—their husbands' ability to provide for their children. After three weeks of striking, they went along with their husbands to protest the use of scabs. But under priestly advice, they encouraged their husbands to return to work after the contractors granted a pay increase. The political goal of the strike, a closed shop, did not concern them; their children did. Similarly, their two-hundred-strong protest against the police was motivated by the jeopardy in which their children had been placed by armed officers. They presented themselves to the police chief, after all, as mothers accompanied by young children, not as militant union women. Despite Socialist efforts to appeal to them on the basis of their family sentiments, the evidence does not suggest that some new political consciousness moved these women any more than it had moved rioting cannery women who were protesting management's efforts to keep their underage children out of the work sheds. Like many working people of eighteenth- and nineteenth-century Europe, they took to the streets attempting to adjust some wrong done to them. The fact that women did involve themselves in such activities should not surprise us, for they were the family members most closely involved with putting food on the table and caring for the young. The style of political expression they chose was entirely consistent with their determination to fulfill conventional expectations, and it did not necessarily produce a conflict of roles or confusion. If their behavior was not political in the modern sense, we cannot designate it apolitical either; these former peasant women, like many preindustrial people, believed they

[90] "La fine dello sciopero," *IC*, June 18, 1910; "Lo sciopero dei manovali," *La F*, June 18, 1910.

were acting to protect prerogatives that rightly belonged to them and their families.[91]

Where else can we look for evidence of changes in social behavior? The relationships between the first and second generations can tell us a good deal about the adjustments and tensions faced by immigrant newcomers. Despite external pressures, the parent-child relationship changed little; at least the older generation had a clear idea of what their role should be. According to one observer, Italian fathers had the "greatest love" for their children and sought life's advantages for them.[92] But the Italian notion of doing all that is possible for one's children must be distinguished from those of other ethnic groups.[93] The Jewish idea, "Alles für die Kinder," typically meant that a child's education and personal achievements received priority, even if this required young ones to study or work away from home. We have seen that Italians in Buffalo often placed a higher value upon the purchase of a home than upon the education of their children. Italian peasants also tended to view education as a possible threat to the family. An Italian proverb put it well: "Never make your children better than you are."

When Italians encouraged occupational mobility for the second generation, they approved accomplishments that were consistent with the family's needs and interests. If children were to be educated, the family concentrated its resources on the boys. The privileged son who received an education generally entered a practical occupation which he could pursue locally—medicine, law, business, or pharmacy were favorites. Other Italians in Buffalo did their utmost to leave some business interest for their children to inherit or share. As one contemporary noted, "the father desires above all things to have a business in which the sons may become partners."[94] In these ways the

[91] See E. P. Thompson, "The Moral Economy of the English Crowd in the Eighteenth Century," *Past and Present*, No. 50 (1971), pp. 76–136.

[92] Stewart, "Rapid Fire Rises of Buffalo Italians."

[93] Strodtbeck, p. 151; Nathan Glazer and Daniel P. Moynihan, *Beyond the Melting Pot: The Negroes, Puerto Ricans, Jews, Italians, and Irish of New York City* (Cambridge, Mass., 1963), pp. 197–198 draw interesting contrasts between Italians and Jews.

[94] Stewart, "Rapid Fire Rises of Buffalo Italians."

family could tie its children to the local community, and at the same time benefit from their prestige and position.

The biographies of professional school and college graduates from 1904 to 1929 reveal that strong family feelings tied the second generation to the first. Few Italians graduated from colleges and professional schools during these years; almost everyone enrolled attended local institutions. And those who studied at out-of-town colleges usually absented themselves only temporarily. Victor Valanti earned his degree at the University of Pennsylvania but returned to Buffalo as his "proud family" wished. Lawyer Philip Catalano attended Cornell, but also returned home to practice. Charles Leone enrolled in a Baltimore medical school for a time, but soon transferred to the University of Buffalo. Although she won two scholarships to out-of-town schools, Amalia Lanza's father would not permit her to accept them. Instead, she and her mother saved enough to get her through a local college. Medical internships in other cities, over which students had less control, constituted the chief reason for leaving the city, but even these individuals usually established Buffalo practices.[95]

Giuseppi La Placa finally made a success of himself by receiving a higher degree; but he was forced to drop out of school at least once so that he might help his family. His case was typical. Boys commonly disrupted their schooling to work so that a mother or sister could remain at home. If a son completed his education, his parents expected to benefit when they reached old age.[96] The family had sacrificed for the child; the child must sacrifice for the family. For the second generation, Italian-American achievement was less an individual affair than a family venture. If the needs of the child and the needs of the family conflicted, the latter usually won out.

Old World notions favoring male children continued to influence the decisions that had to be made about education and

[95] *IC*, June 24, 1911; Feb. 8, 1913; June 7, 1913; see also Horace Lo Grasso's biography *IC*, July 23, 1924 and Catherine Carnavale's, *IC*, June 20, 1918. Both returned to Buffalo for their medical practices. Amalia Lanza's story applies to a later period.

[96] *IC*, June 5, 1915; Welcome Hall, *Annual Report, 1923*, p. 12; A. Pappalardo, "La moralità paragonata con l'utilità."

child-rearing. Adolescent boys enjoyed considerably more freedom than their sisters, who had heavy household responsibilities. One reporter described thirteen-year-old Antonia, "executive officer" of her family, who could "cook a meal for her father, scold Pietro, her smaller brother, to order almost as volubly as mother can. . . . Her back is bent with carrying little Giuseppe, the next to the youngest in the family, who is not yet able to run around himself." [97] Others described young girls as "little mothers." One, not yet twelve, "trudges patiently up and down carrying a wee *bambino* in one arm and supporting a line of three with the other. All day long the little mother's attention does not relax, and if the *madre* is at her work and the money for the day nursery cannot be saved out of the day's earnings, Margarita or Rosa abandons fun and keeps watch over the little ones." [98]

The child, especially the young girl, had not been liberated from tradition. At the urging of health reformers, some parents permitted their children the luxury of athletics and outdoor play, but working-class parents put their young to work at an early age and saw no practical need for such childish diversions.[99] Most Italians simply had not incorporated American concepts of adolescence. A schoolteacher writing in 1923 supported this suggestion—the contrast she drew between Italian and American childrearing practices is striking: "They [Italian children] come from large families where a spoiled child is not only unheard of but impossible. . . . Unlike many of our little Americans, they are not put on exhibition at home for company. Their word is not law, nor are their clever sayings noted. Self-consciousness, self-satisfaction, and the desire to show off are far removed from their natures." [100]

Some softening of customary attitudes did occur. The growing concern for children's health which accompanied the increased awareness of women's health produced similar liberalizing results. The concern for women and children remained

[97] "Buffalo's Little Italy," *Express*, May 4, 1902.

[98] "Picturesque City Corner," *Express*, Aug. 21, 1908.

[99] *IC*, June 22, 1901; "1,200 fanciulli," *IC*, July 29, 1911; "Che fare del tempo," *IC*, July 9, 1921.

[100] Quoted in Stewart, "Soul of Italian Race."

paternalistic, but a shift in Old World attitudes occurred because some immigrants began to recognize them as people with special needs. Some immigrants began to view childhood in a way that peasants never understood it—as a distinct period of life. For certain Italians, the movement toward the American-style, child-centered family had begun. According to the Italian press, by the 1920's more liberal attitudes toward children were emerging. *Il Corriere,* for example, blamed juvenile misbehavior upon parents, not upon children. While the paper prescribed a return to stricter, more reliable methods, some families moved to even greater permissiveness. Editorial reactions confirm this. One writer chided the older generation for its failure to provide either proper example or sound advice. To parents who replied that children must have more freedom, he countered that such "false freedom" ended in the courtroom, not in happiness.[101] Another commentator speculated that Italian families suffered misfortune because they gave children too much freedom. He claimed the young drew families into their childhood quarrels. If offspring lured parents to their defense, they demanded and received more recognition than peasant children did. The second generation did not always acknowledge its privileges gracefully. When asked by their elders to do an errand, some Italian children would reply, "Go to hell!" Shocked by this juvenile arrogance, *Il Corriere* advised parents to instill honor and admiration among their young.[102]

Considerable anxiety accompanied these changes in the parent-child relationship, just as it had attended the changes in the marital bond. A youthful disregard for ethnic origins, for example, caused parents some dismay. When *Il Corriere*'s editor interviewed Italian children, they insisted upon speaking English, stating, "I am an American." The editor's reproof was that the second generation, "like certain students, professionals, and those who marry non-Italians, has no warm feeling for Italy and is ashamed of its origins." The exposure of young Italians to one of America's most popular cultural media, the movies, also

[101] A. Pappalardo, "Dovere è esempio?" *IC*, Nov. 30, 1907.
[102] Editorial, *IC*, June 20, 1903.

caused concern; some observers believed that they fostered delinquency and family disputes.[103]

A few children entertained themselves with delinquent activities. Chief of Police Regan warned Italian parents of an unruly gang which used the cross bones, skull, and dagger as its symbol. And an *Il Corriere* editorial disapproved of the fact that, especially during summer vacations, young Italian children eight years and over hung about "like vagabonds" on the streets and corners of Little Italy.[104] Typically, immigrant families could not adequately orient their children to new social situations and more individualized values. Hence, the confused young turned from the family to various peer groups and gangs which either aided their absorption into the new society or expressed their rebellion against it.[105] Both tendencies operated in Little Italy, first in the Italian children who succinctly expressed their desire for conformity by reminding their interviewer "I am an American," and second in the skull and cross bones group, which assumed a negative character. The extent of juvenile delinquency in Little Italy at this time is difficult to determine. Published juvenile court records are not particularly informative. *Il Corriere* and an Italian social worker claimed that Italian children usually behaved themselves; on the basis of this evidence, it would appear that rebellious youth presented only minimal problems. The reasons for this bring us back once again to effective kin and neighborhood controls.[106]

If strict child-rearing attitudes began to loosen, reverence for the community's aged remained unquestioned. As late as the 1920's, old age was "honored above all things." [107] The care and attention lavished upon the elderly bordered upon veneration,

[103] "La negazione del patriottismo," *IC*, Feb. 18, 1911; "La perniciosa influenza del cinematografo," *IC*, Sept. 14, 1912.

[104] *IC*, Aug. 3, 1907; June 20, 1903.

[105] Shmuel Eisenstadt, *From Generation to Generation: Age Groups and Social Structure* (Glencoe, 1956), pp. 174–175, discusses this topic.

[106] Children's Court Records for Buffalo are at best fragmentary, and they are inconsistent in their classifications over the years. See City of Buffalo, *Annual Report of the Children's Court, 1912–1930;* see also *IC*, May 25, 1907; De'Rossi, "Le donne ed i fanciulli," p. 5 claims that Italian children rarely misbehaved, and if they did, neighbors and relatives took care of the delinquents.

[107] Stewart, "Soul of Italian Race."

especially if those in question were grandparents. The Italians considered longevity a blessing, particularly if the venerable relative presented no burden.[108] Grandmothers who cared for children and helped with household tasks were highly valued family members.

The evidence cited earlier on family size and birth rates suggested that traditional attitudes favoring large families gradually softened. But by the 1930's first- and second-generation Italians still had the highest birth rate of any ethnic group in the city. Comparatively low illegitimacy rates provided another indication of persisting Old World values.

Traditional marriage rituals remained deeply embedded in the immigrant culture. The bride and her female relatives provided her trousseau. The groom provided only her wedding finery, consisting of a simple veil, orange blossoms, and a dress. The Italian wedding represented an important occasion for both families. Celebrated with a High Mass and an elaborate banquet extending late into the evening, it included plenty of food and Italian and American dancing. Wealthier Italians adopted the American custom of the honeymoon, but most, even as late as the 1920's, did not believe in its propriety. Instead, the young couple remained at home for a week after the wedding to receive guests.[109]

Because of their strong provincial loyalties, Italian parents discouraged their children from marrying into families from different regions or villages. In one case, a woman's Sicilian-born parents approved their daughter's marriage to a non-Sicilian, but on the night before the wedding her brother exercised his prerogative as his sister's protector, wounding the groom-to-be. Apparently, even if his parents approved of the marriage, he could not bring himself to do so. Regionalism and *onore di famiglia* both played a part in determining his behavior. These traditions maintained enough vitality to cause *Il Corriere* to

[108] "Italian Colony in Buffalo," *Courier*, May 8, 1898.

[109] Stewart, "Soul of Italian Race," 1923, contains descriptions of wedding customs; a wedding announcement in *IC*, June 20, 1903 mentions a honeymoon, but this was unusual.

decry what it considered seriously divisive sentiments.[110]

If this impressionistic evidence seems insufficient, statistics tell us something more definite about continuing traditional marriage patterns. In the early days, few Italian-born persons married non-Italians: in 1905 slightly more than 6 percent of all families (150) contained husbands or wives not born in Italy.[111] One hundred and twelve of these were American-born persons who may have had Italian ancestry, so that even this small percentage may be an exaggeration of out-group marriage. As early as 1905, moreover, the male tendency toward exogamy was greater. Eighty percent of those marrying non-Italians were men; only 20 percent were women.

But Italians did eventually marry into other ethnic groups, chiefly people of Polish and Irish descent.[112] (This occurred infrequently until late in the community's history.) According to an analysis of marriage licenses in 1930, about 75 percent of all Italians married Italians. In 1930, 25 percent of Italian men, 15 percent of Polish women, 7 percent of the Italian women, and 5 percent of the Polish men married outside their group. Italian women started out slowly; not until 1950 did they surpass the Polish women.[113] Obviously, Italian women approached exogamous unions much more hesitantly than their brothers did. *Il Corriere* observed this trend as early as 1915, noting that although several Italian men married American girls, very few Italian women married "prominent" American males.[114] The use of the word "prominent" when referring to the women suggests that those who did marry outsiders did not choose partners above their social class. The Italian male apparently

[110] *IC*, Jan. 26, 1907. Another *vendetta* incident is reported in "Un feroce fatto di sangue," *IC*, Jan. 29, 1910. A. Pappalardo, "una parola ai lettori," *IC*, Nov. 23, 1907, disapproved of such acts.

[111] All 1905 figures are from NYSMC.

[112] City of Buffalo, *People of Buffalo*, p. 30.

[113] In 1960, 27 percent of all Italians and 33 percent of all Poles still married within their own ethnic group. See B. R. Bugelski, "Assimilation through Intermarriage," *Social Forces*, 40 (1961–62), 148–153, based upon newspaper listings of marriage licenses. Last names were the sole criteria for determining ethnicity.

[114] Marriage announcement, July 10, 1915.

married outside his ethnic group more readily and perhaps could achieve a higher social station through such a union.

This phenomenon can be explained partly by the relatively higher percentage of men residing in Little Italy.[115] In every age group, moreover, Italian women were more likely to be married than men. Women usually married earlier than men, and the abnormal sex ratio reinforced the custom.

Demographic features ultimately made universal endogamous marriage unlikely. When ethnic intermarriage occurred, therefore, it did not necessarily result from eroding parental control. Italians relinquished their cultural identity slowly. In 1930, after all, roughly three-quarters of all Italians were still marrying Italians. Then, too, Italian males consistently exercised greater independence in this area than their sisters had. This independence, of course, also had its roots within Italian tradition.

In conclusion, the evidence suggesting adjustments in either norms or family behavior requires careful assessment. Most first-generation Italians accepted liberal ideas about child-rearing, education, marital relationships, and woman's place more hesitantly than middle-class and radical journalists did. This should not surprise us, for the ordinary Italian and the ordinary Italian journalist were two very different people. The chief signs of liberalization appeared among a small segment of first-generation Italians—specifically among middle-class men and women and Socialists. Even they approached family change with uncertainty. *Il Corriere*, for example, the voice of the Italian bourgeoisie, sometimes took conservative positions on family issues. Such statements may have indicated sincere concern; they could also have been politically motivated, a reflection of elite efforts to retain the cultural solidarity and uniqueness of a community upon whose integrity its authority and power depended.

Differences in class, in education and in living standards probably explain the variations in values and behavior between a privileged minority and the majority of laboring men and

[115] The ratio for Italians in 1910 was 144.4; for the entire city, it was 100.6; for the native born, 96.2; for the foreign born, 112.9. *Thirteenth Census of the United States, 1910, Population,* p. 871.

women. Certainly, working-class family behavior cannot be inferred from elite perceptions of or prescriptions for that behavior. Evidence concerning child labor, female work patterns, the marital relationship, and attitudes toward charity organizations indicated that working-class Italians retained many of their conservative traditions. On the whole, they maintained strict sex role definitions and an adult-centered family structure. Most of these families also resisted outside pressures toward independence and individualization of their members. The Italians from Buffalo were not unique in this; many working-class ethnic groups have shown similar family characteristics. It is possible that these similarities result from shared class experiences and comparable adaptations by a variety of peasant cultures to these experiences, which only a comparative study will show.

Conclusion

The Italian families who immigrated to Buffalo successfully adjusted their old-country ways to this industrial city. The low rates of divorce, illegitimacy and desertion, the styles of family work and migration, the patterns of self-help among kin and *compari,* and the persisting traditional attitudes toward marriage, women, and sex, all provide evidence for the cohesion of both nuclear and extended families. These families participated in an urban life style whose components included new industrial work patterns, female employment outside the home, high male unemployment, political involvement, and support from charity agencies. Italians also shared with thousands of other city dwellers the experience of immigration itself. They withstood difficulties that might easily have provoked family crises—first the actual immigration, often with temporary family separations, then a wife's decision to work, the husband's frequent unemployment and the death of many children; the Italians in Buffalo interpreted these new experiences and acted upon them in ways entirely consistent with their Old World culture. Their tradition provided the interface between Old World and New, lending coherence to the crisis of adjustment. Comparisons of Italian and Polish immigrants suggest that cultural differences determined their patterns of adjustment. Finally, the particular time, place and economic conditions that these Italians encountered in Buffalo between 1880 and 1930 limited the directions of their particular adaptation.

Are some ethnic groups more successful than others in maintaining Old World traditions? Is there anything peculiar or special about any one group? These questions appear over and over in discussions of the Italian family. A kaleidoscope of stereotyped images flashes by: the indulgent Sicilian mother overly concerned with feeding her children, the submissive yet powerful wife, the silent yet assertive father, the major family crises that result when a child leaves home or a relative fails to attend a marriage or return a favor. But are these behavioral patterns peculiarly Italian-American? Some social scientists emphasize that many ethnic groups share such patterns, and that they seem to stem from similar class situations, both in the Old World peasant society and in America, rather than from any ethnic peculiarity. Indeed many studies (the most germane being Herbert Gan's recent analysis of second-generation Italian-Americans) posit the existence of a working-class subculture which cuts across ethnic lines.[1] But the evidence presented in this book indicates that ethnic differences existed among first-generation working-class groups. These require explanation and deserve attention. Because this is a case study of only one ethnic group in a single geographical and temporal context, I have not been able to test this proposition thoroughly. The evidence suggests that the Italian families in Buffalo were more adult-centered, more familistic, and more insistent upon sex differences than either the Americans or Poles of the same social class. They also had occupational patterns which distinguished them from other working-class groups. One can, I believe, convincingly argue that these differences derived from stronger Italian traditions of male superiority and familism. Only a thorough comparative study, however, could prove that Italian peasants had a special capacity to sustain their family traditions. In any case, the explanation for Italian family stability need not rest solely upon the successful transmission of a strong heritage. We can understand this stability equally as a successful adaptation of Old World patterns to new situations.

The ethnic community played an important role in this process. Providing a stable reference point after the shock of immigration, it helped immigrant families to make the transition

[1] Gans, *Urban Villagers, passim.*

from rural peasants to urban workers.[2] It was "urban villages," not the entire society, that absorbed the Italians and other national groups. While substantially different from the villages abroad, they still supplied a familiar orientation. Most important, they embraced those networks of kin relationships and friendships which were so necessary for the preservation of family traditions. In the ghetto, the Italians and others like them learned to cope, to search for new ways of life in a society that as yet had little meaning for them.

Within the ethnic community, several networks operated to maintain the old familial culture or to build a new one.[3] The kind of social control exerted by these networks differed from that provided by the peasant community, which had been a small, territorially based organization that monitored all family activities and values. In the United States the family received support from neighborhood friends and relatives and from a variety of social agencies. Some of these groups—kin, peers, Church—were familiar to the former peasants. Others, such as the voluntary and political organizations, the unions, insurance and burial societies, and city neighborhoods, were less so. Though this dispersed network had certain more specialized components than the peasants had known before, it assisted their adaptation and adjustment. Close bonds between relatives and friends knit this social network together. The continued existence of these bonds helps to explain the persistence over time of inherited values and attitudes.

The findings of this book concerning the nuclear and the extended family, relationships between family and community and, finally, geographic mobility underscore the shortcomings of historical explanations and conclusions based solely or primarily on quantification. The inaccuracy and inconclusiveness of the data represent only one part of the indictment. Other evidence shows that cultural meanings cannot be inferred from quantifiable experiences. Form, in other words, does not deter-

[2] Marc Fried, "Functions of the Working-Class Community in Modern Urban Society: Implications for Forced Relocation," *Journal of the American Institute of Planners*, 33 (March 1967), 90–103.

[3] Bott, *Family and Social Network*, discusses urban kin networks.

mine cultural content. The meanings that Italians gave to women's work, to the separations required by immigration, to extended family roles and geographic mobility could not be inferred from quantifiable experiences.

If form does not determine cultural content, neither can it clarify process, which is the essence of historical experience. Census data describing the general outlines of the nuclear family, the extended family, and neighborhood patterns in Little Italy support this conclusion. Statistical descriptions of these characteristics and institutions, when unsupported by literary and oral sources, will provide us with a distorted image of change. To take the nuclear family first: census and charity agency reports describe the short-term periods of upheaval caused by temporary family separations and the clearer long-term patterns of stability. By themselves, statistical data cannot explain these alternate periods of break-up and cohesion bridged by an intermittent period when family bonds adapted to new circumstances. If we were to deduce possible family stress from statistical descriptions of female work patterns, the eventual bankruptcy of Old World attitudes toward women's work outside the home would be the predicted ultimate outcome. Yet literary evidence and oral sources suggest that Italians themselves ascribed different, more conventional interpretations to women's work peculiar to Italians as a group. Both Polish and Italian families saw women enter the work world, but each group found different options consistent with their own set of cultural attitudes. This tells us that the same form—the nuclear family—adjusted differently to the same socioeconomic circumstances. It is not enough simply to measure female labor force participation: awareness of the particular cultural meanings that each group gave to women's work is needed to complete our understanding of their situations.

The story of the extended family is similar. Even though statistical information based upon censuses underestimates the existing kin ties within households and neighborhoods, it does allow us to verify their importance. We know that the extended family performed important social functions in the old country, but statistics alone cannot indicate how this network assumed new roles in America. Again, census data give only an incomplete picture of how kin helped each other find jobs, homes, husbands, and wives. And some kinds of kin support defy measurement. Emotional bonds, sexual controls, affection, and charitable impulses do not countenance quantification. Further, there are important questions which the census data alone do not permit us to ask. Without a different set of questions provided by broader anthropological and sociological viewpoints, for example, we would not know that extended family ties operated beyond the urban neighborhood and household, that they cemented an entire community and enveloped the Niagara Frontier region.

The evidence on population turnover and geographic mobility provides perhaps the clearest example of the narrowness of interpretations based upon quantification. We have questioned the accuracy of data concerning population turnover, as well as the conclusions drawn from them. Literary and oral testimony tells us that Italians interpreted their geographic mobility differently from contemporary historians. It should not surprise us that their interpretations of their own mobility were rooted in their own experience and cultural attitudes. Many contemporary historians infer from high population turnover among working-class people rootlessness, anonymity, and community instability.[4] But Italians understood their situation differently. We have seen how two-way chains of immigrants related by blood, *comparraggio,* or village ties extended across the ocean and continued to operate. Family and village ties monitored the entire migration process; they tied thousands of men and women together, irrespective of where they lived at a particular moment; and they provided an entry into local communities. Given these facts, the notion that community stability and class consciousness are somehow inextricably bound to geographic propinquity is an oversimplification. For Italian immigrants, community was not a place but a spiritual, emotional, or blood tie.

[4] See, for example, Stephan Thernstrom, "Urbanization, Migration and Social Mobility in Late Nineteenth Century America" in Herbert G. Gutman and Gregory S. Kealey, eds., *Many Pasts,* II (New York, 1973), 110–124.

The objective situation in Buffalo and other American cities is critical to our understanding of these families. But one-dimensional statistical descriptions fail to elucidate the quality of their lives. Historians interested in process and consciousness—such essential parts of the experience of these immigrants—will not find them in the census reports. If socioeconomic conditions and statistics describe the "objective conditions" of immigrants' lives, they fail to illuminate the subjective reality. The core of historical analysis lies in comprehending the tension between the two. If empirical measurement fills out one half of the historical dialectic, culture provides the other. Without both, we shall never understand the immigrants, or the society they helped to create.

Bibliography

UNPUBLISHED WORKS

Manuscripts

City of Buffalo, N.Y., City Assessment Roll, 1925.

Saint Anthony of Padua Church. Marriage Registers, 1909–1920, 1925, 1928, 1930.

Manuscript Censuses

New York State. Manuscript Census, Buffalo, N.Y., 1905, 1925.

United States Bureau of the Census. Federal Manuscript Census, Buffalo, N.Y., 1900.

Letters

Bell, Rudolph M. New Brunswick, N.J. Letter, March 5, 1976, to the author.

Claflin, Charlotte I. Letter to Dr. Stephen Gredel. Oct. 16, 1961. Buffalo Historical Society, Letter File.

Shelton, Brenda. Buffalo, N.Y. Letter, June 27, 1969, to the author.

Interviews

Interview with Rose Angelico, Buffalo, N.Y., April 16, 1973.

Interview with Thomas Angelico. Buffalo, N.Y., April 16, 1973.

Interview with Marion Callendrucci. Buffalo, N.Y., April 17, 1973.

Interview with Vincent De Bella. Buffalo, N.Y. April 20, 1973.

Interview with Richard Ferranti. Buffalo, N.Y. April 16, 1973.

Interview with Frank Iannuzzi. Buffalo, N.Y. April 16, 1973.

Interview with Isabella Iannuzzi. Buffalo, N.Y. April 16, 1973.

Interview with Amalia Lanza. Buffalo, N.Y. April 17, 1973.

Interview with Dante Pellegrino. Buffalo, N.Y. April 16, 1973.

Interview with Roberta Salerno. Buffalo, N.Y. April 16, 1973.

Interview with Mary Sansone. Buffalo, N.Y. April 16, 1973.

Dissertations and Papers

Alessi, Samuel C. "The Coming of the Italians to Chautauqua County." Chautauqua County Historical Society, Westfield, N.Y., August 6, 1960.

Augello, Michael. "A History of Italian Immigrants in Buffalo, 1880–1925." M.A. thesis, Canisius College, Buffalo, N.Y., 1960.

Bell, Rudolph M. "Old World Influences on New World Experiences: The Demography of Italo-American Migration." Rutgers University, 1975.

Briggs, John W. "Italians in Italy and America: A Study of Change within Conformity for Immigrants to Three American Cities, 1890–1930." Ph.D. dissertation, University of Minnesota, 1972.

Briggs, John W. "Return the Immigrant to Immigration Studies: A New Appeal for an Old Approach." Delivered at the Conference of the Canadian Association of American Studies, 1972.

Chazanof, William. "The Sicilians of Fredonia." American Community Life Class, New York State University College at Fredonia, May 15, 1961.

Covello, Leonard. "The Social Background of the Italo-American School Child: A Study of the Southern Italian Family Mores and Their Effect on the School Situation in Italy and America." Ph.D. dissertation, New York University, 1944.

"The Early History of Census Tract 12 (Ward 4)." Unpublished Report, Department of Sociology of the University of Buffalo and the Buffalo Foundation, Buffalo, 1930.

Fenton, Edwin. "Immigrants and Unions, A Case Study: Italians and American Labor, 1870–1920." Ph.D. dissertation, Harvard University, 1957.

Golab, Caroline. "The Impact of the Industrial Experience on the Immigrant Family: The Huddled Masses Reconsidered." Delivered at the Eleutherian Mills Historical Society Conference on Immigrants in Industrial America, Nov. 1973.

Gorman, Patricia M. "The Life and Work of Dr. Charles R. Borzilleri." Thesis, D'Youville College, Buffalo, N.Y., 1967.

Gredel, Stephen. "Italian Pioneers of Buffalo." Buffalo and Erie County Historical Society, March, 1961.

Huganir, George H. "The Hosiery Looper in the Twentieth Century: A Study of Family Occupational Processes and Adaptation to Factory and Community Change, 1900–1950." Ph.D. dissertation, University of Pennsylvania, 1958.

Iorizzo, Luciano John. "Italian Immigrants and the Impact of the Padrone System." Ph.D. dissertation, Syracuse University, 1966.

Kearns, Karen. Unpublished paper on New York City domestic workers. City University of New York Graduate Center, Fall, 1974.

[McLaughlin, Virginia Yans. See Yans-McLaughlin.]

Ognibene, Samuel W. "Italians in Buffalo, New York: 1890–1910." Unpublished paper, State University of New York at Buffalo, 1965.

Pane Pinto, Nina J. "Post World War II Immigration to the United States: A Case Study of Italian Female Immigration." M.A. thesis, State University of New York at Buffalo, 1967.

Scott, Joan W., and Louise Tilly, "Women's Work and the Family in Nineteenth Century Europe." Manuscript, University of North Carolina at Chapel Hill and the University of Michigan, 1973. (Subsequently published in *Comparative Studies in Society and History,* 18 (1975), 36–64.)

Shelton, Brenda K. "Social Reform and Social Control in Buffalo, New York." Ph.D. dissertation, State University of New York at Buffalo, June 1970.

Tilly, Charles. "From Mobilization to Political Conflict." Manuscript, University of Michigan, 1970.

Tilly, Louise. "Comments on the Yans-McLaughlin and Davidoff Papers." Delivered at the Anglo-American Conference on Comparative Labor History, New Brunswick, N.J., April, 1973.

Triller, Thomas Wayne. "The History of the Development of the International Institute in Buffalo, New York." M.A. thesis, University of Buffalo School of Social Work, Feb., 1952.

Yans-McLaughlin, Virginia. "Like the Fingers of the Hand: The Family and Community Life of First-generation Italian-Americans in Buffalo, New York, 1880–1930." Ph.D. dissertation, State University of New York at Buffalo, 1970.

Documents and Reports

Buffalo Municipal Housing Authority. "Report," Part I. Buffalo, 1935. (Microfilm)

Buffalo Municipal Housing Authority. "Report," Part II. Buffalo, 1935.

Coit, Eleanor G. "An Industrial Study, Buffalo, New York." Business and Industrial Department, Young Women's Christian Association, Buffalo, New York, 1922.

"Neighborhood House Reports." Manuscript, State University of New York at Buffalo, Jan., 1930.

Wallens, Pauline D. "Recreation Survey of Tract 12, Ward 4." Department of Sociology of the University of Buffalo and the Buffalo Foundation, 1929.

Young Women's Christian Association (Buffalo, New York), The City Business and Industrial Department and Students of the Department of Sociology, University of Buffalo. "Some Facts Concerning Women in Buffalo Industries." Buffalo, N.Y., 1925.

PUBLISHED WORKS

Census Reports

Associazione per lo Sviluppo dell'Industria nel Mezzogiorno. *Statistiche sul Mezzogiorno d'Italia, 1861–1953*. Rome, 1954.

Italy. *Annuario Statistico, 1905–1907*. Rome, 1907.

Italy (Repubblica Italiana), Istituto Centrale di Statistica. *Comuni e loro popolazione ai censimenti dal 1861 al 1951*. Rome, 1960.

U.S. Department of Commerce and Labor, Bureau of the Census. *Twelfth Census of the United States, 1900: Population*, Vol. I, Pt. 1. Washington, D.C., 1901. Vol. II, Pt. 2. Washington, D.C., 1902. *Special Reports: Occupations*. Washington, D.C., 1904.

——. *Thirteenth Census of the United States, 1910: Population*, Vol. I. Washington, D.C., 1913. Vol. III, *Reports by States*. Washington, D.C., 1912.

——. *Fourteenth Census of the United States, 1920. Population*. Vol. II, Washington, D.C., 1922.

——. *Fifteenth Census of the United States, 1930: Population*, Vol. II, Pt. 2, Washington, D.C., 1932. Vol. IV. *Occupations by State*, Washington, D.C., 1933.

Reports and Proceedings: Buffalo

Buffalo, City of. *Annual Report of the Children's Court of Buffalo, 1912–1930*. Buffalo, 1912–1930.

——. *Annual Report of the Department of Social Welfare for the Fiscal Year Ending June 30, 1929*. Buffalo, 1929.

——. *Annual Report of the Superintendent of Education*. Buffalo, 1917.

———. Department of Public Affairs. *Annual Report of the Bureau of Public Welfare for Fiscal Year Ending June 30, 1926*. Buffalo, 1926.

——. Department of Public Affairs. *Annual Report of the Bureau of Public Welfare for Fiscal Year Ending June 30, 1927*. Buffalo, 1927.

Charity Organization Society (Buffalo, New York). *Annual Report, 1892–1907*. Buffalo, 1892–1907.

——. *Proceedings at the 5th Annual Meeting of the Charity Organization Society of Buffalo, Jan. 18, 1883.* Buffalo, 1883.

Children's Court of Buffalo, New York. *Annual Report*, Buffalo, 1912–1920.

Remington, Mary. *Report of the Remington Gospel Settlement.* Buffalo, 1904.

Welcome Hall. *Annual Reports.* Buffalo, 1894–1930.

Reports: State, National, and Italian

Consumers' League of New York. *Behind the Scenes in the Canneries: Investigation Conducted by the Consumer's League of New York.* New York, 1930.

De'Rossi, Maria Maddalena. Segretariato Femminile per la Tutela delle Donne e dei Fanciulli Emigranti. *Relazione.* "Le donne ed i fanciulli italiani a Buffalo e ad Albion." Rome, 1913.

Italy, *Atti della giunta per l'Inchiesta Agraria e sulle condizioni della classe agricola,* 13, Tomo 2, Fas. 4. Rome, 1885.

New York State. *Preliminary Report of the Factory Investigating Commission, 1912,* I–III. Albany, 1912.

New York State. *Second Report of the New York State Factory Investigating Commission,* I–III. Albany, 1913.

New York State. *Second Report of the Factory Investigating Commission, 1913*, IV, *Testimony and Proceedings.* Albany, 1913.

New York State. *Fourth Report of the Factory Investigating Commission*, IV. Albany, 1915.

North American Civil League for Immigrants, New York–New Jersey Committee. *Report.* New York, Dec. 1, 1909–Feb. 1, 1913.

U.S. Bureau of Education. *Education of the Immigrant.* Washington, D.C., 1913.

U.S. Department of Commerce. *Seasonal Operation in the Construction Industries: Summary of Report and Recommendations of a Committee of the President's Conference on Unemployment.* Washington, D.C., 1924.

U.S. Congress. Senate, 61st Cong., 2d sess. *Reports of the Immigration Commission*, Vol. XVIII, *Immigrants in Industries.* Pt. 22, *The Floating Immigrant Labor Supply.* Washington, D.C., 1911. Vol. XXII, *Immigrants in Industries*, Pt. 24, *Recent Immigrants in Agriculture, II.* Washington, D.C., 1911. Vol. XXVI, *Immigrants in Cities, I* Washington, D.C., 1911. Vol. XXVIII, *Occupations of Immigrants.* Washington, D.C., 1911.

——. 61st Cong., 3d sess. *Reports of the Immigration Commission,*

Vol. IV, *Emigration Conditions in Europe*. Washington, D.C., 1911. Vol. XXIV, *Immigrants as Charity Seekers, I*. Washington, D.C., 1911. Vol. XXX, *The Children of Immigrants in Schools, II*, Washington, D.C., 1911.

Journals

Buffalo Foundation Forum. 1922, 1926.

Charities. Vol. 6–15, 1901–1905.

Charities and the Commons. Vol. 15–21, 1905–1909.

Italy. Ministry of Foreign Affairs. *Bollettino dell'Emigrazione*. 1901–1926.

Survey. Vol. 22–41, 1909–1926.

Newspapers

Buffalo *Courier*. 1901–1923.

Buffalo *Express*. 1891–1905.

Buffalo *Times*. 1903–1927.

Il Corriere Italiano. Buffalo, New York. April 2, 1898–July 6, 1899; May 25, 1901–Dec. 28, 1950.

La Fiaccola. Buffalo, New York. Aug. 7, 1909—Dec. 1, 1912.

Articles

Addams, Jane. "Foreign-Born Children in the Primary Grades." Originally published in 1897; reprinted in *The Nation Transformed*. Edited by Sigmund Diamond. New York, 1963. Pp. 42ff.

Bailey, Samuel. "The Italians and the Development of Organized Labor in Argentina, Brazil, and the United States, 1880–1914." *Journal of Social History*, 3 (Winter 1969), 123–134.

Baxter, Celena. "Sicilian Family Life." *The Family*, 14 (May 1933), 82–87.

Bendix, Reinhard. "Tradition and Modernity Reconsidered." *Comparative Studies in Society and History*, 9 (1967), 292–346.

Bugelski, B. R. "Assimilation through Intermarriage." *Social Forces*, 40 (1961/62), 148–153.

Byington, Margaret F. "The Family in a Typical Mill Town." *American Journal of Sociology*, 14 (1909), 648–659.

Campisi, Paul J. "Ethnic Family Patterns: The Italian Family in the United States." *American Journal of Sociology*, 53, (1947–48), 443–449.

Cancian, Frank. "The Southern Italian Peasant: World View and Political Behavior." *Anthropological Quarterly*, 34, (1961), 1–18.

Carpenter, Niles. "Nationality, Color, and Economic Opportunity in the City of Buffalo." *The University of Buffalo Studies*, 4, No. 4. Buffalo: University of Buffalo, 1927.

Clough, Shepard B., and Carlo Levi. "Economic Growth in Italy." *Journal of Economic History*, 16 (1956), 334–349.

Davis, J. "Morals and Backwardness." *Comparative Studies in Society and History*, 12 (July 1970), 340–353.

Fried, Marc. "Functions of the Working-Class Community in Modern Urban Society: Implications for Forced Relocation." *Journal of the American Institute of Planners*, 33 (March 1967), 90–103.

Friedman, F. G. "The World of 'La Miseria.'" *Partisan Review*, 20 (March–April 1953), 218–231.

Geertz, Clifford. "Ritual and Social Change." *American Anthropologist*, 59 (1957), 32–54.

Gettleman, Marvin E. "Charity and Social Class in the United States, 1874–1900." *American Journal of Sociology and Economics*, 22, Nos. 3–4 (July–Oct. 1963), pp. 313–329, 417–426.

Goody, Jack. "Forms of Pro-parenthood: the Sharing and Substitution of Parental Roles." In *Kinship*, edited by Jack Goody. Middlesex, England, 1971.

Gredel, Stephen. "Immigration of Ethnic Groups to Buffalo, Based upon Censuses of 1850, 1865, and 1892." *Niagara Frontier* (Summer 1963), 42–56.

Habakkuk, H. J. "Family Structure and Economic Change in Nineteenth-Century Europe." *Journal of Economic History*, 15 (1955), 1–12.

Klaczynska, Barbara. "Why Women Work: A Comparison of Various Ethnic Groups—Philadelphia, 1910–1930." *Labor History*, 17 (Winter 1976), 73–87.

Litwak, Eugene. "Geographic Mobility and Extended Family Cohesion." *American Sociological Review*, 25 (1960), 385–394.

——. "Occupational Mobility and Extended Family Cohesion." *American Sociological Review*, 25 (1960), 9–21.

McDonald (*sic*), John S. "Italy's Rural Social Structure and Emigration." *Occidente: Rivista di Studi Politici*, 12 (Sept.–Oct. 1956), 439–456.

MacDonald, John S., and Leatrice D. MacDonald. "Chain Migration, Ethnic Neighborhood Formation, and Social Network." *Milbank Memorial Fund Quarterly*, 42 (Jan. 1964), 82–97.

——. "Institutional Economics and Rural Development: Two Italian Types." *Human Organization*, 23 (Summer 1964), 113–118.

Magnani, Ferdinand. "The Italian Population in the History of Buffalo." *Catholic Union and Times, Centenary Edition.* June 26, 1931.

Mintz, Sidney W., and Eric R. Wolf. "Ritual Co-parenthood." In *Kinship*, edited by Jack Goody. Middlesex, England, 1971, 346–362.

Moss, Leonard W., and Walter H. Thomson. "The South Italian Family: Literature and Observation" *Human Organization,* 18 (Spring 1959), 25–41.

[McLaughlin, Virginia Yans; see Yans-McLaughlin]

Oppenheimer, Valerie Kincade. "Demographic Influence on Female Employment and the Status of Women." *American Journal of Sociology*, 58 (Jan. 1973), 946–951.

Parsons, Anne. "Is the Oedipus Complex Universal." In *Magic and Anomie: Essays in Psychosocial Anthropology.* Glencoe, Ill., 1969. Pp. 16–53.

Parsons, Talcott. "The Kinship System of the Contemporary United States." *American Anthropologist*, 45 (1943), 22–38.

Pitkin, Donald S. "Land Tenure and Family Organization in an Italian Village." *Human Organization*, 18 (Winter 1959–60), 169–173.

Rose, Arnold M. "A Research Note on the Influence of Immigration on the Birth Rate." *American Journal of Sociology*, 48, (Jan. 1942), 614–621.

Scott, Joan, and Louise A. Tilly. "Woman's Work and the Family in Nineteenth Century Europe." *Comparative Studies in Society and History*, 18 (1975), 36–64.

Shepard, Mrs. Frederick J. "The Women's Educational and Industrial Union in Buffalo." *Buffalo Historical Society Publication*, 22 (1918), 147–200.

Silverman, Sydel F. "Agricultural Organization, Social Structure, and Values in Italy: Amoral Familism Reconsidered." *American Anthropologist*, 70 (Feb. 1968), 1–20.

Sprey, Jetse. "The Family as a System in Conflict." In *Intimate Life Styles*, edited by Joann S. DeLora and Jack R. DeLora. Pacific Palisades, Cal., 1972. Pp. 184–195.

Strodtbeck, Fred. "Family, Interaction, Values and Achievement." In *Talent and Society*, edited by David McClelland, et al. Princeton, 1958. Pp. 135–191.

Taussig, Ellen. "The Polish Community." Buffalo *Evening News*, Nov. 13, 1971.

Thernstrom, Stephan. "Urbanization, Migration and Social Mobility in Late Nineteenth Century America." In *Many Pasts*, II, edited by Herbert G. Gutman and Gregory S. Kealey. New York, 1973. Pp. 110–124.

Thernstrom, Stephan, and Peter Knights. "Men in Motion: Some Data and Speculations on Urban Population Mobility in Nineteenth Century North America." *Journal of Interdisciplinary History*, 1 (1970), 7–35.

Thompson, E. P. "The Moral Economy of the English Crowd in the Eighteenth Century." *Past and Present*, No. 50 (1971), 76–136.

Tilly, Louise A. "Comments on the Yans-McLaughlin and Davidoff Papers." *Journal of Social History*, 7 (1974), 452–459.

Tipps, Dean C. "Modernization Theory and the Comparative Study of Societies: A Critical Perspective." *Comparative Studies in Society and History*, 15 (1967), 199–226.

"Uncle Sam's Debt to the Italians." *Il Pensiero Italiano, Giornale della Colonia di Utica, New York*, No. 13, Sept. 26, 1914.

Valetta, Clement. "The Settlement of Roseto: World View and Promise." In *The Ethnic Experience in Pennsylvania*, edited by John Bodnar. Lewisburg, Pa., 1973. Pp. 120–143.

Vecoli, Rudolph J. "*Contadini* in Chicago: A Critique of *The Uprooted*." *Journal of American History*, 51 (Dec. 1964), 404–417.

Vecoli, Rudolph J. "Peasants and Prelates: Italian Immigrants and the Catholic Church." *Journal of Social History*, 2 (Spring 1969), 217–268.

Whyte, William F. "Sicilian Peasant Society." *American Anthropologist*, 46 (Jan.–March, 1944), 65–74.

Wirth, Louis. "Urbanism as a Way of Life." *American Journal of Sociology*, 44 (July, 1938), 1–24.

Yans-McLaughlin, Virginia. "Italian Women and Work: Experience and Perception." In *Class, Sex, and the Woman Worker*, edited by Milton Cantor and Bruce Laurie. Westport, Conn.: Greenwood Press, 1977.

——. "A Flexible Tradition: Immigrant Families Confront New Work Experiences." *Journal of Social History*, 7 (1974), 429–445.

——. "Patterns of Work and Family Organization: Buffalo's Italians." *Journal of Interdisciplinary History*, 2 (1971), 299–314.

Books

Adams, Myron. *The Buffalo Newsboy and the Street Trades Bill*. Buffalo, 1903.

Anderson, Michael. *Family Structure in Nineteenth Century Lancashire*. London, 1971.

Arensberg, Conrad, and Solon Kimball, *Family and Community in Ireland*. Cambridge, Mass., 1940.

Banfield, Edward C. *The Moral Basis of a Backward Society*. New York, 1958.

Barton, Josef J. *Peasants and Strangers: Italians, Rumanians, and Slovaks in an American City, 1890–1950*. Cambridge, Mass., 1975.

Bianco, Carla. *The Two Rosetos*. Bloomington, Ind., 1974.

Blok, Anton. *The Mafia of a Sicilian Village, 1860–1960: A Study of Violent Peasant Entrepreneurs*. New York, 1974.

Bott, Elizabeth. *Family and Social Network*. London, 1971.

Breckinridge, Sophonisba P. *New Homes for Old*. New York, 1921.

Buffalo, City of. *The People of Buffalo*. Buffalo, 1947.

Burber, H. E. *Industrial Analysis of Buffalo*. Buffalo, n. d.

Calhoun, Arthur W. *A Social History of the American Family*. Vol. 3. New York, 1946.

Chafe, William H. *The American Woman: Her Changing Social Economic and Political Roles, 1920–1970*. New York, 1972.

Chapman, Charlotte Gower. *Milocca: A Sicilian Village*. Cambridge, Mass., 1971.

Church of Saint Anthony of Padua. *Golden Jubilee, 1891–1941*. Buffalo, 1941.

Cronin, Constance. *The Sting of Change: Sicilians in Sicily and Australia*. Chicago, 1970.

DeCapite, Michael. *Maria*. New York, 1943.

De Forest, Edward, and Lawrence Veiller, eds. *The Tenement House Problem*. 2 vols. New York, 1903.

Dickinson, Robert E. *The Population Problem of Southern Italy*. Syracuse, 1955.

Eisenstadt, Shmuel. *From Generation to Generation: Age Groups and Social Structure*. Glencoe, Ill., 1956.

Felt, Jeremy. *Hostages of Fortune: Child Labor Reform in New York State*. Syracuse, 1965.

Firth, Raymond. *Two Studies of Kinship in London*. London, 1956.

Foerster, Robert. *The Italian Immigration of Our Times*. Cambridge, Mass., 1919.

Gans, Herbert J. *The Urban Villagers: Group and Class in the Life of Italian Americans*. Glencoe, Ill., 1962.

Geertz, Clifford. *Peddlers and Princes: Social and Economic Modernization in Two Indonesian Towns*. Chicago, 1963.

Glazer, Nathan, and Daniel P. Moynihan. *Beyond the Melting Pot: The Negroes, Puerto Ricans, Jews, Italians, and Irish of New York City*. Cambridge, Mass., 1963.

Gredel, Stephen. *Pioneers of Buffalo—Its Growth and Development*. Buffalo, 1966.

Hale, Nathan. *Freud and the Americans*. New York, 1971.

Handlin, Oscar. *The Uprooted*. 2d ed. Boston, 1973.

Hildebrand, George H. *Growth and Structure in the Economy of Modern Italy*. Cambridge, Mass., 1965.

Hill, Henry W. ed., *Municipality of Buffalo, New York: A History, 1720–1923*. Vol. 2. New York and Chicago, 1923.

Hill, Richmond C. *Twentieth Century Buffalo*. Pt. 1. Buffalo, 1902.

Horton, John T. "Old Erie." *History of Northwestern New York. New York, 1947.*

Hutchinson, E. P. *Immigrants and Their Children*. New York, 1956.

Ireland, Bertram. *The Little Child in Our Great Cities*. New York, 1925.

Korman, Gerd. *Industrialization, Immigrants and Americanizers: The View from Milwaukee, 1866–1921*, Madison, Wis., 1967.

Lantz, Herman. *The People of Coaltown*. New York, 1958.

Larned, J. N. *A History of Buffalo*, Vol. 2. New York, 1911.

Lieberson, Stanley. *Ethnic Patterns in American Cities*. Glencoe, Ill., 1963.

Livi Bacci, Massimo. *L'immigrazione e l'assimilazione degli Italiani negli Stati Uniti secondo le statistiche demografiche americane*. Milan, 1961.

Lopreato, Joseph. *Peasants No More: Social Class and Social Change in an Underdeveloped Society*. San Francisco, 1967.

Lubove, Roy. *The Professional Altruist: The Emergence of Social Work as a Career, 1880–1930*. Cambridge, Mass., 1965.

Magnani, Ferdinand. *La città di Buffalo, New York e paesi circonvicini e le colonie italiane*. Buffalo, 1908.

Malcolm, James, comp. *A Record of Failure: History of Asphalt Pavements in Buffalo*. Buffalo, n.d. [1901?].

Mangold, George B., and Lillian B. Hall, *Migratory Child Workers*. New York, 1929.

Mitchell, Juliet. *Women's Estate*. New York, 1971.

Monroe, Day. *Chicago Families: A Study of Unpublished Census Data*. Chicago, 1932.

Nelli, Humbert S. *The Italians in Chicago: 1880–1930*. New York, 1970.

Neufeld, Maurice F. *Italy: School for Awakening Countries, The Italian Labor Movement and Its Political, Social, and Economic Setting from 1800 to 1960*. Ithaca, N.Y., 1961.

Nienberg, Bertha. *The Woman Homemaker in the City of Rochester, New York at the Census of 1920*. Washington, D.C., 1923.

Odencrantz, Louise C. *Italian Women in Industry: A Study of Conditions in New York City.* New York, 1919.

Park, Robert E., and Herbert A. Miller. *Old World Traits Transplanted.* New York, 1921.

Queen of the Lakes, Buffalo. Souvenir of the Tenth Convention of the National Association of Builders. Buffalo, 1896.

Radin, Paul. *The Italians of San Francisco: Their Adjustment and Acculturation.* Vol. 2. San Francisco, 1935.

Roberts, Peter. *The Foreign Population Problem in Buffalo* (extracts). Buffalo, 1908.

Rudolph, Lloyd I., and Susanne Hoeber Rudolph. *The Modernity of Tradition.* Chicago, 1967.

Schachter, Gustav. *The Italian South.* New York, 1965.

Schiavo, Giovanni. *Italian-American History*, Vol. 2, *The Italian Contribution to the Catholic Church in America.* New York, 1949.

Smelser, Neil J. *Social Change in the Industrial Revolution: An Application of Theory to the British Cotton Industry.* Chicago, 1959.

Smuts, Robert. *Women and Work in America.* New York, 1971.

Società Italiana di Mutuo Soccorso. *Fratellanza di S. Antonio di Padova.* Buffalo, n.d. [1903?].

Sonnino, Sidney. *La Sicilia nel 1876*, Vol. 2, *I Contadini.* Florence, 1877.

Suttles, Gerald D. *The Social Order of a Slum: Ethnicity and Territory in the Inner City.* Chicago, 1968.

Sylos-Labini, Paolo, ed. *Problemi dell'economia siciliana.* Milan, 1966.

Taylor, Philip. *The Distant Magnet.* New York, 1971.

Thernstrom, Stephan. *Poverty and Progress: Social Mobility in a Nineteenth Century City.* Cambridge, Mass., 1964.

Thomas, William I., and Florian Znaniecki. *The Polish Peasant in Europe and America*, Vol. 2. 2d ed. New York, 1958.

Van Kleeck, Mary. *Artificial Flower Makers.* New York, 1913.

Verga, Giovanni. *The House by the Medlar-Tree.* Translated by Mary A. Craig. New York, 1890.

Villari, Luigi. *Italian Life in Town and Country.* London, 1902.

Ware, Caroline F. *Greenwich Village, 1920–1930: A Comment on American Civilization in the Post War Years.* New York, 1965.

Warner, W. Lloyd. *The Social Systems of American Ethnic Groups.* Vol. 3. The Yankee City Series. New Haven, 1945.

Weir, L. H. *Recreation Survey of Buffalo.* Buffalo, 1925.

Whyte, William F. *Street Corner Society: The Social Structure of an Italian Slum.* 2d ed. Chicago, 1955.

Williams, Phyllis H. *South Italian Folkways in Europe and America.* New Haven, 1938.

Woods, Robert A. and Albert J. Kennedy. *Young Working Girls: A Summary of Evidence from Two Thousand Social Workers.* Boston and New York, 1913.

Index